Michael Schulz

Understanding Calisthenics

For questions and suggestions
support@kingofweighted.com

Disclaimer
This book is written for educational purposes only. It is not a substitute for individual medical advice and should not be used as such. If you wish to seek medical advice, consult a qualified medical practitioner. The King Of Weighted GmbH and the author are not liable for any negative effects directly or indirectly related to the information contained in this book.

First printing, 2023
ISBN 979-8-85-772641-9
ISBN 978-3-00-075605-4 (ebook)

Vertrieb:
King Of Weighted GmbH
Petersburger Str.28
10249 Berlin

Illustrations, Photos: Michael Schulz
Layout: Mia Sommerhalder
Laura Michelle Maske (Laura Maskings)
Cover: Camilo Edison Riano Galviz
Translated into English: Michael Schulz

Index

4. Dynamic lever skills

5. About the author

Reference List

Foreword

I thought long about whether I wanted to write a book like this. My main concern about doing so was that I would change my mind on some issues and probably see things differently in a few years. I am constantly learning and getting better with every plan I write, every education I take, and every new client I coach. In the process, I am always getting new information, and data, and most importantly, meeting other experts who provide me with new insights.

«You are allowed to stand 100% by your current opinion, and it is also allowed to differ from the opinion once the book was written. You are developing and, normally, things will change. We are not politicians who always have to be right. We are scientists and practitioners who are always looking for a new „right" ». – Alexander Pürzel after I told him about my concerns.

In the process, it also happens that I have to admit to mistakes and change my opinion on a subject. Once this book is printed and in your hand, everything remains there as it was printed, whether my opinion or the data situation has changed or not. I want to assure you that I have written every line to the best of my ability and knowledge. However, I would also like to point out to you that there is little to no evidence for much of the content and that it is based mostly on my experience, and observations. Should evidence appear in the future that refutes or relativizes statements of mine, there is therefore no conflict. It pushes the sport and we should accept that as a natural progression. If you are very interested in this sport, I would like to encourage you to perhaps become the next author of a book, study, article, or other technical paper for our sport.

1.

Fundamentals

1.
Fundamentals

The first chapter of this book is intended to provide you with the necessary basics of human anatomy and biomechanics that you will need to fully understand the following chapters. Feel free to start with the other chapters and use this chapter as a reference if you have trouble understanding any part of this book. Since this book cannot replace an anatomy book, the explanation of anatomy is kept to a minimum in table form. So if you are an anatomically trained reader, please forgive that many facts are presented somewhat simplified at this point for the sake of clarity. For example, functional units such as the elbow are grouped into one joint rather than listing and explaining all the partial joints individually. This section does not replace self-study of human anatomy but only provides the necessary foundation for a better understanding of the explained exercises in the following chapters. With the help of the tables, you will be able to assign the correct anatomical terms and the corresponding muscles to human movements in the future.

Elbow movements

Movement	Explanation	Muscles
Flexion	Bending of the arm	M.Biceps Brachii, M.Brachialis, M.Brachioradialis
Extension	Straightening of the arm	M.Triceps Brachii, M.Anconeus
Supination	Outward rotation of the hand, back of the hand is turned backward	M.Biceps Brachii, M.Supinator
Pronation	Inward rotation of the hand, back of the hand is turned forward	M.Pronator quadratus

Movements of the shoulder/arm

Movement	Explanation	Muscles
Flexion	Lifting the arm forward (sagittal view)	M.Deltoideus, M.Biceps Brachii, M.Coracobrachialis, M.Pectoralis Major, M.Serratus Anterior
Extension	Lifting the arm backward (sagittal view)	M.Deltoideus, M.Triceps Brachii, M.Latissimus Dorsi, M.Pectoralis Major, M.Teres Major
Abduction	Moving the arm away from the center of the body (frontal view)	M.Trapezius, M.Deltoideus, M.Biceps Brachii, M.Serratus Anterior, M.Supraspinatus
Adduction	Moving the arm to the center of the body (frontal view)	M.Deltoideus, M.Infraspinatus, M.Teres Minor
External rotation	Rotation of the arm away from the center of the body	M.Deltoideus, M.Infraspinatus, M.Teres Minor
Internal rotation	Rotation of the arm towards the center of the body	M.Pectoralis Major, M.Latissimus Dorsi, M.Deltoideus, M.Teres Major, M.Subscapularis
Protraction	Forward leading of the shoulder	M.Pectoralis Major, M.Serratus Anterior, M.Pectoralis Minor
Retraction	Pulling back the shoulder	M.Trapezius, M.Latissimus Dorsi, M.Rhomboideus Major & Minor
Elevation	Raising the shoulder upwards (elevation of the arm = raising the arm)	M.Trapezius, M.Deltoideus, M.Biceps Brachii, M.Serratus Anterior, M.Supraspinatus
Depression	Lowering the shoulder downwards	M.Trapezius, M.Latissimus Dorsi, M.Pectoralis Major, M.Pectoralis Minor

Movements of the shoulder blades

Movement	Explanation	Muscles
Abduction (protraction)	Spreading the shoulder blades away from the center of the body	M.Serratus Anterior, M.Pectoralis Minor
Adduction (retraction)	Bringing the shoulder blades together towards the center of the body	M.Trapezius, M.Latissimus Dorsi, M.Rhomboideus Major & Minor
Upward rotation	Rotation of the shoulder blade upwards when moving the arm overhead	M.Trapezius, M.Serratus Anterior
Downward rotation	Rotation of the shoulder blade downwards when lowering the arm	M.Levator Scapulae, M.Pectoralis Minor, M.Rhomboideus Major & Minor
Elevation (translation cranial)	Lifting the shoulder blade upwards	M.Levator Scapulae, M.Trapezius
Depression (translation cranial)	Leading the shoulder blade downwards	M.Latissimus Dorsi, M.Trapezius, M.Pectoralis Major, M.Pectoralis Minor

Movements of the thoracic spine

Movement	Explanation	Muscles
Flexion	Bending (sagittal view)	M.Rectus Abdominis, M.Obliquus Externus Abdominis, M.Obliquus Internus Abdominis, M.Linea Alba, M.Psoas Major & Minor, M.Transversus Abdominis
Extension	Straightening (sagittal view)	M.Longissimus, M.Iliocostalis, M. Interspinales, M.Multifidus, M. Semispinalis, M.Spinalis

Lateral flexion (sideways tilt)	Sideways tilt (frontal view)	M.Obliquus Externus Abdominis, M.Iliocostalis Lumborum, M. Obliquus Internus Abdominis, M. Intertransversarii, M.Linea Alba, M.Longissimus, M.Mutlifindus, M.Psoas, M.Quadratus Lumborum, M. Spinalis, M.Transversus Abdominis
Rotation	Turning the spine around it's axis	M.Obliquus Externus Abdominis, M.Obliquus Internus Abdominis, M. Rotatores, M.Transversus Abdominis, M.Semispinalis, M.Multifidus

When analyzing the terms and movements involved, it becomes evident that the shoulder, shoulder blades, and arms are interconnected during complex movements. Specific arm movements within the shoulder joint require corresponding movements of the shoulder blades. The shoulder joint is the most mobile ball-and-socket joint in the human body, which necessitates a significant amount of stability.

When you apply load to the shoulder, it is crucial for the upper arm to be centered within the socket of the shoulder joint. This optimal alignment allows for efficient force transfer and even distribution of load on the muscles, tendons, ligaments, fascia, and other passive structures within the joint. If the upper arm is not properly centered, the incoming force will act unevenly on the shoulder, exerting greater strain on specific muscles and passive structures involved in stabilization. Therefore, when moving the shoulder, the surrounding muscles play a vital role in ensuring that the upper arm remains centered and secure within the socket of the shoulder joint.

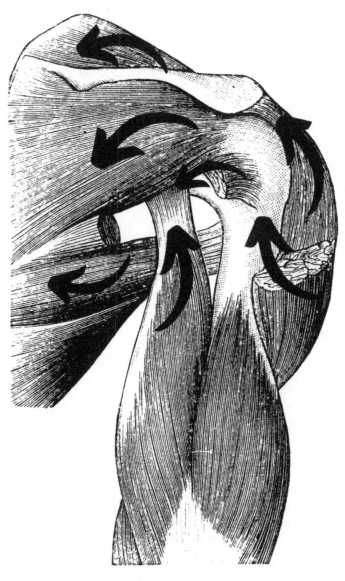

Compression and stabilization of the shoulder joint by the adjacent muscles.

The socket of the shoulder joint is formed by the scapula, also known as the shoulder blade. Visualize the shoulder blade as the foundational support for your arm. When the shoulder blade lacks stability while bearing load, the upper arm will not remain stable within its socket. Therefore, it is crucial for the shoulder blade to provide support and move in tandem with the arm, ensuring optimal centering of the upper arm within the shoulder socket.

In order to achieve this, the shoulder blade must participate in the arm's movements, coordinating its motion to guarantee the best possible centering of the upper arm. For instance, when you push your arm forward, the shoulder blade should also move forward. Conversely, when you pull your arm backward, the shoulder blade should move or rotate backward accordingly. When raising your arm overhead, the shoulder blade must rotate upward as well. This coordinated interaction between the shoulder and scapula during overhead movements is referred to as scapulohumeral rhythm.

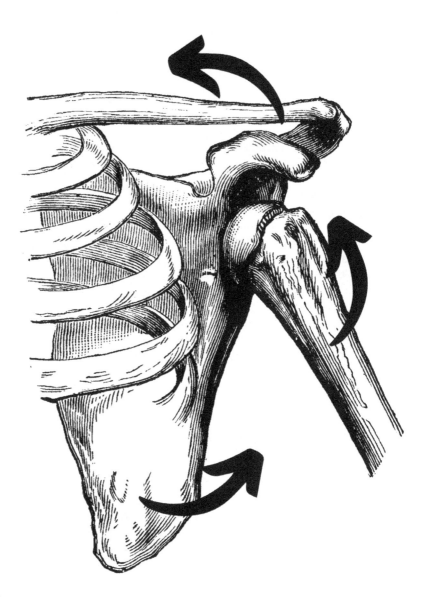

Scapulohumeral rhythm

In order for the scapula to effectively stabilize arm movements, it must be securely attached to the rib cage. Structurally, the shoulder blade forms a joint with the collarbone, which in turn connects to the sternum.

At the back of the rib cage, the shoulder blade is positioned with the help of sliding bearings, allowing it to glide along the rib cage. To ensure proper movement of the scapula on the rib cage, it is important to have adequate mobility and flexibility in the thoracic spine and rib cage. If the thoracic spine and ribs do not move correctly during a planned movement, the scapula may not be able to assume its optimal position in many cases.

Therefore, when moving the arm, it is necessary for the thoracic spine, rib cage, shoulder joint, scapula, and collarbone to move in the appropriate manner and be stabilized against the forces acting upon them. While this explanation is simplified, understanding this concept can help minimize the risk of shoulder problems resulting from incorrect exercise techniques during your workouts. With the knowledge you now possess, you can determine how to properly control your shoulder during each exercise by considering the movements you perform and the direction of the forces you need to stabilize against. The book you mentioned provides detailed explanations for the specific exercises it covers.

1.0.1

Torque

Why does a dip at 90° elbow flexion feels heavy but light in the support hold, despite the weight remaining constant? The answer lies in the concept of torque. Torque refers to the force exerted on a lever around a rotational axis. In the case of the human body, the rotational axis is a joint, the lever is a bone, and the force is applied by a contracting muscle.

The magnitude of the torque depends on two factors: the force applied and the length of the lever. The force is represented as a vector, with its length indicating its magnitude and its direction indicating its working direction. The line along which the vector is located is called the line of action. In this context, force vectors are used qualitatively to give a sense of the loads involved in an exercise, without representing actual measured or calculated forces.

The length of the lever is the normal distance between the point where the force is applied and the rotational axis. The longer the lever, the greater the resulting torque. The normal distance is the shortest connection between the force and the rotational axis, which can be found geometrically by drawing a right-angled connection between the line of action of the force and the rotational axis. The approximate position of the joint serves as the rotational axis.

In mathematical terms, considering only vertical forces and levers, the torque (M) can be calculated using the formula:

$$M = F \times r$$

Where F represents the force and r represents the lever length.

Understanding torque helps explain why a dip in the support hold feels light. In this position, the lever arm is shorter, resulting in a smaller torque despite the same force being applied. On the other hand, at 90° elbow flexion, the lever arm is longer, leading to a larger torque for the same force. This is why the support hold position feels relatively lighter, even with heavy loads. By considering torque, you can better understand the factors influencing the difficulty of exercises in different positions and optimize your training accordingly.

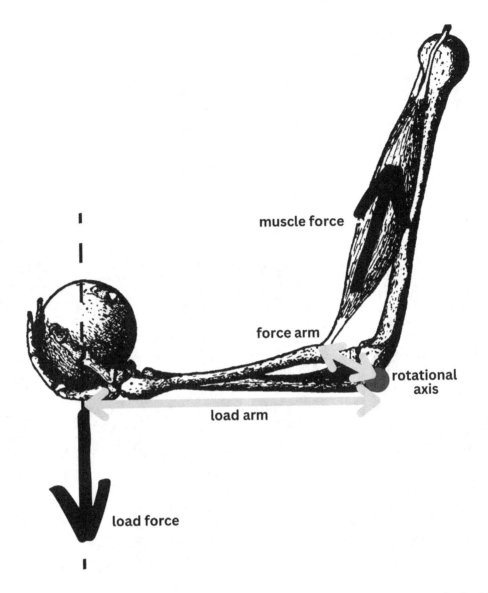

muscle force

force arm

rotational axis

load arm

load force

The ball exerts a downward force due to its weight. This force acts on the line of action (dashed line). The normal distance to the elbow joint, i.e. the connecting between the line of action and the elbow, represents the lever that the ball has on the elbow joint (load arm). To prevent the ball from extending the arm, the biceps must apply a counterforce. However, this has a much smaller lever (force arm) available for this purpose. This means that the biceps must apply a greater force than the ball exerts because it possesses a smaller lever if it wants to stabilize the forearm.

In this book, there are two important types of torques that are essential for a deeper understanding. The first type involves the torques exerted on your joints by external loads. These torques are generated when you apply loads such as your body weight, additional weights, barbells, or similar equipment during exercises. The lever is automatically created when there is a distance between the line of action of the force and the joint, which serves as the rotational axis. Levers resulting from external loads are referred to as **load arms.**

The second type of torque focuses on the internal torques acting on your joints. Whenever a muscle contracts and causes a joint to rotate, a torque is produced within the joint. The force applied by the muscle determines the strength of the contraction, and the lever is defined by the distance between the imaginary line of action of the muscle and the imaginary rotational axis of the joint. Thus, the force exerted by the muscle and the length of the associated lever determines the magnitude of the torque generated in the joint, consequently affecting the ability to move external loads. In this context, the levers created by muscles are known as **force arms.**

"Passive" load transfer in the dip support hold and active load transfer in the lower reversal point of the dip.

To analyze the dip exercise further, let's examine the load arms at different positions. First, let's focus on the support hold position. Since you're neglecting body weight for this example and considering only the additional weight, draw a line to represent the line of action of the force exerted by the additional weight (dashed line). The joints of interest are the shoulder joint and the elbow joint.

In the support hold position, both the shoulder joint and the elbow joint are in close proximity to the line of action of the force. This means that the normal distance between the rotational axes of these joints and the line of action is very small. When this distance is small, the value of "r" in the torque formula ($M = F \times r$) is very small as well. As a result, the torque exerted on these joints is minimal. This is why it feels relatively easy for you to hold the support hold position. This minimal torque is referred to as passive load conduction, although in reality, the torque is never exactly zero but rather very small.

Now, let's analyze the lower reversal point of the dip. Draw the load arms acting on the shoulder and the elbow, and you'll notice that they are no longer small. In fact, at the lower reversal point, the torque exerted on the shoulder joint is maximum because the arm is positioned at a right angle to the line of action of the force, resulting in the maximum load arm. This explains why the lower reversal point is more challenging since it is where the external load exerts the greatest torque on the shoulder joint.

It's important to note that this method of visualizing approximate ratios of acting forces using load arms works best when the movement primarily occurs in one plane (sagittal or frontal). In cases where there are significant changes in motion across different planes, a two-dimensional view in a single plane may not be sufficient, and additional considerations of other planes are necessary for a comprehensive analysis. An example of this would be a strong abduction of the elbows due to the internal rota-

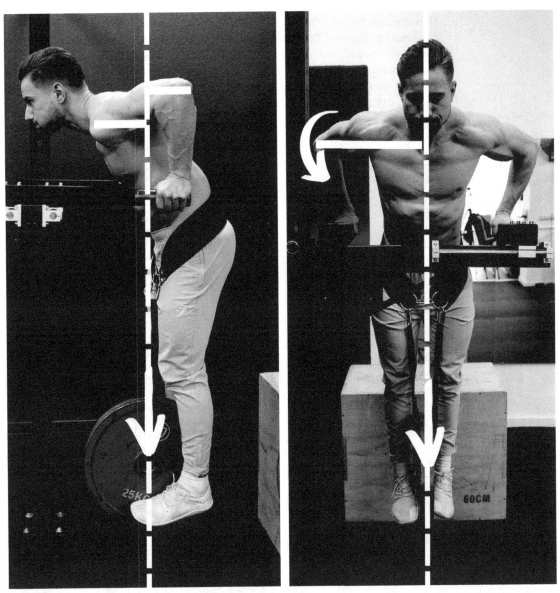

Load shifts between the planes during strong internal rotation and abduction of the elbows.

tion of the arm during a dip exercise. The position of the upper arm plays a crucial role in determining the load on the shoulder joint. When viewed sagittally (from the side), the load arm on the shoulder joint decreases as the effective length of the upper arm decreases. However, when viewed frontally (from the front), the distance from the elbow to the line of action increases, resulting in an increased torque on the adductor muscles of the upper arm in the shoulder. This leads to a shift in the load ditribution.

In this case, there is a deloading effect sagittally, while a stronger load is observed frontally. This load shift indicates that the body is attempting to compensate for a strength deficit in the deltoids and triceps, which are in a biomechanically disadvantageous position. By increasing abduction, the body aims to shift the load to the chest, which is an adductor of the arm, to better handle the load. It's important to note that this is a simplified biomechanical perspective, and caution should be exercised in drawing absolute conclusions. A comprehensive understanding requires more information and analysis.

Nevertheless, this simplified biomechanical view can be helpful in identifying strengths and weaknesses in complex multi-joint exercises such as dips or pull-ups. It allows you to identify which structures are exposed to larger torques and which structures experience reduced torques in different positions of the exercise. By identifying these patterns, you can work on strengthening your strengths and addressing your weaknesses, ultimately improving your overall strength and performance.

Example of load shifting from shoulder to elbow. In the left picture, the shoulder moves away from the line of action and the elbow does not. In the right example, the shoulder is moved closer to the line of action, and the elbow is moved away, thus shifting the load.

You have observed that during the negative phase of the dip, the torque on the shoulder joint increases, reaching its peak when the upper arm is parallel to the floor. By pushing your elbow backward during this phase, you can shift the load distribution between the shoulder and elbow joints. This can help alleviate some of the stress on the shoulder while placing more load on the elbow and wrist. This knowledge is valuable for both you and your coaches, as it allows for technique optimization and informed training decisions.

One possible approach is to focus on paused reversal points during training, which can help reduce the load shift and allow for better shoulder positioning. If you have longer upper arms, being conscious of pushing the elbow back can create a more favorable shoulder-to-elbow load ratio for you. Alternatively, adjusting your grip width to shorten the effective length of your upper arm can also be beneficial, as it reduces the need to move the elbow and allows for better utilization of the chest muscles.

The versatility of interpretation options in analyzing torque distribution provides you with valuable insights. Mastering this form of analysis allows for significant optimization of training and exercise selection within a short period of time. It's important to note that the ability of a muscle to generate and apply torque in a joint is influenced by various factors, including bone position, muscle insertion, and muscle length relative to its resting length.

Understanding and analyzing both external torques exerted by external loads and internal torques generated by your own muscles are key factors in comprehending movement. If the internal torque generated by your muscles is insufficient to counterbalance the external torque, you may struggle to perform a specific movement or maintain a particular position. It's worth noting that there are three different lever arrangements in your body, each with specific points where muscle force and external load act relative to the axis of rotation. Being aware of these lever arrangements can further enhance your understanding of movement mechanics.(15)

First-Class Lever

In this setup, the rotational axis is located between the point of application of the external load and the muscle force. You can find this placement, for example, when extending your elbow through your triceps. In this arrangement, a mechanical disadvantage occurs when the external load has a larger load arm than the muscle has a force arm. As a result, the muscle must generate significantly more force to move the external load. (15)

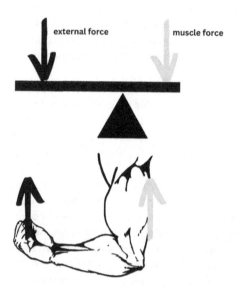

First class lever using the triceps extension as an example. The external force pulls the arm into flexion. The muscle force tries to extend the arm against the external force. In this arrangement, a mechanical disadvantage is created. The force arm of the triceps is significantly smaller than the load arm of the external load.

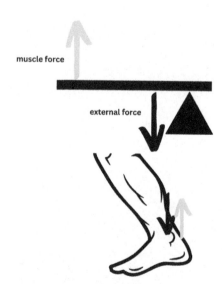

Second-Class Lever (load arm < force arm)

In this arrangement, the force application points of the muscle force and the external load are on the same side of the rotational axis. A second-class lever is additionally defined by a mechanical advantage. The mechanical advantage arises from the fact that in this setup the load arm is smaller than the force arm. Thus, in this arrangement, the muscle must apply less force than the external load to overcome it because it has a mechanical advantage due to the larger force arm. An example of this is plantar flexion in the foot, which is lifting your heel when you stand on your toes. (15)

Second class lever using plantar flexion in the foot as an example. The force arm of the calf muscles is greater than the load arm of gravity acting on the body. A mechanical advantage is created.

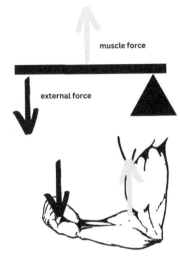

muscle force

external force

Third-Class Lever (load arm > force arm)

In this arrangement, as with the second-class lever, the force application points of the muscle force and the external load are on the same side of the rotational axis. A third-class lever is additionally defined by a mechanical disadvantage. The mechanical disadvantage arises from the fact that in this arrangement the force arm is smaller than the load arm. An example of this is arm flexion at the elbow through your biceps brachii. (15)

Third class lever using the biceps curl as an example. The external load wants to extend the arm. The muscle force of the biceps works against it. The biceps has a smaller force arm than the external load. A mechanical disadvantage is created.

1.0.2

Mechanical properties of the muscular system

Muscles are remarkable structures that have the ability to contract and generate force, converting chemical energy into mechanical energy. Understanding the mechanical properties of muscles is crucial in comprehending the force they can exert in different positions.

To delve deeper into these characteristics, let's focus on the muscle-tendon complex, which is a simplified model of a skeletal muscle that helps explain its mechanical properties. This complex comprises three key elements: the muscle itself, its associated tendon, and the muscle-tendon junction that connects the muscle to the bone. Additionally, the entire complex is surrounded by connective tissue.

When a muscle is stretched, it generates what are known as **passive muscle forces.** These forces arise from the elastic properties of the connective tissue within the muscle. You can visualize this phenomenon as a spring-like effect: when you pull the muscle apart, the connective tissue generates a force that opposes the extension. Consequently, the more a muscle is stretched, the greater the passive muscle forces generated by the stretching of the connective tissue.

Thus, the force a muscle can produce is influenced by its length. In addition to passive muscle force, muscles can generate **active muscle force** through contraction. Similar to passive force, the active muscle force also depends on the length of the muscle. This relationship is described by the **force-length relationship.** At the resting length of a muscle, the active muscle force is greatest.

If you're interested in further understanding the underlying reasons for this relationship, you can explore the theory of sliding filament, which elucidates the mechanism of muscle contraction. However, to avoid digressing too much, I won't delve further into it at this point.

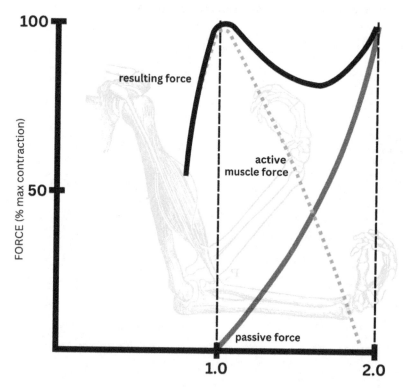

Force-length relationship of a skeletal muscle.

If a muscle undergoes lengthening or shortening from its resting length (represented by the dashed line at 1.0), the active force it can generate decreases accordingly (15). To determine the resulting total force, both the active force and passive force need to be combined. This relationship is commonly illustrated using a force-length diagram, where the y-axis represents the muscle force as a percentage and the x-axis represents the muscle length relative to the resting length (16).

However, it's important to note that the resting length of a muscle is not always at the natural joint position in the human body. For instance, the biceps muscle has a resting length at approximately 90° flexion in the elbow. Nonetheless, the key takeaway from this illustration is that a strongly shortened muscle can exert less force compared to a muscle at its resting position or a stretched muscle. This understanding becomes relevant when considering compensation movements during exercises, as the body often tries to adjust the muscle length through compensatory movements in order to regain increased force (15) (16).

Apart from fiber length, muscle force is also influenced by the contraction speed of the muscle. As the speed of muscle contraction increases, the force it can generate decreases, and conversely, at lower contraction velocities, the muscle can apply greater force. It's important to emphasize that this relationship is not linear (15).

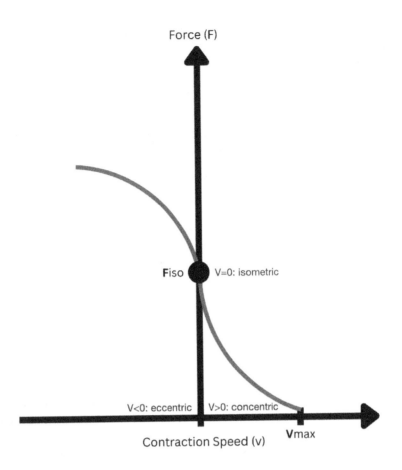

Force-velocity relation according to A.V. Hill

This **force-velocity relationship**, as described by A.V. Hill (17), gives rise to the three working modes of muscles. When the contraction speed approaches zero (V=0), the force generated by the muscle is known as **isometric force or isometric muscle work** (Fiso). In this mode, the muscle length remains constant during contraction, and the muscle force is equal to the external force acting to stretch the muscle.

As the contraction speed decreases further, becoming negative (V<0), the muscle's capacity to generate force increases. This is referred to as **eccentric muscle work**, where the muscle is stretched under load, and the external force exceeds the force the muscle can apply.

Conversely, when the contraction speed increases above zero (V>0), it is referred to as **concentric muscle work**. The faster the muscle contracts, such as when accelerating an external load, the lower the potential muscle force. Concentric muscle work involves the shortening of the muscle under load, with the muscle force exceeding the external force (15).

These principles are directly applicable in practice. For instance, when performing only the negative phase of a pull-up, you can handle significantly more weight compared to pulling yourself up from the bottom or holding the weight isometrically. Similarly, in a muscle-up where the aim is to pull up quickly, the amount of additional weight needed is considerably less than in a standard pull-up. This highlights the clear manifestation of the force-velocity relationship (15).

1.0.3

Explanation of terms

Should you come across one or the other term in the course of the book that raises question marks for you, there is a very high probability that you will find it in this list. In the following, you will find short definitions or explanations for the technical terms used in this book. The terms are sorted alphabetically for a better overview.

1.0.3.1

Anthropometrics

Your anthropometrics, or physical characteristics, can have a significant impact on your performance in weight training. Some of the factors that are affected by your anthropometrics include height and weight, build, body segment lengths, joint mobility, and size. So depending on your anthropometrics, you may have advantages or disadvantages for certain exercises, strength ranges, or other athletic qualities.

1.0.3.2

Assistance exercises

Assistance exercises are exercises that are specifically designed to strengthen certain muscle groups, techniques, movements, or joints that are important for the better execution of the main exercises. Assistance exercises can be divided according to their purpose for the main exercise. Strength assistance has the purpose of increasing the maximum strength for the main exercise, hypertrophy assistance aims to increase the muscles involved in the main exercise, and health assistance provides for reducing the risk of injury during the main exercise.

1.0.3.3

Equilibrium

Equilibrium is actually a term from physics that describes the balance condition of a system. In general, equilibrium means that there is no change in the position or motion of a system. In terms of the human body and strength sports, equilibrium refers to the condition in which a particular body part or the entire body system is in a balanced, stable, and equilibrated state.

Frequency

1.0.3.4

The training frequency tells you the frequency with which you load a particular muscle or muscle group. The training frequency usually refers to the number of training sessions for a specific muscle or muscle group or exercise per week.

Intensity (absolute)

1.0.3.5

The absolute training intensity tells you how heavy the training weight you use is in relation to your maximum weight for this exercise. This is done using a percentage of one rep max (1RM or ORM), which is the weight you can move for a maximum of one repetition.

Intensity (relative)

1.0.3.6

In contrast to absolute intensity, the relative intensity does not indicate the weight moved. The relative intensity indicates how close you are to muscle failure, i.e. the point at which you can no longer perform any technically acceptable repetitions. The relative intensity is therefore a subjective indication of how you feel the load. In weight training, various scales are used to better indicate and assess relative intensity. The most relevant are the RPE scale and the RIR scale.

Main Lift/Exercise

1.0.3.7

Main exercises are the exercises in your training plan that you train with the highest priority. Usually, the main exercises are basic exercises, competitive exercises, or in the context of calisthenics, skills that you want to learn with the highest priority. These exercises form the foundation of your training plan. All other exercises will be based on the main exercises and the related goals.

1.0.3.8 Mind Muscle Connection

The Mind Muscle Connection refers to the connection that exists between your nervous system and your muscles. It is about consciously focusing on the contraction of your muscles to gain better control, and a better "feel" towards the muscle to achieve a more effective and efficient exercise performance. With a good Mind Muscle Connection, it is possible for you to feel a muscle more consciously during an exercise and therefore to contract it more consciously.

1.0.3.9 1RM / e1RM

The 1RM represents the weight you can move for a maximum of one repetition of a given exercise. If the 1RM is preceded by an "e", it stands for the estimated 1RM. Fortunately, you don't have to estimate the e1RM, but you can calculate it relatively accurately. There are several formulas you can use. These formulas calculate the estimated e1RM resulting from a training set of an exercise. The higher the absolute intensity of the set you use to calculate an e1RM, the more accurate the result. On our website, we have provided such a calculator for you for free.

1.0.3.10 RPE

RPE stands for "Rate of Perceived Exertion" and is a scale you can use to assess your subjective effort during physical activity, especially weight training. The use of RPE in weight training refers to the use of the scale to determine the relative intensity of an exercise or training set. The scale ranges from 0 to 10, with RPE0 being "no effort" and RPE10 being "maximum effort." You can use RPEs to rate your effort during an exercise on a scale of 0 to 10, and thus decide whether you should perform the exercise with more or less weight or repetitions, depending on the relative intensity you originally planned for that exercise. RPEs allow you to subjectively evaluate your effort and adjust it accordingly.

1.0.3.11 RIR

RIR refers to the number of reps you could still do after completing the intended number of reps for a particular exercise in a set. For example, if you planned to do 8 reps for an exercise, but you are able to do 10 reps before reaching muscle failure, then you have 2 reps in reserve (RIR = 2).

1.0.3.12 RIR or RPE

You can use both RIR and RPE to determine the intensity of an exercise. Both scales have different strengths and weaknesses. RIR is a more objective measure of intensity because it relates to a specific number of repetitions. However, it can be quite difficult to evaluate the exact number of repetitions you could still do. Especially for sets with many repetitions, it becomes almost impossible. RPE, on the other hand, is a slightly more subjective measure of intensity, but that makes it more flexible because you are basing your RPE estimates on subjective ratings of effort. For example, a heavy single may have an RIR=0, but an RPE of 9. So you wouldn't be able to do another repetition but would be perfectly capable of using even more weight for a repetition. So when to use RIR or RPE depends a bit on your personal preferences and goals. Some strength athletes prefer to use RIR to get an objective measure of intensity, while others prefer to use RPE to allow for more flexibility and adaptability. So it may be helpful for you to use both concepts to gain a better understanding of the intensity of an exercise. Depending on your repetition range and goals, you can then use one scale or the other. For moderate repetition ranges of 5–12, experience has shown that RIR works very well. For low and high ranges, RIR estimation becomes very difficult and inaccurate, as there are many other psychological factors involved. For these ranges, I recommend using RPE. Whenever I explain RPE or RIR to someone, the next question I get is why you need it or even plan to use it instead of just always training for muscle failure. With that being said, especially for you as a strength athlete, it's not recommended to always train to RPE10 because it can lead to your body being overstressed. This can lead to injuries or non-functional overload. Continuously training to maximum effort, which is an RPE10 or RIR0, can also result in your body not having enough time to recover and regenerate, which can lead to a loss of performance and limitation of progress. So your strength training should include a combination of high, as well as sub-maximal intensities to sufficiently challenge your body, but at the same time give you enough time to recover and recuperate to avoid injury and overuse. Therefore, I recommend you use RPE values of 7 to 8 for most of your exercises in the strength range (< 6 reps) to ensure sufficient effort, but at the same time give you enough room to recover. However, it is important to note that everyone's body can tolerate different loads and also everyone's body reacts differently to certain loads. Therefore, it is important here that you plan your loads in such a way that you get stronger in the long run without exhausting yourself.

1.0.3.13 Range of motion

Range of motion (ROM) refers to the maximum distance a joint or set of joints can move within their physiological limits. The maximum ROM of an exercise usually requires the joint to use its full range of motion in such a way as to achieve the maximum stretch and contraction of the target muscles involved.

1.0.3.14 Sticking point

The sticking point of an exercise refers to the point in the movement where execution becomes particularly difficult or stagnates. This usually occurs when the muscles responsible for execution are working at their maximum strength capacity and are no longer able to fully move the weight. A sticking point can be due to a variety of factors, including lack of strength, pre-fatigue, poor technique, improper joint positions/leverage ratios, or even inadequate control of movement patterns.

Tempo 1.0.3.15

In weight training language, tempo refers to the speed at which you perform an exercise. The tempo is stated in terms of the time it takes to complete a single repetition. It is usually divided into three to four phases. These are the concentric phase, the eccentric phase, and the upper and lower reversal point of an exercise. The phases are given in seconds. The following notation is often used: A/B/C/D or A:B:C:D, where the letters here are examples of seconds. An "X" usually stands for execution with maximum effort, i.e. the greatest possible acceleration that is possible with this weight in this phase of the exercise.

"A" stands for the eccentric "negative' phase, "B" for the lower reversal point, "C" for the concentric "positive" phase, and "D" for the upper reversal point. So a 1/2/1/1 dip means you go down for one second, at normal tempo, pause there for 2s and go up at normal tempo and after a short reset at the upper reversal point of 1s, initiate the next repetition. Of course, it is not necessary to precisely define each exercise in all four phases.

Variations 1.0.3.16

Variations of a main exercise refer to a variation or modification of the main exercise to focus more or differently on certain muscle groups, ranges of motion, or joints. You can achieve a variation through changes in grip/stance, equipment, or speed of execution. Variations are used to improve muscle building or strength development by creating new stimuli for your body and counteracting the conditioning to the main exercise that occurs through habituation. Additionally, variations are helpful in preventing injury. Variations allow you to put less stress on certain muscle groups or joints while continuing to challenge others, thus avoiding overloading certain structures without unnecessary time off.

Valgus position

Valgus position (from Latin valgus "crooked") in the context of limbs, refers to a misalignment where the part further away from the body is pointing beyond normal from the midline. (31)

Volume

Volume, also called training volume, is the sum of your completed training. The volume is usually given in working sets per exercise per week. However, the volume is more precisely defined by the workload. This is the product of sets x weight x repetitions. This is important to understand because you can increase your volume without increasing the number of sets.

Working set

A working set is any set in your workout that is high enough in intensity to stimulate strength or muscle growth. So if you do several light warm-up sets before you start your work sets, you don't count them toward your training volume.

Athlete Timo Wunnenberg, Final Rep World Championships 2022, Photo: dedicatedsports

Weighted Calisthenic

2.
Weighted
Calisthenics

Weighted Calisthenics exists as long as the basic calisthenics exercises themselves do. It also seems natural to load an exercise when it becomes too light to set the intended stimulus. In basic terms, that's exactly what Weighted Calisthenics is, as paradoxical as the composition of those words may sound at first. You use extra weight as a tool to progressively load a calisthenics exercise. You can't scale your body weight to meet your goals, so it's only logical to load the exercises externally. This component adds to classic calisthenics training exactly what it has been missing: A meaningful, long-term scaling possibility for the intensity of exercises without changing movement patterns. Where before you had to position yourself differently or change your angle to gravity, you can now simply add 2.5kg to your weighted belt and improve. This new way of training ‚calisthenics' and especially making it comparable and measurable, led relatively quickly to new competition formats, as athletes now have the chance to compete on the additional weight moved during an exercise. The format that has gained worldwide acceptance is the so-called 1RM (one rep max) weighted calisthenics or street lifting. Athletes are divided into different weight classes and have three attempts each to move as much additional weight as possible during muscle ups, weighted dips, weighted chin/pull ups, and the barbell back squat with one repetition. The winner is the person who has moved the most weight in their weight class summed over all four lifts. This sum is called the total. Only the heaviest repetition declared valid by the competition judge is totaled. Sounds cool, and is also cool. Everyone benefits from this systematization and professionalization of the sport through competitions. New, optimized, more sustainable techniques of exercises, new training systems, and improved, optimized equipment are created. All athletes benefit from this knowledge, even those who are not interested in competitions but still want to use elements from competitive sports for their own training. For example, it can help an athlete learn a front lever faster because the knowledge from competition sports around pull ups and chin ups has allowed them to increase their performance in this area very quickly and the carryover from that could improve progression in the front lever. So if you're reading this now and thinking, I don't need competition, take the explanations and techniques of the basic exercises of competitive sports to heart anyway, because they can also have a huge added value for your training if applied correctly.

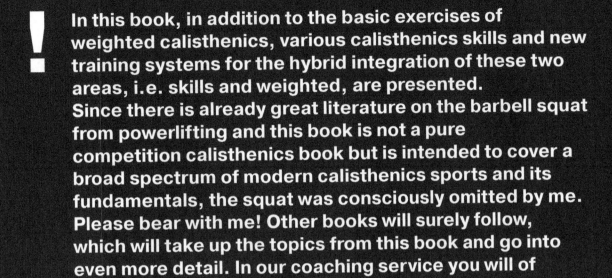

! In this book, in addition to the basic exercises of weighted calisthenics, various calisthenics skills and new training systems for the hybrid integration of these two areas, i.e. skills and weighted, are presented.
Since there is already great literature on the barbell squat from powerlifting and this book is not a pure competition calisthenics book but is intended to cover a broad spectrum of modern calisthenics sports and its fundamentals, the squat was consciously omitted by me. Please bear with me! Other books will surely follow, which will take up the topics from this book and go into even more detail. In our coaching service you will of course also get the best advice on the squat!

2.0.1

Weighted belt

All three of the following competitive exercises have one thing in common. All three are loaded via a weighted belt, also known as a dip belt. The weighted belt connects the athlete, therefore you, with the additional weight. This connection needs to be set as stable and beneficial as possible. To avoid repeating myself in the exercise chapters, let's first take a look at what is important when buying a weighted belt and how to put it on and adjust it correctly.

2.0.1.1

Load capacity

A weighted belt should be able to handle the load you plan to put on it. So when buying, pay attention to the indication of the load capacity. Keep in mind that you should plan for a certain degree of safety. Belts often break if you let off the dip or pull-up bar with the weight uncontrolled and the additional weight is therefore strongly accelerated. High peak forces act here, which is why your belt should be generously designed. However, even with a stable belt, I advise you not to let yourself off uncontrollably from training devices, safety first.

Length

2.0.1.2

The belt should be long enough so that when wrapped around the hips, it can be closed comfortably with one, or if necessary two, carabiners. However, it should also not be too long, so that it overlaps strongly in front of the body. If it is too short or significantly too long, the fabric will twist, impinge skin or otherwise interfere with training. As a guide, you can measure the distance on which the belt should sit later: This means the circumference from the pubic bone, over your pelvic bones, around your lower back, and back to the other pubic bone. If the length of the belt is approximately the same as the measured length, it will fit you well. A few centimeters difference is not a problem at all. You can move the belt a little on your hips and make it tighter or looser by using different closure techniques. However, too much deviation is not recommended.

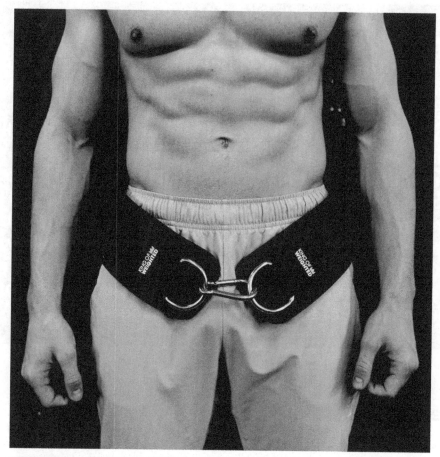

Optimal belt length (King Of Weighted belt L with 95cm length)

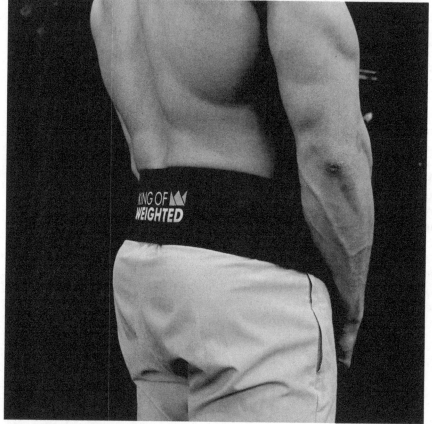

Optimum belt width

| 2.0.1.1 | **Width** | **Chain/Rope** | 2.0.1.4 |

A belt should be wide enough so that the load on your hips is well distributed without the material cutting into your skin too much. If possible, avoid belts with a large back pad. The load should be distributed laterally on your hips and not concentrated on your lower back. This can make it harder for you to stabilize your hips properly during pull ups and dips because the belt pushes you into a hollow back via the large back pad. In some competitions, the width of the approved belt is standardized. This is because the belt is used to check the depth of the hips during a dip. For this to work fairly for each athlete, all belts must be the same width.

The chain should be long enough to allow your desired weight positions. A length-adjustable chain is advantageous. Three carabiners are optimal for individual adjustment and easy handling (1x close, 1x per end of the chain). Chains made of nylon are much more comfortable and easier to handle than steel chains. They make less noise in the gym and the whole belt is easier to store. If you train with very wide plates, you should plan with a longer chain than if you train with thin steel plates. A good orientation here is a 1.10m–1.70m chain length.

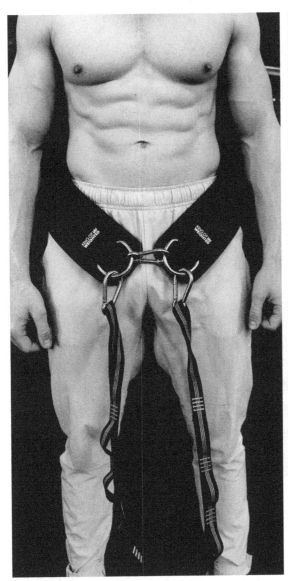 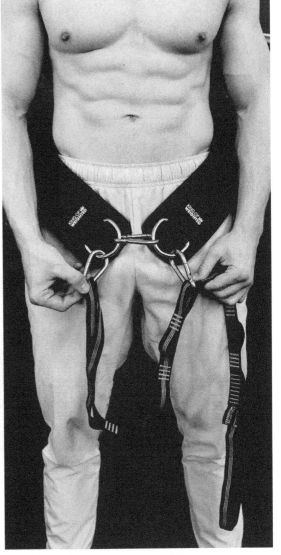

Adjustment possibilities of a daisy chain with three carabiners

2.0.1.5   **Belt position**

As already mentioned, the belt should sit on your hips. The belt rests on the side of your pelvic bones and your back at the transition from your lumbar spine to your butt. Close the belt in front of your body with a carabiner. Make sure the belt is centered in front of your body and sits the same height on the left and right sides. The same applies to the additional weight attached to it. This is the only way to ensure symmetrical weight allocation later on throughout the exercise.

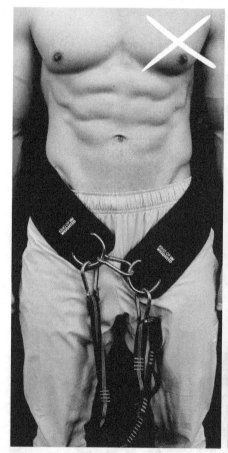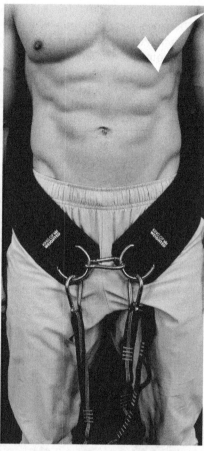

Centered vs. uncentered arrangement

! **You are still looking for a suitable belt? I developed the King Of Weighted belt, especially for weighted calisthenics athletes. It offers you all the important adjustment options, is light, comfortable, and can be loaded up to 300 kg. You can find more information about this product at www.kingofweighted.shop.**

THE NEW COMPETITION STANDARD.

Forget the metal chain. Forget heavy, inflexible, and inconvenient belts. It's time to introduce the next generation. The King Of Weighted Belt.

The King Of Weighted Belt is designed for weighted calisthenics athletes. It comes with three carabiners and a chain that is long enough to hang the weights between your feet. The belt can hold more than 300kg while being super light and flexible. It is available in different lengths to guarantee the best fit for all athletes.

Order your belt at
www.kingofweighted.shop
Free worldwide shipping

Weighted Dips

2.1
Weighted Dips

In this book, you will look at the dip as a competitive exercise in the Weighted Calisthenics-1RM sport. To classify exercise executions as ‚useful' or ‚not so useful', the context and the goal you are pursuing with this execution are crucial. So, in order for you to make classifications in this book, the goal of moving maximum weight with one repetition is defined. So the form that will be discussed below is optimized for just that function. This does not mean that other executions of the dip are automatically worse or less useful. It is the context that decides.

In order for athletes to compete in a standardized manner, there must be a set of rules that establish minimum requirements for exercise execution. Only with this, it is possible to compare the performance of different athletes. In Weighted Calisthenics, a very young sport, a final definition with international scope has not yet been reached. This book is based on the current European standard. The competition rules that are important for you are quoted from the current Final Rep rulebook of the DACH Championship 2023:

"Once the first signal ("Platform ready!") is given, the athlete may step onto the platform. The athlete fastens the weight belt to the hip. Now the athlete moves on the box and then takes the start position with arms fully extended and hips almost fully extended. It is allowed to keep the legs slightly bent or fully extended as long as the knee angle changes minimally during the attempt. The start position is considered to be taken as soon as the athlete has fully extended the elbows (180° joint angle) and is in a support hold. It is not allowed to initiate the attempt during the swing. The spotters can therefore help the athlete to stop the weight during the support hold on request. The athlete waits for the start signal ("Go!") and can perform the attempt after the given signal. The arms must be bent so that the highest point of the back shoulder is visibly lower than the highest point of the elbow. The highest point from the bottom of the belt must be at least level with the highest point of the bar. Wearing light or other colored tops is recommended for better visibility. If both the depth of the shoulder and the hip are not clearly visible due to very dark clothing, in case of doubt the attempt will be scored as "No Rep". The athlete then stretches the arms until the start position has been reached again with the arms fully extended. As soon as the athlete reverses the movement and finds himself back in the start position, the athlete must wait for the signal "Box!" to finish the attempt. After the last signal is given, the athlete may climb back onto the box. The spotters help to lift the weight discs back onto the box. The attempt is now finished. The judges then decide if the attempt was valid and the athlete is allowed to leave the platform.

1. **Fail: The athlete does not complete the attempt with arms fully extended.**

---

2. **Bent Arms: The athlete begins the dip with bent arms. In certain cases of anatomically limited mobility (e.g. not being able to extend the elbows through 180°), it is up to the athlete to tell and show this to the judges before entering the platform for the first attempt.**

---

3. **Depth Shoulder: The athlete does not reach the required depth with the back shoulder.**

---

4. **Depth Hip: The athlete does not reach the required depth with the hip. Furthermore, the valid depth of the hip and shoulder must be reached before initiating the concentric movement phase.**

---

5. **Kipping/Kicking: The athlete generates momentum with an excessive tilting motion in the pelvis or with a kicking motion of the legs, which helps to finish the attempt. A minimal change in knee and hip angle that does not give the athlete an advantage is allowed.**

---

6. **Loss of Control: The athlete falls into an excessive hyperextension of the spine and loses control of the weight. If the box is touched before the last signal ("Box!"), the attempt is considered invalid.**

---

7. **Downward Movement: the direction of the movement reverses before it is completed. A short pause during the attempt is allowed.**

---

8. **Signal: The athlete misses or disregards a signal from the judges.(1)"**

valid shoulder height

valid hip/belt height

Valid hip and shoulder height

Your task as a competitive athlete is to find a form that allows you to move maximum additional weight in a safe way, in accordance with the rules. To do this, you take the classic execution of the dip as a basis to optimize this technique step by step concerning the competition requirements. The classic dip, as you see it printed in thousands, performed on YouTube and Instagram, is usually performed like this:

1. **The chest is pushed out in the support hold, and the shoulders are pulled back and down**

2. **The legs are bent and crossed.**

3. **The movement is initiated downward, with simultaneous flexion in the elbow and extension in the shoulder joint.**

4. **During the downward movement, the shoulders are guided into a slight elevation to allow for greater extension in the shoulder joint.**

5. **The dip is performed to about 90° flexion in the elbow joint.**

6. **After the lower reversal point, press back to the starting position.**

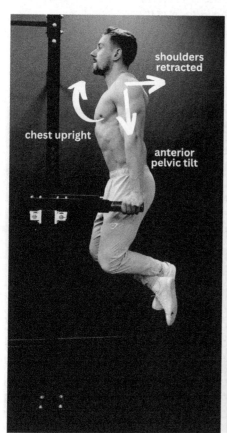
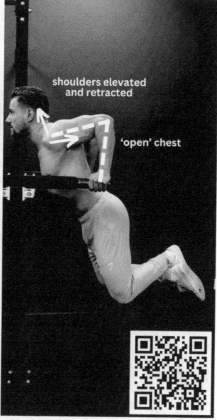

Common execution of dips

Throughout this book, you will embark on a journey to optimize the dip exercise specifically for your 1RM weighted calisthenics goals. Building upon the foundation of the standard technique, your aim will be to fine-tune the exercise, ensuring that you can lift the maximum amount of additional weight while minimizing the risk involved. This entails refining the range of motion to meet the precise requirements of the competition. In each step of the process, you will delve into the reasons behind these modifications and explore the advantages they bring to enhance your performance.

2.1.1

Expansion to compression

One of the initial adjustments you'll make to tailor the dip for the requirements of the 1RM sport is the compression of the "proud chest" or expanded chest during the downward movement. To achieve this, you engage your abdominal muscles and retract and depress your ribs. By reducing the angulus infrasternalis, which is the angle between the left and right rib cartilages at the bottom of the sternum, you slightly lower your sternum in the starting position of the dip (2). Simultaneously, your shoulders move forward into protraction, and your core muscles become tense. This particular position is often referred to as the hollow body position in the dip.

To familiarize yourself with this posture, stand up and take a deep breath, then exhale slowly for approximately 10 seconds. As you exhale and compress your ribcage, you will notice a lowering of your ribs and sternum, a tightening sensation in your abdomen, and a slight backward rotation of your pelvis (posterior pelvic tilt). Later on, you will assume this compressed position in the starting position of the dip to establish a stable foundation for initiating the negative phase.

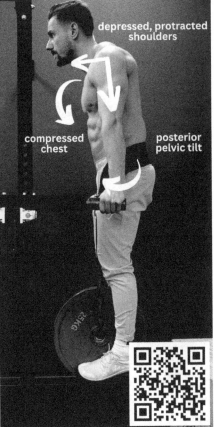

Optimized start position of the dip (hollow body position).

47

2.1.2

Constant depression and protraction

The second significant modification you make in comparison to the "classic" dip is the emphasis on anchoring the shoulder in a depressed position throughout the entire range of motion, in addition to protraction. The aim here is not to completely eliminate shoulder elevation but rather to minimize it as much as possible. By depressing the shoulder blades, you greatly limit the potential extension of your arms. You can easily test this yourself by actively pushing your shoulder down and then attempting to extend your arm backward without allowing the shoulder to elevate again. You will notice a significant reduction in the range of motion compared to extension with unanchored shoulder blades.

To achieve a stable depression, you need to engage your chest and latissimus muscles, generating strong tension. This tension in the chest typically results in a slight protraction of the shoulder. Additionally, try to activate your serratus anterior muscles by gently spreading your shoulder blades apart. This action promotes the compression strategy and creates more tension in the chest and shoulder area, facilitating better control and deceleration of heavy loads during the negative phase of the movement.

The incorporation of compression and constant shoulder depression introduces you to important changes with several benefits:

Alignment of the chest muscles in the direction of movement

a. The lowered sternum alignment during the downward movement of the dip directs the pectoral muscles in the direction of motion. This alignment enables better deceleration and control of the negative movement by engaging the muscle fibers of the lower and middle chest. The protracted position further enhances this effect.

b. By sinking the sternum and maintaining shoulder depression throughout the negative movement, you achieve the required shoulder depth (rear shoulder below elbow) while significantly reducing shoulder extension. This means that you attain the necessary shoulder height with less vertical movement of the weight and a reduced range of motion in your shoulder.

c. The compression maintained during the negative movement ensures that your pelvis remains in a posterior pelvic tilt. This prevents excessive arching of the lower back during the negative phase. As a result, the hips move backward and downward, facilitating a very vertical weight path. The greater the additional weight relative to your body weight, the more vertical the path of the weight will be, optimizing your movement efficiency.

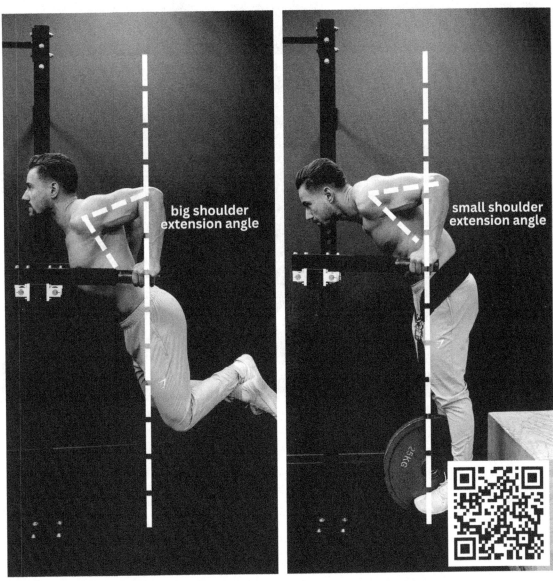

Optimized dip with less extension in the shoulder at nearly the same dip depth and a very vertical weight path.

big horizontal movement

more vertical weight path

Horizontal movement of the legs/additional weight during the negative movement and the possible resulting pendulum movement.

By transitioning from ribcage expansion to ribcage compression during the negative movement of the dip, you have effectively achieved a reduction in the active range of motion while maintaining sufficient dip depth. This change has resulted in a decreased angle of shoulder extension, thereby reducing the load on the active and passive structures of your shoulder in the final position and, consequently, the risk of dip-related injuries. By minimizing shoulder extension, you also reduce the stretching of the shoulder capsule, reducing the potential for injury to that structure. Additionally, the constant shoulder depression and slight protraction contribute to decreased activity in the upper trapezius and increased activity in the lower trapezius and serratus anterior. This increased activation promotes a stable shoulder and scapula position, thereby reducing the risk of impingement injuries (3).

Furthermore, by maintaining a vertical path of motion for the additional weight, you have eliminated the backward movement of the legs, allowing for a relatively straight downward weight path. This modification minimizes pendulum motion, enhancing your control over the movement. A vertical weight path not only reduces the distance the weight travels but also minimizes the sagittal distance between the weight, your own center of mass, and your shoulder joint. This reduction in distances translates to decreased torque on your shoulder joint. Particularly at the lower reversal point, where the distance is already maximized due to the position of the upper arm, it is important to avoid any further increase through pendulum-like movements.

The role of the chest has undergone a significant change with the new technique. In a traditional dip, the emphasis is on stretching the chest by pulling the shoulders back and expanding the ribcage, similar to the bench press. This aims to maximize the growth stimulus for the chest muscles. However, with the optimized technique, the goal is to avoid excessive changes in the length of the chest muscles. Instead, the chest becomes one of the primary stabilizers during the dip. In the negative movement, along with the front shoulder, the chest's role is to control the angle between the upper arm and the torso, allowing only the necessary range of motion as dictated by the competition rules. As a result, the active range of motion of the chest is reduced. However, it's important to note that due to the compression technique, more chest muscle fibers are aligned in the direction of movement, leading to increased activation and stimulation of the chest muscles. This optimized technique also allows for greater weight to be moved during the exercise. Unfortunately, there is currently no available data on the specific extent to which the stimulus to the chest is reduced, increased, or remains the same when comparing different variations of the dip. However, it's worth mentioning that this discussion may be less relevant to you as a strength athlete, as the primary objective of performing the exercise in a competitive setting is to maximize performance rather than solely focusing on maximizing chest growth. If your goal is chest hypertrophy, there is nothing wrong with adapting the technique to incorporate more chest stretch and provide additional growth stimulus as needed. For more information on variations of the weighted dip, please refer to the "Variations for Weighted Dips" section.

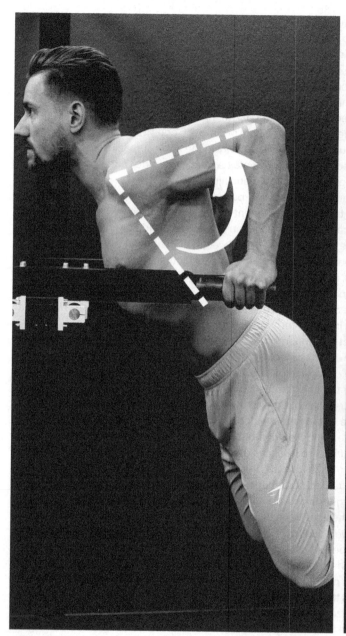
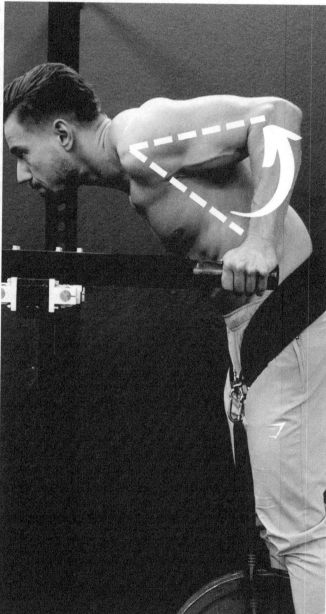

Reduced stretch on the pectoral muscles due to a reduction in shoulder extension.

2.1.3

Compression to expansion

With your optimized dip technique, you have reached the bottom reversal point of the movement. In order to perform a valid repetition in competition, you need to return from the bottom reversal point to the starting position. To achieve this, you must reverse the movement of the negative phase. This entails transitioning gradually from compression back to expansion. As you press upward, you intentionally extend your thoracic spine by lifting your sternum. Instead of maintaining compression, you consciously straighten yourself during the ascent.

This results in the following advantages:

a. **By expanding the rib cage, the chest muscles undergo a stretch, which optimizes their force-length relationship. This increased stretch allows the chest muscles to generate more force during the positive phase of the dip, leading to a more effective execution.**

b. **The expansion of the rib cage, occurring after the lower reversal point, reduces the normal distance between the line of force from the additional weight and the shoulder joint. This reduction in distance decreases the torque exerted on the shoulder joint by the added weight, resulting in reduced stress on the active and passive structures of the joint. This transition from compression to expansion allows for the elevation of the chest and shoulders, facilitating the opening of the elbow joint with minimal vertical movement of the additional weight. As a result, the shoulder joint is capable of moving more efficiently than the additional weight within the same time frame.**

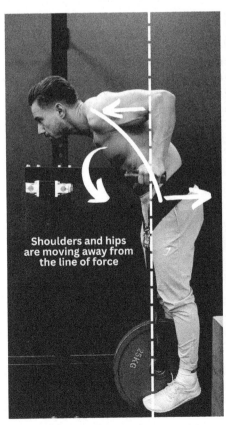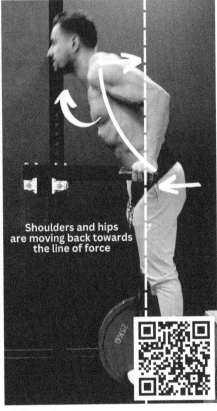

Expanding the ribcage after the lower reversal point.

So you can efficiently move to a more favorable position by straightening your chest after the bottom reversal point. This action helps to reduce the leverage of the external load and enhance the strength effect of your chest muscles. In the context of weighted calisthenics, the terms "open" (expansion) and "closed" (compression) chest are often used to describe this concept. They essentially refer to the same idea. To successfully complete a repetition, you need to extend your spine, bring your hips forward, and fully extend your elbows. Once you have achieved full extension at the elbows, you can return to the starting position. To accomplish this, utilize the compression technique once again, bringing yourself and your shoulders back into an optimal position.

2.1.4

Common weighted dip mistakes

It is important to acknowledge that mistakes are common when performing complex exercises like the weighted dip, both in training and in competition. To help you identify and address these mistakes, here is a list of common errors to watch out for. By recognizing and correcting these mistakes through proper training, you can improve your technique in the short to medium term:

2.1.4.1   **No downward movement of the hip**

Newcomers to the sport of 1RM calisthenics often struggle with the technique, often swinging between two extremes. One common error is overly focusing on compression, causing the movement in the spine to compensate excessively for the movement in the hips (vertically) and shoulders. Consequently, the additional weight barely moves, and the hips remain stationary. If you find yourself in this situation, ensure that during the negative movement, you maintain shoulder extension by bringing the elbows backward and keeping your upper body more upright. The highest point of your belt from the bottom should be at least level with the highest point of the bar. (1)

"Jackknife" dip with insufficient hip height due to too much crunching

2.1.4.2   **Vertical movement initiation**

Not initiating the movement with a slight lowering of the sternum inevitably results in increased scapular elevation, leading to a greater range of motion in shoulder extension. This inefficient technique poses a higher risk of injury when dealing with additional weight that exceeds the conditioned range of motion. To address this issue, it is important to actively anchor your shoulders in a depressed position during the initiation of the movement and focus on gently lowering your sternum as

you descend. Imagine actively preventing excessive stretching of your chest during the initial phase. Incorporating controlled and slow negative movements into your training can enhance your perception of the correct technique. Additionally, if you find that your current dip bar lacks sufficient frontal space for compression and forward-downward movement initiation, it is advisable to seek an alternative option.

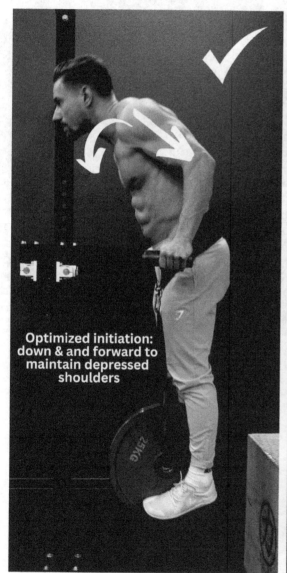 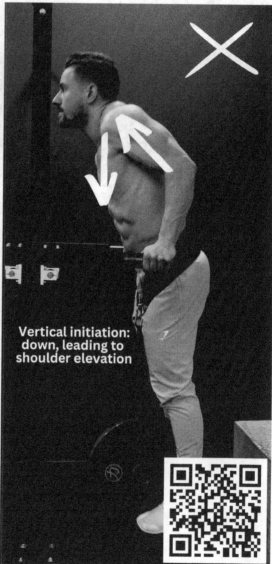

Vertical motion initiation (right) compared with optimized motion initiation (left).

Leaning forward instead of compressing

Athletes often exhibit a preference for either expansion or compression strategies, although this tendency is typically subconscious (2). Athletes who lean towards an expansion strategy often encounter difficulties in adopting and maintaining proper compression. Consequently, compensation occurs during the negative movement. Rather than compressing, these athletes lean excessively forward and hyperextend their spines, guiding the hips backward instead of downward in an effort to limit the range of motion imposed by the weight. This, however, increases the leverage of the additional weight on the shoulders due to the greater normal distance. Moreover, the range of motion for the positive movement becomes excessive as the shoulders are pushed far back and the hips are brought forward. To rectify this, incorporating slow and controlled negative movements, as well as positive movements, can aid in acquiring the correct movement pattern and effectively engaging the abdominal muscles. Additionally, athletes experiencing significant compression issues are advised to include various compression exercises, such as Knee/Leg Raises or Hollow Body Holds, in their training regimen. (2)

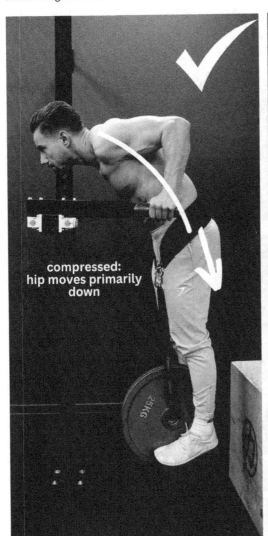
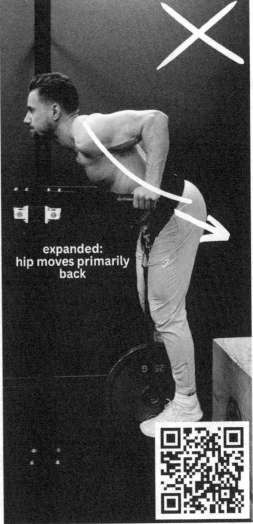

compressed:
hip moves primarily
down

expanded:
hip moves primarily
back

Reduction of the weight path through a hollow back instead of compression.

2.1.4.4

Loss of depression/compression around the lower reversal point

As the weight of the dip increases, maintaining shoulder depression and compression around the lower reversal point becomes more challenging. When compression and/or depression are lost at the bottom reversal point, the angle between the upper arm and torso opens up. This premature elevation of the ribcage occurs due to the forward movement of the additional weight. As a result, the weight descends in proportion to the change in spine length. A loss of depression has a similar effect, with the weight moving downward as the shoulder rises. It is crucial to avoid unintended, additional range of motion at the heaviest point of the dip, where the shoulder experiences the greatest leverage (upper arm approximately parallel to the floor). Athletes with relatively weak pectoral muscles often exhibit this type of movement compensation. The maintenance of depression and compression relies heavily on the tension in your chest. If the chest fails to sustain this tension at the reversal point, expansion and/or elevation may occur. To address this, incorporating paused dips at the lower reversal point can be beneficial. Additionally, for long-term improvement in chest strength, it is recommended to focus on chest-dominant assistance exercises.

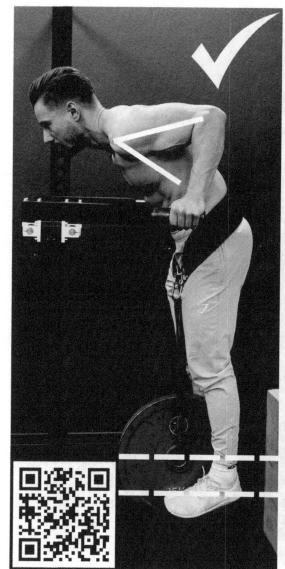

Loss of compression/depression around the lower reversal point.

Too early expansion

At the lower reversal point of the dip, applying the expansion strategy prematurely, before extending your elbows slightly, can lead to unfavorable outcomes. The angle between your upper arm and torso opens too early, and although your sternum straightens, it doesn't rise sufficiently. While this approach may increase chest strength potential, it also increases leverage on the shoulder without adequate upward movement. Consequently, you are unable to fully benefit from the expansion strategy, and may even create a mechanical disadvantage.

Several factors contribute to this issue. It could be a matter of timing, which can improve with practice and conscious training of the technique's timing. Specifically, you might be transitioning from compression to expansion too soon after the bottom reversal point. Additionally, a weak chest could play a significant role. Insufficient chest strength may cause your body to enter the expansion phase prematurely, as it lacks the necessary support for lengthening. Another possible factor is a deficit in triceps strength. If the triceps fail to sufficiently extend the elbow at the inversion point, the body may compensate by initiating chest expansion.

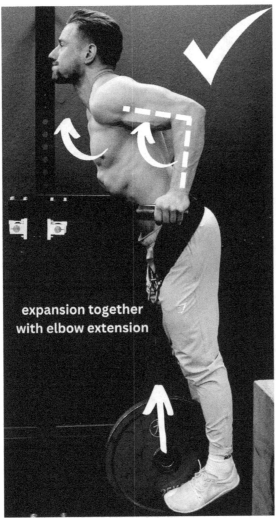
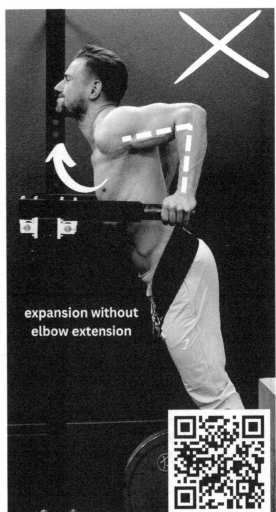

expansion together with elbow extension

expansion without elbow extension

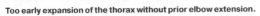
Too early expansion of the thorax without prior elbow extension.

2.1.4.6

Hyperextension of the lumbar spine

During the positive phase of the dip, if you observe the movement from the front, you will notice that you are not only performing shoulder flexion but also shoulder adduction as you ascend. The chest and latissimus muscles primarily contribute to shoulder adduction and depression. When dealing with maximum loads or higher levels of chest fatigue, the influence of the latissimus becomes more prominent. This can result in a more pronounced hyperextension of the lumbar spine.

The latissimus muscle is connected to the pelvis through the thoracolumbar fascia. When it contracts forcefully, it can extend or hyperextend the spine and tilt the pelvis forward. However, it is important to minimize excessive hyperextension. As the lumbar spine hyperextends, the center of gravity shifts further away from the shoulder in the sagittal plane.

Therefore, you are increasing the load on your shoulder at a time when you may not want additional stress on the shoulder joint. To provide resistance for your latissimus, it is crucial to ensure that your hips remain stable. You can achieve this by re-engaging and maintaining tension in your abdominal muscles after straightening the sternum during the upward movement. This stabilizes the hips and allows the latissimus to provide support without the disadvantage of excessive lumbar spine hyperextension.

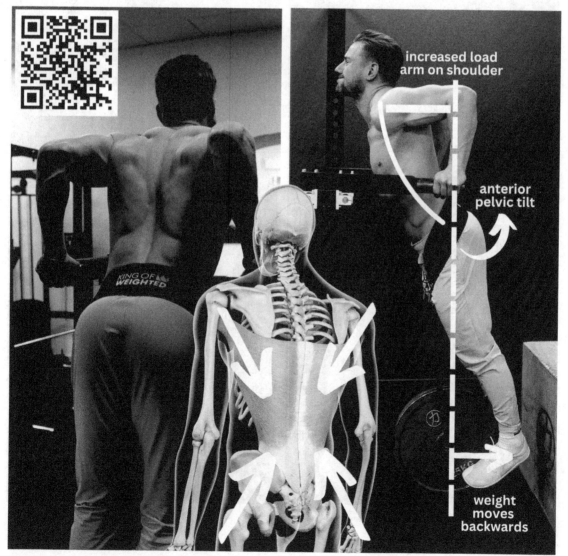

increased load arm on shoulder

anterior pelvic tilt

weight moves backwards

Hyperextension of the lumbar spine by the latissimus.

Strong shoulder internal rotation

Compensation movements tend to emerge when dealing with heavy loads or significant fatigue. As you initiate the positive movement after the lower reversal point, the body employs internal rotation to abduct the arm, effectively reducing the load arm on the shoulder joint, particularly around the sticking point at approximately a 90° elbow angle. This transition shifts the movement from the sagittal plane to the frontal plane, transforming shoulder flexion into adduction. In this position, the partial shift into adduction proves to be a more efficient strategy, as both the triceps and shoulder can exert less torque on elbow flexion and shoulder flexion when the posture becomes more upright. The chest assumes a crucial role from this point onward, ensuring the successful completion of the dip through the adduction of the upper arm. Thus, we emphasize that internal rotation of the upper arm, accompanied by a slight resultant abduction, is an effective strategy to overcome the sticking point after the lower reversal point.

However, a problem arises when excessive internal rotation and abduction are induced in the upper arm. Therefore, the dosage of these movements becomes crucial. Failure to limit internal rotation results in shifting the sticking point to the frontal plane. The distance between the elbow and the line of force from the additional weight reaches its maximum. Consequently, your triceps and front shoulder find themselves in an unfavorable position, while your chest experiences maximal (or excessive) loading. Essentially, you replace one sticking point with another, albeit with a significantly higher risk of injury. The shoulder becomes more challenging to depress, the subacromial space becomes more constricted, and your overall body position becomes unstable, as you struggle to compensate for horizontal movements caused by the additional weight. Therefore, it is essential to allow the appropriate amount of internal rotation while maintaining a controlled approach that is sufficiently high to avoid extreme positions.

 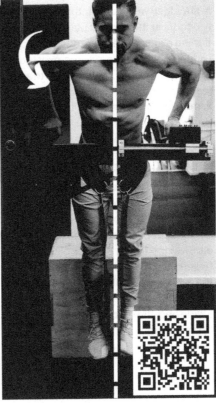

Reducing the effective upper arm length by a slight internal rotation (left) is beneficial. Excessive internal rotation (right) can force a new ‚sticking point' due to the strong abducted position of the upper arm.

Individualization
of the technique

If you take a closer look at the top ten ranked Weighted Calisthenics athletes in the world, you'll notice that each athlete employs a unique dip technique. This is because they have different body characteristics such as anthropometry, muscle development, centers of gravity, muscle attachments, and orientations. Therefore, it wouldn't make sense for every athlete to use the exact same technique given their individual circumstances. Now, let's explore how you can personalize your dip technique based on your specific needs. To understand how you can adapt your technique, let's consider some key parameters that can be customized. The first factor to consider is your grip width, which, similar to adjusting your stance in a squat, can affect the load distribution and target different areas of your body. So, how does grip width impact your dip? Let's examine two extreme scenarios: an extremely narrow grip and an extremely wide grip.

2.1.5.1

Narrow grip

When using a narrow grip, approximately shoulder-width apart, the dip primarily occurs in the sagittal plane. This positioning aligns the elbows and shoulders, reducing the outward force exerted by the added weight. As a result, there is less stress on shoulder adduction, which is the movement required to counteract this force. This narrow grip decreases the stability demands on the shoulder, allowing for easier compensation for movements of the added weight in the sagittal plane. In the frontal plane, when examining the two-dimensional force and load arms, it becomes evident that a narrow grip minimizes the load on the elbows due to the shorter distance between the arms and the body. However, the situation is different in the sagittal plane. Visualize the dip from above: with a wide grip, the elbows are positioned far from the body at the bottom reversal point, resulting in a shorter upper arm

length when viewed from the side. On the other hand, a narrow grip keeps the elbows closer to the body, resulting in a longer upper arm length. With a close grip, the shoulder undergoes a larger range of motion, and the load arm on the shoulder in the sagittal plane is maximized. This makes the dip movement predominantly flexion-based. As a consequence, the chest cannot effectively assist in extending the arms and facilitating dip straightening through upper arm adduction. The movement becomes more reliant on the shoulder and triceps, shifting the dominance away from the chest. For beginners, a relatively tight grip is more suitable as the sagittal plane's dominant movement aids in shoulder stabilization and reduces the risk of impingement injuries due to the lower abduction of the arm.

Dip with a narrow grip (shoulder width).

2.1.5.2   **Wide grip**

When using a very wide grip, the dynamics of the dip change. The abducted position of the arm causes a significant shortening of the upper arm in the sagittal plane, reducing both the load arm on the shoulder and the range of motion for dipping. In the frontal plane, a larger force component pushes your arms outward, resulting in a greater challenge in shoulder adduction. Additionally, the abduction angle of the arms creates a force that acts on the shoulder at that specific angle, making it more difficult to maintain stable depression and protraction in the shoulder compared to a tight grip.

Furthermore, the arm abduction necessitates more shoulder internal rotation during the downward phase of the dip. To achieve sufficient depth, you will need to allow for more shoulder elevation compared to a narrower grip. This increased range of motion in the shoulder contributes to the wider grip feeling more challenging to stabilize and maintain control.

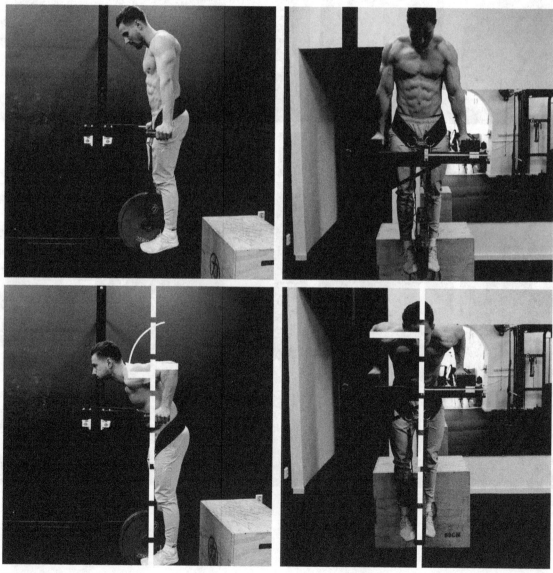

Dip with a very wide grip.

wide grip with more upright posture

narrow grip with more compression

Upright posture and reduced shoulder path due to the wider grip (left) compared to the narrow grip (right).

With a wide grip, the load arm on the elbows becomes greater in the frontal plane. This places increased demand on the arm adductors. However, as you become stronger, the reduced range of motion that comes with a wider grip can work to your advantage, as stability is likely to no longer be a limiting factor. The upper arm becomes shorter and the overall posture more upright, resulting in a smaller shoulder path.

The wide grip offers the advantage of allowing your chest to provide better support for extending your arms and straightening your body. With your hands fixed, the chest can assist in elbow extension through traction in adduction. The effectiveness of this assistance depends on the chest's ability to adduct and contribute to arm extension. This effect is less pronounced with a tighter grip. Therefore, the wide grip is stronger but also carries more risk. To determine the appropriate width, you can use a guideline of forearm length plus 3–5 fingers when your hand is outstretched.

2.1.5.3   Elbow position

In the sagittal plane, you have the ability to redistribute the load between your shoulder joint and elbow joint by adjusting the position of your elbow. Moving the elbow backward reduces the load on the shoulder joint while increasing the load on the elbow joint. This adjustment also decreases the required compression and results in a slightly more upright posture.

From a frontal plane perspective, you can position your elbow inward or outward relative to the wrist. Outward movement of the elbow shortens the effective length of the upper arm in the sagittal plane, reducing the lever on your shoulder. This allows you to compensate for the potential drawbacks of a tighter grip. Additionally, it promotes slight internal rotation of the shoulder and abduction of the upper arm, creating a better angle for the chest to exert pulling force. Conversely, moving the elbows inward over the wrists increases the effective length of the upper arm sagittally. Although this position stretches the chest more, its fibers are not optimally aligned with the direction of motion. In this position, the chest and latissimus have limited ability to assist in elbow ex-

Displacement of the load on the elbow in the sagittal plane (right).

tension through adduction. Therefore, an excessive form this position does not offer any significant advantages and should be avoided.

In summary, from a frontal perspective, your elbow should be positioned above or slightly outside your wrists, while from a sagittal perspective, it should be above or slightly behind your wrist.

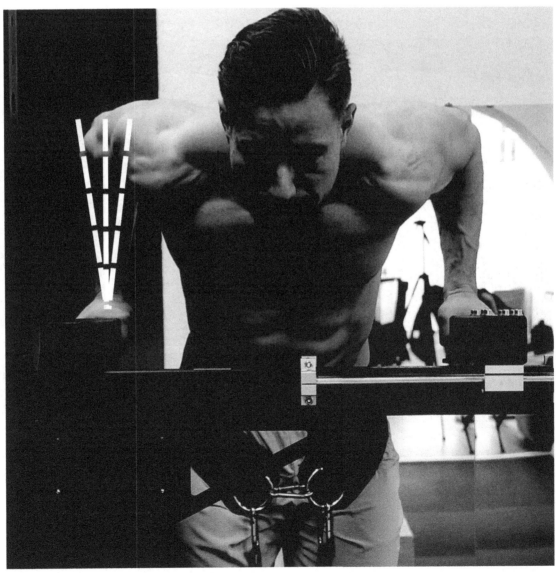

Range of good elbow position in relation to the wrist (frontal)

2.1.5.4   **Degree of compression**

As mentioned earlier, the trajectory of your shoulder joint in the sagittal plane and the movement of your hip are important factors to consider. It's crucial to minimize both of these paths for optimal technique. By "minimal," I mean the smallest range of motion that still adheres to the competition rules. This approach maximizes the efficiency of each repetition. One way to control these paths is by adjusting the level of compression during the downward movement. Increasing compression, which involves tilting your sternum towards the floor, causes your shoulders to move forward and your hips to move backward. Simultaneously, greater compression limits the depth of your hip movement. The goal is to find a balance or "sweet spot". You should aim for a technique that minimizes the trajectory of your shoulder joint while achieving the necessary hip depth. In other words, you want to maintain an upright position at the bottom reversal point while keeping the movement of the added weight to a minimum. It's important to note that more compression does not necessarily equate to better technique.

Ascending upright posture with increasing vertical range of motion, but decreasing horizontal range of motion from left to right.

Weight path

The most direct path for the movement of the added weight is a vertical one. This implies that the weight should ideally move in a vertical trajectory. However, this statement is only partially true. The added weight and your body together form a single object that needs to be moved. This object has multiple partial centers of gravity and a total body center of gravity. For an efficient dip, it is important for the overall body center of gravity to move as vertically as possible. As the weight becomes heavier and its proportion to your body weight increases, the total body center of gravity will be closer to the added weight. This means that the technique slightly changes as the weight increases. When performing heavy dips, it becomes more crucial to maintain a vertical path for the weight. The swinging motion of the weight becomes harder to regulate and control with increased weight, and therefore, a vertical path is preferred. However, it's important to note that when using smaller added weights, a slight horizontal movement is natural and doesn't necessarily need to be prevented.

When it comes to individualizing the technique, you can refer to the following list as a starting point. However, keep in mind that it is just a guideline, and you should continue to refine and optimize your technique based on your own needs. One of the key factors to consider is the length of your arms, as it can greatly influence your technique. Whether your arms are long or short, you can choose a technique that capitalizes on your strengths and compensates for any weaknesses you may have.

 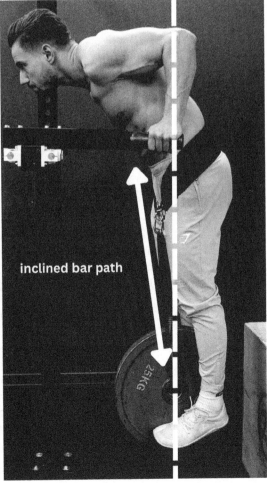

vertical bar path   inclined bar path

Weight path at 79kg body weight with 107.5kg (left) and 50kg additional weight (right).

2.1.5.6 **Short upper arm**

If you have a shorter upper arm, opting for a tighter grip (approximately forearm length with fingers extended plus maximum 1-2 fingers) can be beneficial. This allows you to maintain a relatively upright posture and requires less compression. Since the short upper arm naturally limits the range of motion, excessive compression is not required. Throughout the dip, you can aim to keep your elbows relatively vertical above your hands.

2.1.5.7 **Long upper arm**

If you have longer upper arms, you should choose a wider grip (forearm length with fingers extended plus 3-5 fingers), so that you can somewhat relativize the strong compression required due to the long upper arm. If you want to choose a tighter grip for sensible reasons, let your up-

per arm move backward during the negative movement (wrist ulnar abduction). A slight shoulder internal rotation can also help you correct the disadvantages of your long upper arm, especially with tighter grips.

You can also adjust your technique in favor of stronger movement patterns. If you are very strong in adduction or rather flexion of the shoulder, you can adjust the dip through grip width and elbow position.

Flexion dominant **2.1.5.8**

Choose a tight grip with the upper arms rather close to the body.

Adduction dominant **2.1.5.9**

Choose a wider grip and/or slightly abducted upper arms.

2.1.6

Breathing

Proper breathing during the dip is crucial to maximizing performance. When performing heavy repetitions, it is important to use light compressive breathing to support core stability. This involves inhaling into your stomach at the start position, followed by closing the glottis, pressing your diaphragm down, and tightening your abdominal muscles. To enhance compression, you can exhale prior to the breath used for compressive breathing. This exhalation slightly lowers the ribs, tightens the abdominal muscles, and improves the stability of your starting position. This technique, known as double-bracing, involves exhaling to prepare your position and then inhaling again for a compressive breath. It is essential to hold your breath until the end of the repetition and then exhale. Exhaling prematurely may result in a loss of tension in your core. For easier repetitions, you can maintain a consistent breathing cycle for several reps. When performing slow-tempo variations of the dip, you can consider breathing in at the bottom of the reversal point to prevent dizziness.

2.1.7

Viewing direction

When it comes to body movements, a general guideline is to align your line of sight with the direction of movement. In the case of dips, you can slightly direct your gaze forward and downward during the negative movement, and slightly forward and upward during the positive movement to enhance your performance. However, it's important to note that the impact of this adjustment is limited.

2.1.8

Wrist position

Your hands/wrists play a vital role as they are connecting you to the bar during dips. They transfer the force between your body and the equipment. It is important to optimize this connection for optimal performance. To achieve this, it is recommended to maintain a relatively neutral wrist position. The pressure should be directed through the ball of your palms towards the ulnar side, as this promotes stability and reduces stress on the wrist. While wrist wraps can enhance stability, they are not essential when maintaining a neutral wrist position. They primarily provide a psychological sense of security. Avoid placing your hands too far inward or outward on the bar, as an unstable wrist can quickly lead to an unstable elbow and shoulder position. Use your thumb as a guide for hand placement, ensuring that it is centered on the bar. If your thumb is centered, it indicates that your wrist is also properly aligned with the bar.

 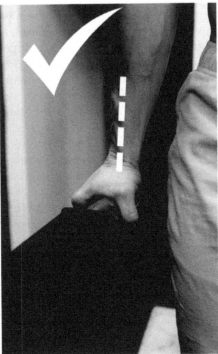 

Wrist placement (left), optimal position (middle), poor position (right).

2.1.9

Set up and entry

A strong dip must be prepared. This starts with the right equipment and the correct construction of your exercise setup and ends with the correct entry into the start position. In the following, you will find reference values and guidelines to help you find your personal, optimal setup.

2.1.9.1

Bar height, width, and grip

Ensure that the height of your bar is sufficient so that when performing the dip with your legs extended, you do not touch the floor in the lowest position. This height is crucial for optimal technique. In the event that your bar is too low and you do not have access to a better option, you can bend your knees and attempt to execute the discussed technique to the best of your ability with bent knees. Moreover, the bar should allow for a customized grip width. A forearm length with fingers extended, plus an additional width if desired, is a suitable guideline. The diameter of the bar should neither be excessively thick, which would require excessive wrist bending, nor too thin, which would result in inadequate pressure distribution and discomfort. A diameter of 50 mm is a recommended standard, commonly used in competitions. Additionally, the surface of the bar should provide sufficient grip. If the bar has a smooth coating, the use of chalk becomes essential. Some bars may be conical or tapered, offering different grip widths within a single assembly. However, it's important to note that such grips tend to force you into a stronger internally rotated posture, potentially compromising the transfer of force from the palm of your hand to the bar. Nevertheless, the differences in this regard are relatively small and negligible for the majority of athletes.

Entry

2.1.9.2

To achieve maximum performance and optimal stability in the dip, it is crucial to enter the movement with minimal effort. This requires an entry point that allows you to begin with fully extended arms and depressed shoulders. It is important to avoid a low entry where you have to push yourself up to the starting position with a partial repetition.

The entry point should be positioned close to your hands, minimizing any strong pendulum motion of the weight during the entry. Here's how you can achieve this: Begin by placing your hands on the bar with your elbows and shoulders in position. Next, bring the weight into the entry point, positioning it between your hands. To control and slow down any potential movements of the weight, place one foot or leg on it. This position also allows you to build tension for the compression phase. Once you are satisfied with your position and stability, lift your second leg off the entry point and finalize your start position.

By following this approach, you can ensure a smooth and controlled entry into the dip, maximizing your stability and setting yourself up for a successful performance.

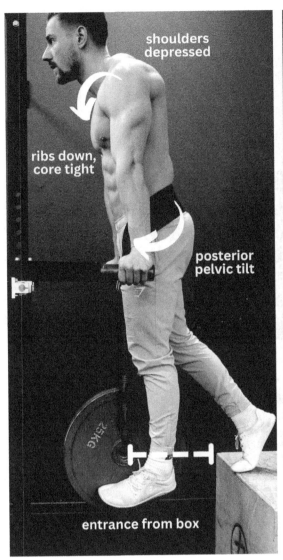 

Recommended entry for weighted dips

2.1.9.3   **Weight position**

For beginners who are using minimal added weight, placing the weight close to the hips tends to feel more natural as it has less impact on the athlete's center of gravity. Additionally, using a shorter chain or attachment helps minimize any swaying motion in the weight, making it easier to stabilize.

On the other hand, advanced athletes benefit from positioning the weight between their feet. This allows them to generate tension effectively against the weight and maintain a stable starting position. It eliminates the need for a wide split with broad plates and enables a smoother dipping motion. The longer pendulum created by positioning the weight between the feet provides greater stability during a few repetitions, as it requires more effort to initiate swinging. However, once the weight starts swinging, it becomes more challenging to stabilize. Nevertheless, for heavier loads, the lower position of the weight is generally superior to a higher position and should be taken into consideration.

Ultimately, the choice of weight positioning depends on the athlete's level of experience and the amount of added weight being used. Beginners may find it more comfortable to position the weight closer to their hips, while advanced athletes can benefit from placing it between their feet for enhanced stability and efficiency in their dip performance.

Has the book helped you this far?
Show it to me! It costs you 60s to leave a review on
our site. It costs you another 60s to write an Insta-
gram story about the book and tag us
@kingofweighted and @micha_bln_!
Thank you so much for your support!

@kingofweighted

@micha_bln_

Hello from the Homegym - Builders!

Our goal is to enrich the lives of athletes and help them reach their full potential.

We focus on excellence in product development, and manufacturing and work closely with elite athletes to understand their needs and solve problems. Our passion for innovation and quality is reflected in products designed specifically for athletes, based on the needs and desires of our customers.

This is also how the „Adjustable Dipholm" was created. A product that is perfectly tailored to your needs and offers you a perfect training experience.
Reach your full potential in Weighted Calisthenics with the Dipholm Adjustable - the perfect bar for dips!

Get more information here:

2.1.10

Variations
weighted dips

By now, you are familiar with the ideal technique for performing dips. You understand the common mistakes to avoid and how to tailor the dip to your specific needs. In the next stage, you will receive a guide that helps you choose the appropriate exercises and exercise categories to elevate your dip training to the next level. You will explore different dip variations and determine which ones are suitable for incorporation into your training routine and why. In the subsequent step, you will extend this analysis to a selection of assistance exercises. This comprehensive approach will enable you to correct any technical errors in your dips and, if necessary, make adjustments to your training regimen to prevent these mistakes in the long run.

2.1.10.1

Tempo Dips

The first category of variations in weighted dips is known as tempo dips. Tempo dips involve intentionally altering the normal speed of your movements. By manipulating the tempo of each phase of the exercise, you can target specific aspects of the movement to improve and strengthen them. In other words, tempo variations allow you to focus on particular parts of the dip by controlling the pace. Given the technical nature of weighted dips, incorporating tempo variations into your training plan is highly beneficial. In the following section, you will be introduced to a 'best practice' guide that outlines different tempo variations, explains when and why they can be used and provides examples. Keep in mind that the presented tempos are not exhaustive, and you are encouraged to experiment with other tempo combinations that may be suitable for your specific circumstances.

Slow negatives 2–3/0/1/1

2.1.10.2

Execution: The negative movement of the dip is performed at a slower pace, taking approximately two to three seconds. The reversal points and positive movement are executed at your normal speed.

Application: This tempo variation is beneficial when you encounter difficulties with initiating the dip correctly. It specifically addresses issues related to shoulder depression, compression, and chest tension. By slowing down the negatives, you can ensure a solid technique when reaching the challenging lower reversal point of the dip. This exercise is particularly valuable during the transition phase from an expansion strategy to a compression strategy. The slower tempo allows for increased concentration and precision in executing the movement. It's important to note that the slower tempo requires reducing the additional weight, preventing the temptation to work at excessively high intensities. Additionally, this tempo variation can serve as a means to artificially limit the amount of additional weight used.

Paused lower reversal point 1/1–3/1/1

2.1.10.3

Execution: The lower reversal point after the negative phase is sustained isometrically for one to three seconds.

Application: This variation is utilized by incorporating short pauses of about one second to promote a clean and controlled execution of the lower reversal point. By pausing at the reversal point, the use of a bounce or stretch-shortening cycle is eliminated. This encourages greater reliance on muscular control rather than passive structures. Longer pauses, typically around two seconds, are often employed to enhance depression and protraction at the reversal point or to intentionally limit the amount of weight used. Holding the position isometrically allows for increased time spent in that specific position, leading to improved activation and familiarity over time. This variation is also beneficial if you struggle with the timing of initiating the positive movement, helping to prevent premature expansion without proper elbow extension. For competitive athletes experiencing difficulties with dip depth, this variation aids in developing a better sense of the correct depth. Moreover, as mentioned previously, it serves as a safeguard against excessive loading at the expense of proper technique.mature expansion without proper elbow extension. For competitive athletes experiencing difficulties with dip depth, this variation aids in developing a better sense of the correct depth. Moreover, as mentioned previously, it serves as a safeguard against excessive loading at the expense of proper technique.

2.1.10.4 Explosive positive 1/0/X/1

Execution: The positive phase of the dip is executed with maximal effort, aiming to accelerate the weight as much as possible. Depending on the chosen weight, this may not always result in an explosive movement but rather a slight increase in speed compared to your regular pace. The main focus should be on generating maximum force per repetition.

Application: This form of dips is employed to enhance your strength capacity without the necessity of working with maximal or submaximal loads. By emphasizing strong acceleration, you aim for a transfer to maximum strength, as it elicits high recruitment and activation of the relevant muscle fibers, similar to working with maximum loads. However, it is crucial to ensure that the increased movement speed does not compromise your technique.

In all tempo variations, the upper reversal point is consistently set at one second. This allows for a controlled reorganization after the negative phase, giving you time to attain a perfect starting position before commencing the next repetition. Particularly in high-intensity sets, this approach helps maintain a higher level of technique throughout the entire set.

Dips with modified resistance profile   2.1.10.5

By manipulating the resistance profile of an exercise, you have the ability to alter the amount of load you encounter at different points and positions during the movement. This allows you to control the perceived heaviness or lightness of the exercise at specific positions. In the case of dips, the load curve is influenced by the effective length of the upper arm, with the load increasing in the downward direction and decreasing in the upward direction. However, it's important to note that individual perception may not always align with this resistance profile, as internal torques within your muscles also change depending on your position. In the weighted dip, there are two common variations where you intentionally modify the resistance profile to serve a specific training purpose.

2.1.10.6   **Dips against a resistance band**

Execution: In this variation, you incorporate a resistance band along with the weight during the dip. The resistance band provides additional tension that increases as it stretches, allowing for a more consistent load throughout the movement and placing greater emphasis on the upper position of the dip. The band can be attached either to the floor and your belt or around your neck, depending on your preference. It may take some time to adjust to the setup. It is recommended to use a relatively light band to make slight adjustments to the load curve and maintain targeted training. Using a very strong band may limit the use of additional weight and deviate significantly from the actual competition exercise.

Application: If you encounter a sticking point during the lockout phase (extension of the arms) of the dip, where you tend to decelerate significantly, this variation can help you overcome it in the future. The band assists in overloading this specific position without fatiguing you excessively from the preceding phases of the dip. Moreover, the band encourages better control of the negative movement, as it prevents rapid acceleration in the downward phase.

 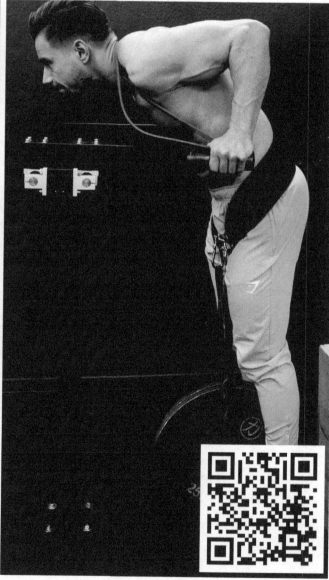

Dips against a resistance band

Dips with dead stop

Execution: In this variation, you position your added weight in a way that it makes contact with the ground or a box at a specific point during the negative movement, resulting in a complete deceleration or "dead stop." The weight momentarily reaches zero load before you push back up from that position.

Application: Typically, you choose the dead stop position at the depth required in official competitions. This helps condition yourself to maintain the appropriate depth according to the rules. The dead stop technique requires precise control during the negative phase to prevent loss of tension when the weight touches the ground. By eliminating the stretch-shortening cycle, similar to a paused variation, this approach enhances your power output through improved self-awareness and technique, particularly around your sticking point.

Dips with a dead stop in the lower reversal point.

 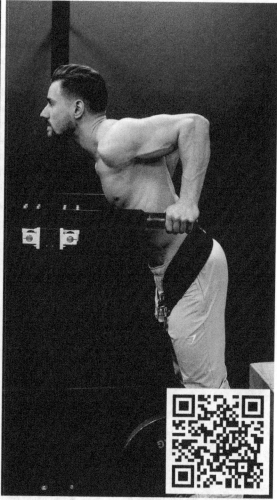

Open chest dips

2.1.10.8

Open chest dips

Execution: In this dip variation, the emphasis is on minimizing or eliminating compression, allowing for an increased range of motion in shoulder extension. It is important to maintain shoulder depression and only permit the necessary elevation based on your planned range of motion.

Application: This variation can be utilized to enhance stability and mobility in the end range of shoulder extension. By training this area with reduced weight in a controlled manner, both your active and passive structures will become more resilient and stronger. This improvement can positively impact your competition technique, reducing the risk of injury and enhancing your ability to withstand technique errors. If you notice a specific muscle group, such as the chest, is more dominant in maintaining an upright position, this variation can be employed as a targeted hypertrophy assistance exercise. However, it is advisable to use light to moderate loads and higher repetition ranges when training this variation.

Partial repetitions

2.1.10.9

Execution: Partial repetitions involve training a reduced range of motion in the dip exercise. This can include focusing on the upper portion, or lower portion, or performing a dip shrug, which involves dynamic execution of shoulder depression in the support position.

Application: Partial reps can be utilized to overload and target specific subsections of the range of motion. By working with heavier weights within the smaller range, you can achieve greater muscle stimulation than during full-range repetitions. Additionally, incorporating partial reps into your training routine can help improve technique and proficiency in the targeted areas through frequent practice.

Ring dips

Execution: In this variation, you incorporate gymnastic rings instead of traditional bars for performing dips. The unstable support provided by the rings constantly challenges your balance and requires continuous adjustments to maintain proper positioning. As your body weight pulls you down and the rings can move laterally, you must engage your chest muscles to generate inward force and stabilize the rings. Consequently, ring dips effectively target and stimulate the chest muscles. Additionally, at the end of each repetition, you have the option to perform a ring turnout by externally rotating the shoulder joint and supinating the forearm.

Application: Ring dips are an excellent choice for enhancing the stability of your dip exercise. The inherent demand for stability makes them suitable as a variation for lighter dip sessions while maintaining a higher frequency of dip training. Moreover, due to the emphasis on chest engagement, ring dips can also serve as an effective hypertrophy assistance exercise for developing the chest muscles.

Ring dips

2.1.11

Assistance exercises for weighted dips

If an athlete is already capable of performing weighted dips across multiple sets, there is typically no need for additional strength assistance exercises in their programming. The intensity of the dips can be adjusted independently by incorporating added weight, eliminating the necessity for further assistance exercises to address the strength component of the training plan for weighted dips as the primary exercise.

2.1.11.1   **Hypertrophy assistance**

Hypertrophy assistance exercises that target the muscles involved in dips can be incorporated into the training plan alongside the main exercise and programmed variations. Depending on the volume already allocated to the main exercise and variations, the inclusion of hypertrophy assistance sets may not be necessary or only require minimal sets. The selection of appropriate hypertrophy assistance exercises allows you to target specific structures that may not be adequately stimulated by the main exercise, the weighted dip, utilizing the concept of the "limiting factor." By conducting movement analysis, closely observing exercise execution, or seeking guidance from an experienced trainer, you can identify these limiting factors. The following list introduces useful hypertrophy assistance exercises and provides explanations for their effective integration based on individual circumstances. While this list is comprehensive, there are other valid reasons to incorporate these exercises as well. A strong and well-defined chest is crucial for achieving a powerful dip. However, due to the limited range of motion involved, the dip alone may not provide sufficient stimulus for many athletes in the long term. Therefore, it is beneficial for most athletes to include additional chest-focused assistance exercises. To maintain movement specificity, it is recommended to prioritize multi-joint exercises. Since the chest works in conjunction with the shoulders and triceps during the dip, exercises that mimic similar movement patterns have greater carryover to the main exercise compared to less related exercises. With these considerations in mind, the following exercises are particularly suitable for integrating more chest-dominant assistance exercises into your training plan.

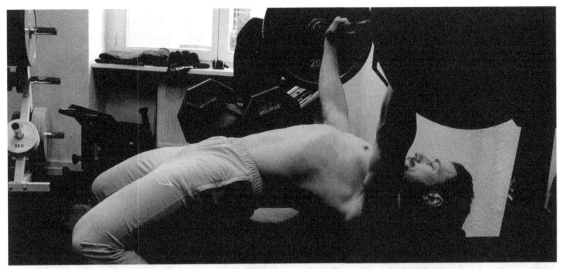

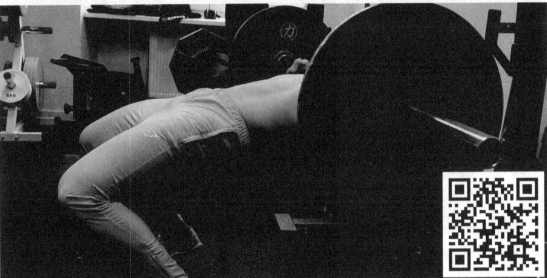

Bench press with a barbell

2.1.11.2

Bench press

Bench press exercises using barbells, as well as variations with dumbbells or machines, should be prioritized as the primary choice for chest-dominant assistance exercises. Unlike the technique used in competitive dips, which emphasizes chest compression, the bench press focuses on creating a strong bridge and maintaining a maximally expanded ribcage. This introduces a crucial element to your training regimen. The bench press effectively targets and loads the chest in its expanded position. To specifically target the chest, it is recommended to work with intensities below 80% of your bench press one-repetition maximum (Fmax). At higher intensities, the activity of the chest does not increase proportionally, as the shoulder and triceps begin to bear a greater portion of the load (4).

If you incorporate higher-intensity bench presses into your routine, it is important to consider the additional stress placed on your shoulders and triceps. Proper workout planning should take into account this cumulative load from both bench presses and dips to prevent potential overloading. Furthermore, if you are unable to perform weighted dips temporarily due to injury or other reasons, high-intensity bench presses can serve as a suitable substitute, as they activate similar muscle groups to weighted dips.

You may be wondering why push-ups or weighted push-ups are not prioritized at the top of the list in a "calisthenics" book. While there is nothing inherently wrong with weighted push-ups, the primary drawback lies in the challenge of progressive loading. Unlike the bench press, which offers simplicity in loading and scalability, push-ups present complexities when it comes to loading through the use of weight vests, bands, or weighted belts. Loading push-ups significantly increases the demand for stability, consequently raising the risk of potential injuries.

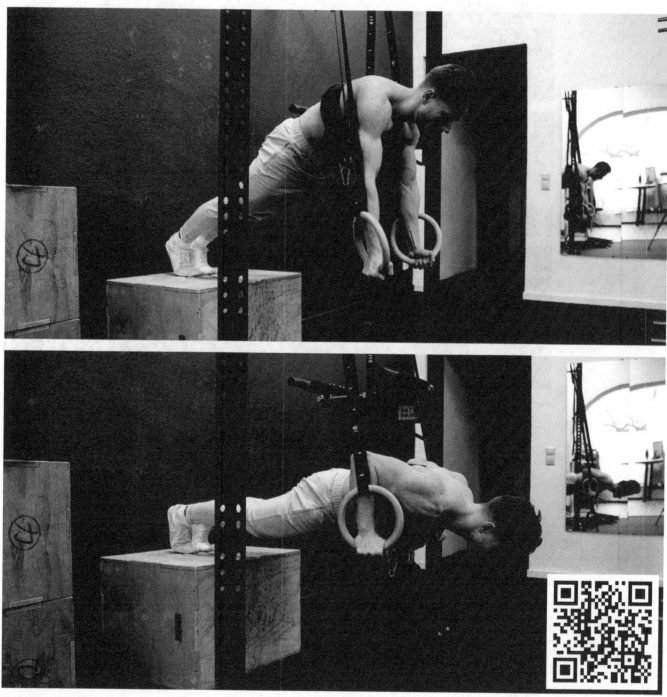

Weighted push ups

! **"Isolation exercises" are in quotation marks, since there is, in fact, no such thing as a pure isolation exercise for a single muscle. Human movements, even if they only take place in one joint, always require a more complex interaction of a broad range of muscles.**

Chest "isolation exercises"

2.1.11.3

If you have a less developed chest, incorporating additional isolation volume for the chest can be beneficial. In this case, it is important to focus on exercises that specifically target the chest while minimizing fatigue in other muscle groups. The purpose of this extra volume is solely to stimulate chest growth, which will ultimately contribute to increased strength potential due to a larger muscle cross-section. It is important to note that chest isolation exercises may not have significant short-term carryover to your weighted dip. However, exercises such as close grip chest presses with a slow tempo and moderate loads can be effective. This exercise allows for a greater range of motion and the moderate intensities reduce the dominance of the triceps and shoulders. Additionally, the slow tempo enables a strong mind-muscle connection, ensuring that the chest is primarily fatigued. Chest flies on butterfly machines or cable towers are also viable options as long as they provide constant tension throughout the range of motion.

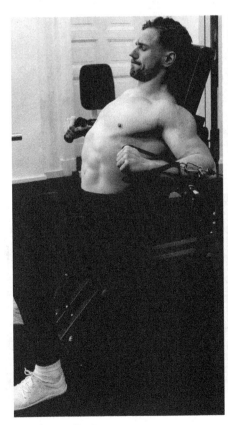 

Example setup chest press

2.1.11.4   Overhead press

Another often overlooked category of assistance exercises for the weighted dip is overhead press exercises. There are several reasons why overhead presses can be highly valuable for improving weighted dips. Firstly, both exercises involve shoulder flexion, making them highly specific and having a strong carryover to each other. The overhead press completes the full range of motion of shoulder flexion, complementing the movement pattern of the weighted dip.

From a holistic training perspective, the overhead press serves as a compensatory movement for the adduction-dominant nature of the weighted dip. The overhead press incorporates abduction movements in the shoulder joint, which helps maintain overall shoulder mobility, stability, and long-term shoulder health.

Many athletes struggle with stability and protraction during the dip due to inadequate activation or strength deficits in the serratus anterior muscle. This can manifest as "scapular winging," where the shoulder blades protrude medially from the body. While weighted dips primarily train the serratus anterior isometrically during shoulder protraction, it is also important to train this muscle through its full range of motion to address any potential deficits. This is where the overhead press becomes beneficial. The overhead press requires upward rotation of the shoulder blades under load, activating and training the serratus anterior muscle.

The choice of overhead press variation depends on your training plan, available equipment, and personal preferences. It is important to select a variation that can be easily scaled and sustained in the long term while ensuring that the target muscles are the limiting factor in the exercise.

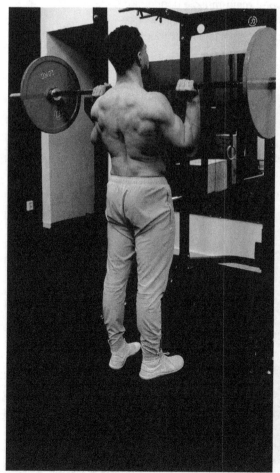 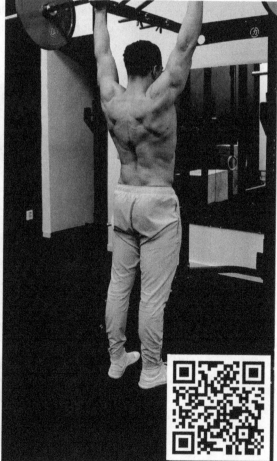

Example set up overhead press with barbell

Arm "isolation exercises"

The dip primarily targets the arms, specifically the triceps (as an extensor) and the biceps brachii (as a shoulder flexor). However, this doesn't mean that additional arm training should be neglected. The arms play crucial roles as stabilizers in the shoulder joint (biceps brachii) and the shoulder blade (triceps brachii). Having strong and well-developed arms is important for elbow resilience, shoulder and shoulder blade stability, and wrist stability.

When training your arms, it's important to incorporate exercises that target both the biceps and triceps in different shoulder positions. This helps enhance the resilience of the structures in your shoulder and elbow against forces from various directions, ultimately promoting joint stability. Additionally, it ensures balanced development of the different heads of the biceps and triceps, as different positions of the upper arm emphasize different muscle heads.

As an experienced athlete, you can handle higher volumes of arm training, potentially up to 32 sets per week (5). However, it's essential to note that this volume already includes the arm work accumulated through exercises like dips, chin-ups, or other movements in your training plan. It's advisable to start with a conservative

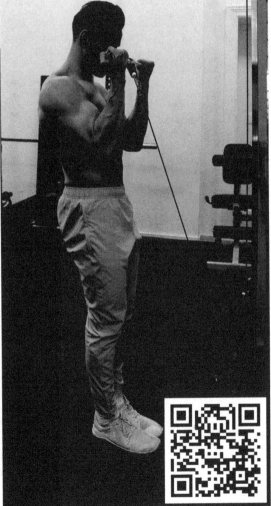

Supinated cable curls

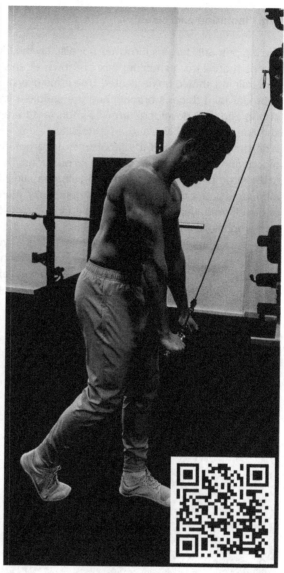

Triceps extensions

2.1.11.6   ## Health assistance

Determining the specific health assistance exercises that are important for you and when they should be incorporated into your training plan is best discussed with an experienced trainer. They can provide personalized guidance based on your individual needs and circumstances. In the following sections, I will introduce you to some exercise categories that have proven to be effective preventive measures in practice. It's important to note that if you perform your main exercises with proper technique, careful execution, and appropriate progression, you'll require less time and effort for health assistance exercises. These exercises serve as a preventive measure, assuming that you are a healthy athlete without any existing injuries or pain. However, if you are dealing with injuries or experiencing pain, it's crucial to consult with an expert and develop an individualized approach to address your specific situation. They can provide guidance on how to adapt your training and incorporate appropriate measures to support your recovery and overall well-being.

Shoulder internal/external rotation exercises

Many athletes today experience deficits in shoulder rotation, often due to repetitive and limited movement patterns in everyday activities such as desk work or specific sports. These rotational deficits can lead to imbalances during the dip exercise, potentially resulting in overloading certain structures and increasing the risk of injury. It's important to distinguish whether these deficits are related to mobility or stability. For mobility deficits, a combination of stretching and end-range training can be effective in addressing them in the short term. This helps to restore and maintain full shoulder mobility. On the other hand, stability deficits require a more long-term and slightly more complex approach. To preventively address these deficits, it is crucial to prioritize maintaining both mobility and stability in your shoulders, including internal and external rotation, through your training routine. As mentioned earlier, the primary way to achieve this is by training your main exercises with a reasonable range of motion and ensuring adequate shoulder stabilization during their execution. However, if you still observe deficits in shoulder rotation, you can consider incorporating specific exercises from the following list to target and improve the areas of concern.

Cross body stretch

Internal rotation:
Cross Body Stretch - with this stretch you open up the back part of your shoulder, which is mainly responsible for external rotation. If you are shortened there, your freedom of movement in the internal rotation can be limited.

Internal Rotation Stretch - with these stretches you will stretch up the external rotators in the shoulder joint as well as the passive structures (ligaments, tendons, shoulder capsule) around the shoulder joint, gaining more range of motion into internal rotation. In this context, a PNF technique is often recommended. To what extent this type of stretching is truly superior remains to be determined (6).

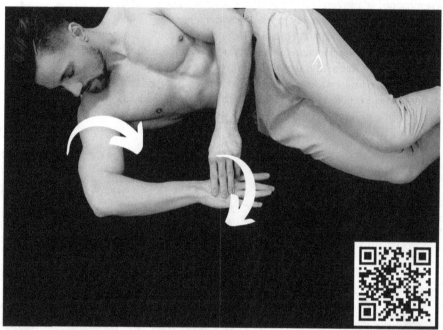

Shoulder internal rotation stretch

Internal rotation walk-out

Internal Rotation Walk Out - In order, for you to be able to stabilize the internal rotation, you can train it with exercises like the internal rotation walkout. To do this, as shown in the pictures, have a resistance band or cable machine pull your arm into the external rotation while you isometrically hold against it. This exercise also works well as a warm-up for the shoulder and chest.

External Rotation:
Supinated Lat Stretch - In many cases, external rotation, especially during overhead movements, is limited by a shortened latissimus. The latissimus is an internal rotator due to its attachment at the front of the upper arm. If you stretch the latissimus, you can get more range of motion in external rotation.

Supinated lat stretch

Shoulder external rotation stretch

External Rotation Stretch - with this stretch you will stretch up the internal rotators in the shoulder joint as well as the passive structures (ligaments, tendons, shoulder capsule) around the shoulder joint, gaining more range of motion into external rotation. Again, a PNF technique is often recommended in the literature.

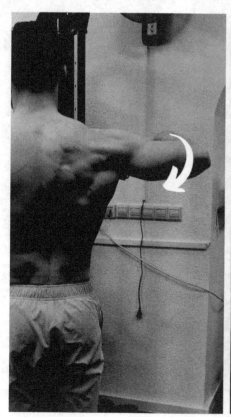
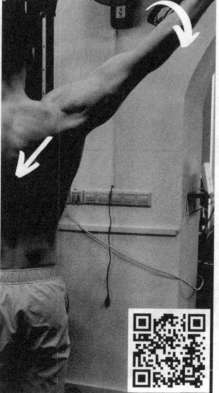

Facepull Trap 3 Raises - Facepull Trap 3 Raises are designed to help you stabilize your shoulder blade through the full range of motion of shoulder abduction and flexion. They will help you to learn to properly active your ascending (lower) fibers of the trapezius muscle and your serratus anterior. Put the cable pulley or resistance band on shoulder height. Stand in front of the cable with your chest facing the cable. Perform a facepull motion until you hit 90° abduction and full external rotation. Engage your serratus anterior (think of pushing your shoulder forward and sideways) to pull your shoulderblade around the rib cage and to let it rotate upwards. Pull with your arm into shoulder flexion while you extend the arm to the side of your body.

Facepull Trap 3 Raises

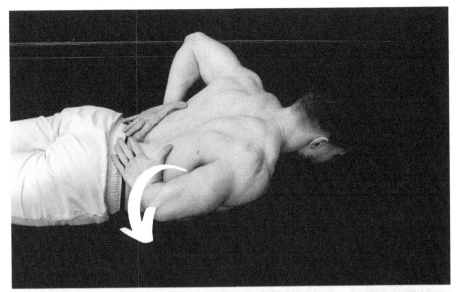

Prone Snow Angels - This exercise is very good as a warm-up for your entire shoulder girdle. The shoulder is moved and stabilized equally through internal and external rotation. In addition, this exercise will help you activate and warm up your trapezius across all three of its fiber orientations. To do this, lie on your stomach on the floor. Raise your chest and head slightly. Extend your arms forward. Then, similar to a snow angel movement, bring your arms back while rotating them inward so that the back of your hands rests on your back in the final position.

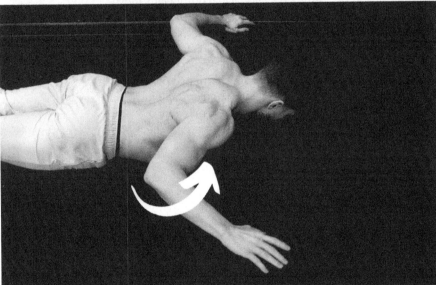

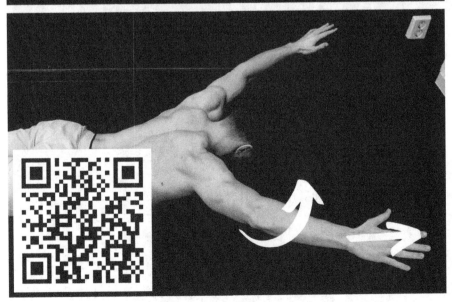

Prone snow angel

2.1.11.8   Shoulder abduction exercises

In addition to the previously discussed overhead exercises, which involve shoulder abduction, it's beneficial to focus on isolated abduction movements such as the classic lateral raise. Performing technically sound and well-executed variations of lateral raises can promote shoulder health in several ways. Firstly, lateral raises help improve the interaction between the supraspinatus and deltoid muscles, which are involved in shoulder abduction. This improved interaction enhances the overall function and stability of the shoulder joint.

Secondly, lateral raises contribute to the proper coordination and interaction of muscles such as the serratus anterior, different parts of the trapezius, and the rotator cuff during abduction. When these muscles work together effectively, they facilitate the centering and compression of the upper arm in the shoulder joint, optimizing the subacromial space. This, in turn, reduces the risk of shoulder

impingement and promotes shoulder health within your training plan (7). By incorporating lateral raises and similar exercises into your routine, you can enhance the overall strength and stability of your shoulders, mitigating the risk of potential injuries and promoting healthy shoulder function. Examples of these are:

Lateral cable raises - To perform this variation, it's recommended to use a wrist sling. Begin by gripping the cable tower and positioning yourself in a sideways stance. This positioning allows for a greater range of motion and shifts the load to the stretched position of the muscle. Start the movement by lifting your arm sideways, avoiding upward movement away from the body. The orientation of the arm should align with the lateral fibers of the deltoid, which don't run perfectly sideways but slightly forward. Throughout the upward movement, focus on keeping your shoulder as stable as possible while moving only your arm. It's important to avoid tensing your neck and

Lateral raises on the cable

instead keep it relaxed while guiding the movement with your shoulder. The movement concludes when your upper arm is approximately parallel to the floor, ensuring that the elbow reaches the highest point of the movement. By following these guidelines, you can effectively target the lateral fibers of the deltoid while maintaining proper form and maximizing the benefits of this exercise variation.

Lu-Raises - The Lu-Raises, named after Chinese weightlifter Lu Xiaojun, provide a different approach to training shoulder abduction throughout its full range of motion. To perform this exercise, you will need two dumbbells or weight plates. Start by holding the weights in your hands and let your elbows guide the movement.

Begin lifting your arms to the sides of your body and continue until they come together above your head. During this motion, allow your shoulder blades to rotate upwards. It's important to note that you should avoid excessive elevation of the shoulder. Instead, focus on keeping your shoulder pulled towards your ears to a minimal degree. This ensures that the movement is controlled and avoids unnecessary strain on the shoulder joint. When performing Lu-Raises, it is recommended to use lighter weights and prioritize proper form and technique. This exercise targets shoulder abduction effectively and allows you to work through the entire range of motion while maintaining control and stability.

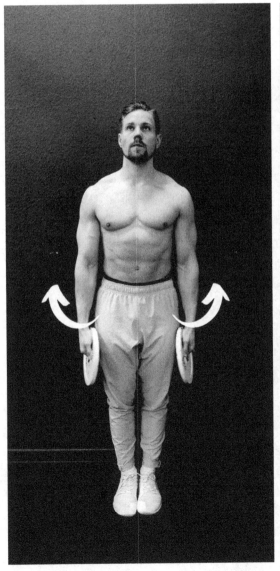

Lu raises

Become a part of the FinalRep Community!

DO YOU WANT TO SHARE YOUR PASSION FOR STREET-LIFTING AND CALISTHENICS WITH LIKE-MINDED PEOPLE?

Then FinalRep is the right choice for you! We offer a **unique community,** where you can exchange ideas with other athletes as well as compete in our professional competitions. Already several hundred athletes have participated at Final Rep! Due to our extensive expertise in streetlifting, we organize epic events that you will never forget.

Our goal is to make our sport more accessible. With a digital infrastructure that enables athletes to participate in competitions easier. **Qualify via our app,** share your training progress, and stay up to date on what successes and records ot-

hers are celebrating. Can't attend an event? Follow them live via our app! Sign up now at FinalRep and **become part of our community!**

You will not only find like-minded people but also a lot of resources and opportunities to prepare for the next competition.

Athlete Michael Schulz, MMC competition 2021, Photo: Patrik Gossen and Nick Reisinger.

Weighted pull/chin ups

2.2 Weighted pull/ chin ups

As with the weighted dip, the pull/chin up will be based on the competition exercise. This chapter aims to find a technique that allows you to perform a repetition with the maximum amount of additional weight, in accordance with the rules, and with the lowest possible risk of injury. For other objectives, deviations from the discussed technique may make sense and are not excluded by this.

For this purpose, we will use the rulebook for Final Rep from 2023 as an example:
As soon as the first signal ("Platform ready!") is given, the athlete may enter the platform. The athlete attaches the weight belt to the hip. Now the athlete moves to the start position on the box, grips the bar in the chosen grip, and moves to the hanging position. It is allowed to use a "semi-false grip". The start position is considered to be taken as soon as the athlete has fully extended the elbows (180° joint angle) and is in the hanging position. It is not allowed to initiate the pulling phase during the swing. The spotters can therefore help the athlete to stop swinging in the hanging position on request. The athlete waits for the start signal ("Go!") and can perform the attempt after the given signal. As soon as the athlete finishes the attempt with the chin visible (vertical) above the bar, the movement may be reversed. As soon as the athlete reverses the movement and finds himself back in the start position, he must wait for the signal "Box!" to finish the attempt. After the last signal is given, the athlete may swing back onto the box. The attempt is now finished. Afterward, the judges decide if the attempt was valid and the athlete is allowed to leave the platform.

Reasons for an invalid pull:
The following list includes violations that result in a "No Rep".

1. **Fail: The athlete does not finish the attempt with the chin visible above the bar.**

2. **Bent Arms: The athlete starts the pull with bent arms. In certain cases of anatomically limited mobility (e.g. not being able to extend the elbows through 180°), it is up to the athlete to tell and show this to the judges before entering the platform for the first attempt.**

3. **Kipping/Kicking: The athlete generates momentum with an excessive tilting motion in the pelvis or with a kicking motion of the legs, which facilitates overcoming the bar. A minimal change in knee and hip angle that does not give the athlete an advantage is allowed.**

4. **Downward Movement I: The direction of the movement reverses before it is completed. A short pause during the attempt is allowed.**

5. **Downward Movement II (stretch-shortening): The athlete may start in an "active hang" (depression in the shoulder girdle). If the athlete changes to a "passive hang" (elevation in the shoulder girdle) after the start signal "Go!" has been given, the so-called "stretch-shortening" is used, which gives the athlete an advantage and simplifies the attempt.**

6. **Signal: The athlete misses or disregards a signal from the judges. (1)"**

The description of the necessary pulling height, the approval of the grip type, and other minor details for initiating the movement may vary depending on the competition. Therefore, it is important for you to have a detailed understanding of the rules specific to your intended competition. This will allow you to adapt your training and, if necessary, modify the form described in this book to ensure optimal preparation for the competition.

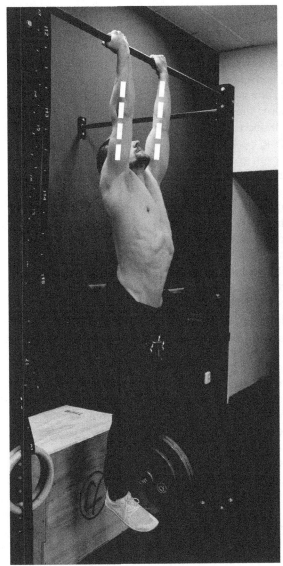 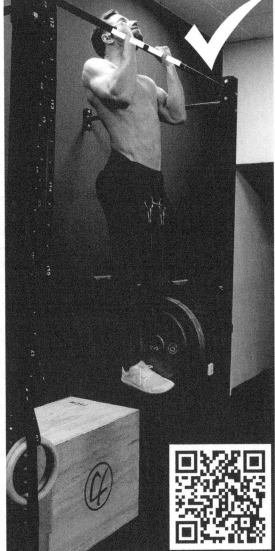

Competition valid chin up

2.2.1

Chin up or pull up

Before delving into the technique, let's first discuss the differences and similarities between chin ups and pull ups. Understanding these distinctions can help you determine which exercise provides greater benefits or improved performance in your training. chin ups are performed with an underhand grip, where the palms face towards you. This grip position is known as supination, which involves the forearm being in a rotated position. On the other hand, pull ups are executed with an overhand grip, where the palms face away from you. This grip position is called pronation, which involves the forearm being in a different rotated position compared to supination.

The main contrast between these two exercises lies in the wrist rotation. It is commonly observed that chin ups place more emphasis on the biceps brachii muscle due to the supinated grip. This observation is supported by findings from electromyography (EMG) studies, which show slightly higher activation of the biceps brachii during chin ups. However, it's important to note that these differences are not significant, as both chin ups (with supinated and semi-pronated grip) and pull ups (with pronated grip) result in high levels of activation in all the muscles responsible for arm flexion.

In summary, while chin ups may have a slight advantage in engaging the biceps brachii due to the supinated grip, both chin ups and pull ups effectively activate the muscles involved in arm flexion. So for now, you can exclude that the main difference is only in the biceps. The reason why a supinated grip does not provide significantly more biceps activation in the chin up is probably that the biceps brachii also performs a flexion (lifting the arm forward) in addition to its arm flexing function in the shoulder joint. However, since extension (bringing the arm backward) is performed during the chin up, the biceps brachii is working as an antagonist (counterpart of a movement) at that moment (8) (9) (10) (11).

Rigidly focusing on a single arm flexor within the context of a highly complex multi-joint exercise is therefore not conducive to providing you with answers regarding which lift is advantageous for you. The more significant differences between the two lifts result from the different grip widths and the resulting elbow position during execution. These factors determine the plane of the movement and how your back muscles will be loaded.

The supination of the forearm often limits the chin up to a rather narrow, shoulder-width grip. On the other hand, the pronation of the pull up allows for a much wider grip. However, you can also use a narrow pronated grip and, depending on your mobility, a wide supinated grip. The grip width determines two important factors for your performance. Firstly, it determines the plane of the pull. A broader grip leads to the movement primarily occurring in the frontal plane, where you perform arm adduction (elbows are guided to the side of the body). Conversely, a narrower grip results in the movement taking place in the sagittal plane, emphasizing shoulder extension (elbows are guided towards the body from the front).

As you widen your grip, two things happen: your upper arm appears shorter when viewed from the side, and the distance between you and the bar decreases. This results in a reduced range of motion required by your shoulder. Additionally, the shorter upper arm length decreases the torque exerted on your shoulder by your body weight and any additional weight. In a chin up, your grip width positions you closer to the bar compared to a pull-up because your wrists are positioned behind the bar in a chin-up and in front of the bar in a pull up. Therefore, if your mobility allows for a wide grip in a chin-up, you can benefit in two ways. This can be compared to the difference between sumo deadlifts and conventional deadlifts.

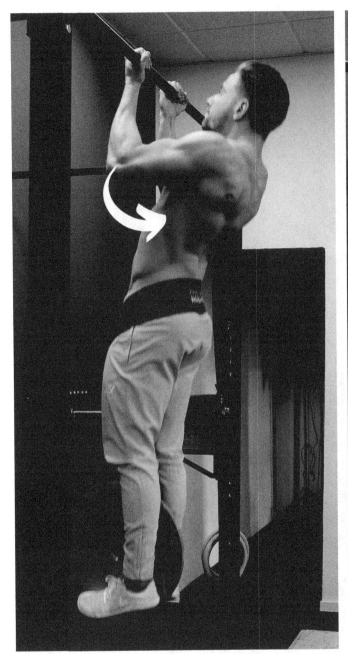
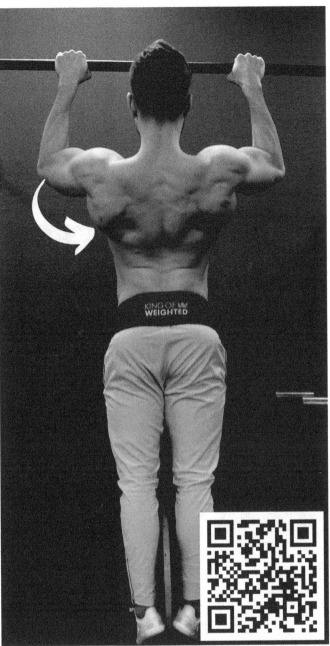

A wider grip, as often used in pull ups, tends to result in adduction in the shoulder joint, and a narrower grip, as often used in chin ups, tends to result in an extension in the shoulder joint.

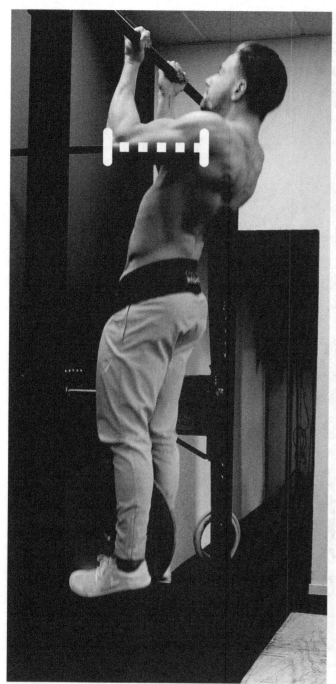
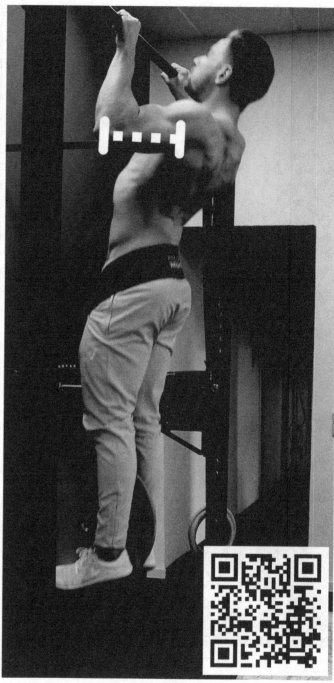

The broader your grip, the smaller the distance to the bar. The shot is slightly rotated, so the difference seems smaller than it would be with a perfect lateral shot, which is unfortunately not possible due to the pillar.

By using a wide grip in pull-ups or chin-ups, similar to sumo deadlifts, you reduce the amount of pulling required per repetition through technique.

However, it's important to note that this doesn't automatically mean that everyone is stronger in sumo deadlifts or should use a very wide grip in pull-ups or chin-ups. The optimal grip width varies for each individual and depends on factors such as mobility, strength, and personal preference.

In theory, a very wide grip in a chin-up would be optimal considering factors such as range of motion and distance to the bar. However, in practice, this is often not the case due to limitations in external shoulder rotation for many athletes. To effectively exert strength throughout the entire range of motion, especially in the upward direction, it

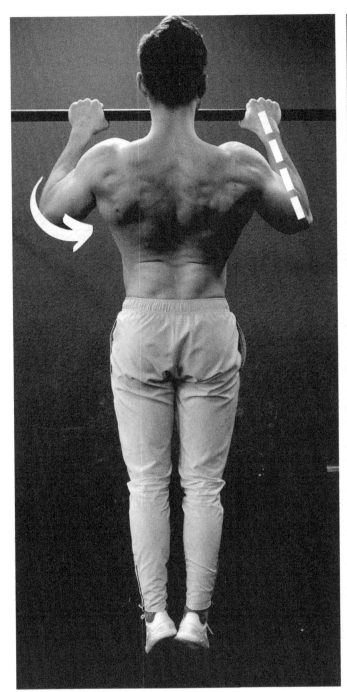 

Comparison of the forearm position with stable external rotation (left) and abduction and extension of the upper arm resulting from strong internal rotation (right).

is crucial for your forearms to remain as vertical as possible beneath the bar. However, this can only be achieved if your shoulder has sufficient mobility and stability in its external rotation.

If your shoulder lacks mobility in external rotation, your forearms will deviate from their vertical alignment due to the fixed position of your hands, and your elbows may move to the side and/or back. This can compromise your form and potentially reduce the effectiveness of the exercise. Therefore, it's important to find a grip width that allows for proper forearm alignment and maintains stability and control throughout the movement. This may vary depending on individual shoulder mobility and should be adjusted accordingly.

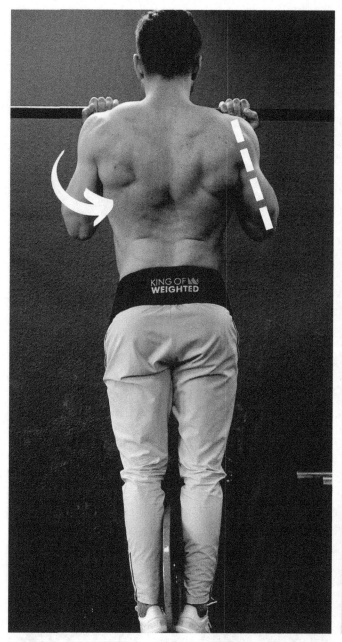 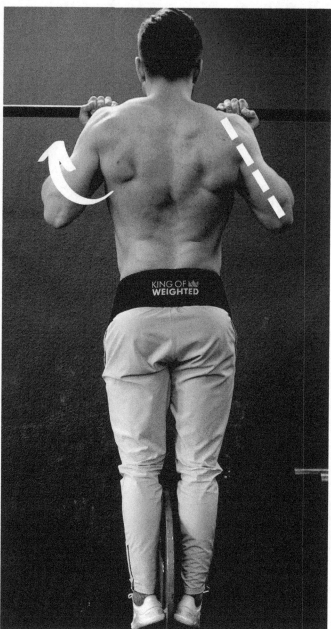

The abduction ability of the wrist limits the possible abduction in the upper arm.

When there are mobility or stability deficits that cause your forearms to deviate to the side, the closing phase of a chin up becomes more challenging. The transfer of strength into the bar is compromised, and you have to rely on generating sufficient acceleration from the lower portion of the movement. On the other hand, the pull-up, with its pronated grip, allows for more flexibility in evading the elbows. As a result, it requires less mobility in external rotation and forearm rotation. In the case of a supinated grip in the chin-up, you are compelled to maintain a strong shoulder external rotation, which leads to greater stability and a more vertical forearm position throughout the entire range of motion. However, this grip significantly restricts the range of motion in your elbows. The limited outward movement of the wrist, around 20° (12), restricts the elbow's range of motion when pulling upward in a chin-up. Consequently, your body has limited capacity to compensate for any mobility deficits in supination and external rotation.

In theory, the chin up grip may appear advantageous due to its ability to promote a better forearm position and minimize evasive movements. However, this perceived advantage can quickly turn into a significant drawback. Forcing the forearm into supination and the shoulder into external rotation can lead to feelings of tightness and potentially result in pain, particularly in certain positions during the lift. The wrists, elbows, and shoulders are particularly susceptible to discomfort. When pain arises during an exercise, the body's natural response is to reduce performance in that specific movement to prevent further pain. In such cases, the practical benefits of the chin up grip become irrelevant when it causes discomfort or pain.

To gain a better understanding of the effects of wide and narrow grips, it is important to consider the internal levers of the muscles involved in the pull/chin-up movement. By examining the average internal torques of the muscles during the closing phase, we can make a more informed evaluation. The values from Kuechele's 1997 study provide a good basis for assessing these lever arms, as they align well with observations from weighted calisthenics (38).

When using a wide grip, the measured values for shoulder adduction in the scapular plane are relevant, while for a narrow grip, the values for shoulder extension in the sagittal plane are considered. The differences in lever arms between the two grips are most notable in the pectoral muscles and the posterior shoulder. During shoulder adduction in the scapular plane, the pectoral muscles have similar lever arms to the latissimus in the examined area. However, in the sagittal plane, this lever arm is only about one-third as large. This means that with a wider grip, the pectoral muscles can contribute more effectively to the movement, while a narrower grip limits their ability to exert strength in the intended direction.

Another significant difference is observed in the lever arms of the posterior shoulder. In shoulder adduction in the scapular plane, the lever arm of the posterior shoulder is, on average, negative, indicating that it acts as an antagonist in this movement and does not exert force in the desired direction. However, for shoulder extension, the lever arm is still nearly 40% as large as that of the latissimus, particularly in the 0–30° range of the closing phase. This highlights the importance of the posterior shoulder during this phase when the lever arms of the latissimus and teres major decrease.

Considering these findings, it is important to note that narrower grips may lead to increased fatigue in the posterior shoulder, while wider grips may result in greater fatigue in the pectoral muscles. Therefore, for optimal performance in these lifts, it is recommended to minimize fatigue in these specific structures through proper exercise alignment and training sequencing.

In summary, the choice of grip width in pull-ups and chin-ups determines the stress placed on shoulder adduction and extension. A wider grip emphasizes shoulder adduction, while a narrower grip places more emphasis on shoulder extension. If your strength lies in shoulder adduction, opting for a wider grip in a pull-up may enhance your performance. On the other hand, if you have limited supination and/or shoulder external rotation, choosing a pull-up grip reduces the risk of injury.

If you possess good mobility in these joints, using a chin-up grip can offer its benefits while still allowing you to adjust the grip width according to your preferred pulling pattern. However, it's important to note that a chin-up grip carries a higher risk of elbow injury for athletes with a large valgus angle in the elbow. The valgus angle refers to the alignment of the upper arm and forearm. If your forearm is positioned to the side rather than in line with your upper arm when your arms are straight next to your body, you have cubitus valgus. In a chin-up grip, this can increase traction on the inner side of your elbow and create greater compression on the outer side, making you more susceptible to injuries in this area, especially when handling heavy loads.

The perfect technique

Now that you have determined which grip style suits you better, you can concentrate on refining your pulling technique to maximize performance and minimize the risk of injury. Compared to the dip exercise, the chin-up/pull-up is less technically complex. This is because the pulling exercise mainly focuses on the concentric phase, which is particularly important in competitions. Therefore, the technical requirements for the chin-up/pull-up are only half as demanding as those for the dip.

To perfect your technique, it is essential to consider your objectives and make initial adjustments accordingly. Firstly, strive to minimize the range of motion within the competition rules and your chosen grip width. By reducing the height and distance of your pull, you can conserve energy while still handling heavier weights. Secondly, concentrate on developing an efficient technique that allows you to minimize the range of motion as much as possible. This involves optimizing your body positioning and alignment at specific moments during the exercise. Thirdly, prioritize sustainability and injury prevention when adapting your technique. Long-term progress can only be achieved if you maintain your overall health. It is not advantageous to repeatedly train in a manner that leads to injuries, even if it means moving slightly more weight in the short term.

By focusing on these aspects of technique, you can enhance your performance in chin-ups/pull-ups while safeguarding your well-being for continued progress.

Reduction of the pull height

In this phase, your focus will be on refining your chin-up/pull-up technique to minimize the range of motion of the exercise, enabling you to handle heavier weights. These adjustments are applicable to both pull-ups and chin-ups and can be implemented regardless of the designated pull up height in competitions.

One method to decrease the pull up height is by making modifications to your grip on the bar. By rotating your wrist upward, you effectively reduce the length of your forearm. As a result, you achieve an increased pulling height for the same range of motion, requiring less effort to pull yourself up. This wrist rotation technique is commonly referred to as a semi false grip.

A false grip, originally used in gymnastics, involves placing the wrist directly on the ring or bar. However, in the case of a semi false grip, the wrist is actively rotated upward and firmly secured to the bar. Several factors come into play to achieve this technique successfully. Firstly, you need a bar with a good grip and sufficient thickness that allows for a full grip, including the pinky finger. Dry and chalked hands are essential to maintain a secure hold, and having strength and flexibility in wrist flexion is also important. Additionally, it's beneficial to have a high entry point on the bar that allows you to grip it fully without needing to jump.

 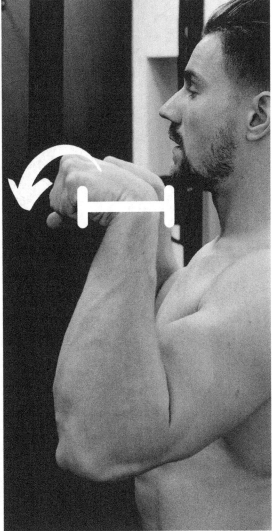

Shortening the forearm with a semi false grip (sagitally) while increasing the distance to the bar.

If your gym lacks a suitable bar or prohibits the use of chalk, it may be worth considering finding an alternative gym or discussing these limitations with the gym management. Such environments can often hinder progress and limit your potential. Once you have addressed these issues, you can focus on overcoming the challenge of active insufficiency in your wrist flexors when attempting to hang in a false grip. This occurs because maintaining a firm grip with a flexed wrist can be difficult due to limited flexibility in the wrist extensors. You can test your flexibility by attempting to make a fist while fully flexing your wrist. If you find that you lack flexibility, you can perform a simple stretch: Make a fist and rest your extended arms on it with your shoulders positioned directly above your wrists. The knuckles of both fists should face each other. Gradually bend your wrists without bending your elbows, and increase the pressure whenever you feel the stretch lessening slightly.

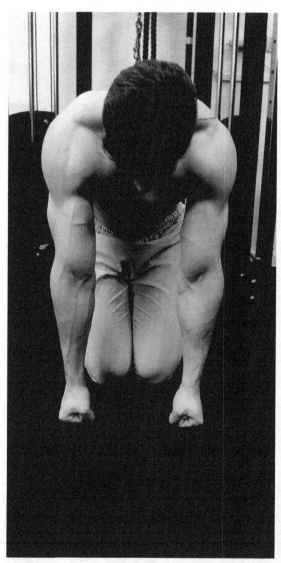 

Stretch for a better semi false grip

To avoid any discomfort or pain caused by the skin pinching during your grip, it is advisable to transition into the semi false grip by starting from above the bar. Reach around the bar as far as possible and firmly squeeze your hand. Then, rotate your hand into the desired semi false grip position and maintain a strong grip to secure it. It is important to note that achieving a solid semi false grip in the chin-up grip may be slightly more challenging due to the supination of the forearm. However, it is still recommended to implement this technique effectively in chin-ups as well.

However, it's worth noting that a strong semi false grip may not be suitable for everyone. If you prefer a narrower pull-up grip, pay attention to whether the semi false grip hampers your performance by increasing the distance to the bar more than it helps you by shortening the forearm. Finding your individual sweet spot of a firm grip and optimal leverage is crucial in this case.

If you find that your hands are too small to securely grip the bar and maintain stability in a semi false grip, an alternative to consider is using a suicide grip. This grip involves placing your thumb on the same side as your fingers, allowing for increased contact area and facilitating upward rotation. The purpose of adopting this grip variation is to achieve a similar effect as with a regular semi false grip.

Grip technique for less skin pinching

Suicide grip for pull ups/chin ups

Another effective technique for reducing the range of motion in chin/pull-ups is adjusting your shoulder position. By pulling your shoulders down and away from your ears while hanging from the bar, you can raise your chin higher and minimize the distance traveled. This becomes particularly crucial in the top position of the exercise, where the proper positioning of your shoulders can determine the validity of a repetition. Correct shoulder positioning can make a difference of several centimeters in pull height. In addition to using the semi false grip, actively depressing your shoulders is crucial. Pulling them down and away from your ears as much as possible helps maintain a stable and advantageous position. If competition rules allow, you can start engaging this shoulder depression even before initiating the chin/pull-up. Holding this position isometrically is much easier than trying to achieve it while under heavy loads during the pulling motion.

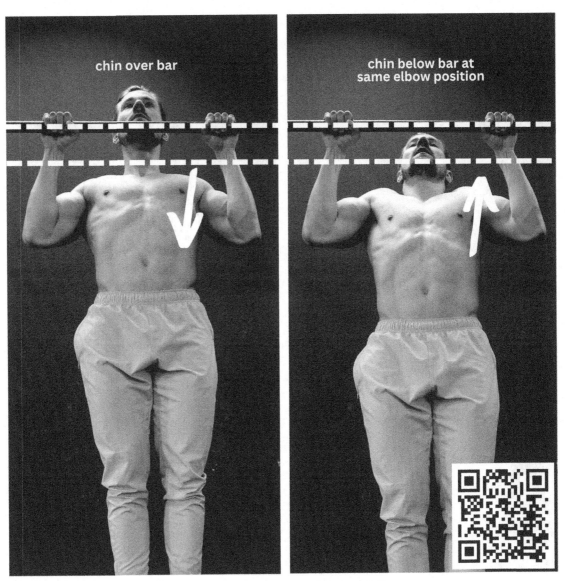

Different chin height at the same elbow position due to an active depression of the shoulder (left).

The correct posture

2.2.2.2

Now that we have already made adjustments to minimize the required pull height, let's shift our focus to efficiently completing the remaining part of the pull-up. The pull phase can be divided into two distinct segments: the lift-off and the closing of the chin/pull-up. These two phases are divided at approximately 90° elbow flexion or when the upper arm is parallel to the floor. During the lift-off phase, your shoulders move away from the bar in a sagittal plane, determined by the effective length of your upper arm. The effective length of your upper arm refers to the resulting length, which varies based on your grip width. It reaches its maximum with a shoulder-width grip.

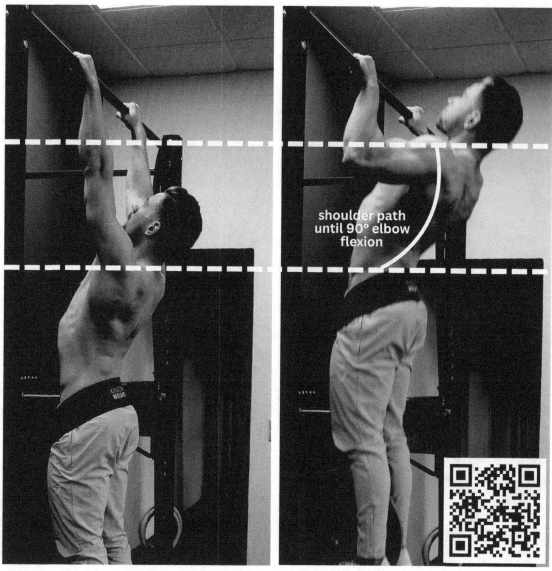

shoulder path until 90° elbow flexion

Lift off to about 90° at the elbow. During the lift-off, you move away from the bar until you reach the maximum distance from the bar at about 90° elbow flexion.

To effectively work in this phase, it is crucial to adjust your posture to meet its demands. One way to achieve this is by initiating the movement with a hyperextension of your thoracic spine, which can be facilitated by your pectoral muscles. By keeping your arms fixed in position, this hyperextension allows your chest to straighten your rib cage, resulting in a specific posture that offers significant advantages.

Compared to a neutral thoracic spine position, the hyperextended posture enables the weight to move more vertically as you lift off, even when your shoulders are moving away from the bar. Additionally, this posture aligns your latissimus, teres major, and posterior shoulder muscles more effectively with the direction of movement. As a result, a greater number of muscle fibers engage in pulling in the desired direction, leading to a more powerful lift-off. Moreover, a slight hyperextension of the spine allows you to achieve shoulder depression while hanging, reducing the risk of impingement.

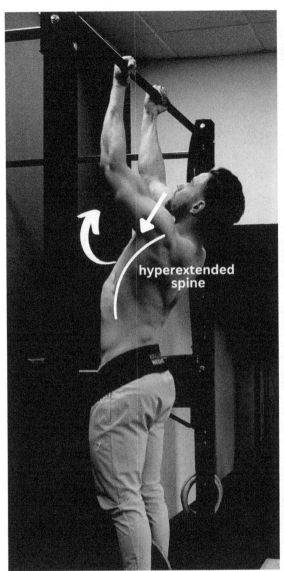 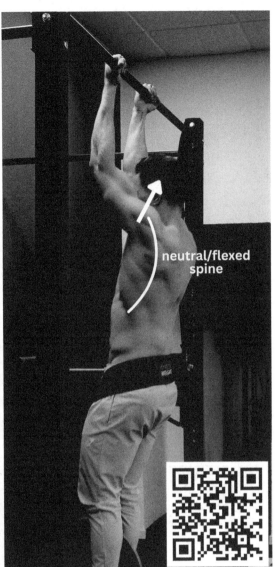

Lift off with spine hyperextended (left) and spine straight/slightly curved (right). The hyperextended position allows for low-risk depression of the shoulder.

After assuming the hyperextension position, it is crucial to pull your shoulders into a depression without adding any additional retraction. Avoiding retraction is important as it would shorten your latissimus muscle, which can have a negative impact on the lift-off. Furthermore, contracting your rhomboids during retraction would somewhat diminish the shoulder depression. Similarly, protracting the shoulders would stretch your latissimus muscle, creating a better length-tension relationship during the lift-off. However, it would also increase the distance to the bar, which can be detrimental. Therefore, during the lift-off, it is recommended to keep your shoulders in a depressed position and approximately in a neutral lateral position, with slight individual variations as

needed. Throughout the entire chin/pull up movement, it is essential to ensure that every centimeter of latissimus contraction results in effective downward movement of the upper arm. The latissimus is a large muscle that originates extensively from the thoracolumbar fascia, ilium, and lumbar spine, among other areas (14). Due to these connections, the latissimus is capable of hyperextending the lumbar spine when your legs are freely suspended and tilting your pelvis forward. To ensure that each latissimus contraction translates into arm movement, it is necessary to stabilize your lumbar spine and hips. Failure to do so can cause the contraction of the latissimus to induce unfavorable movements in the lumbar spine or hips, and the resulting excessive

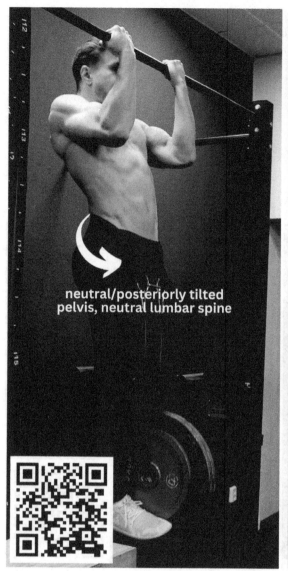 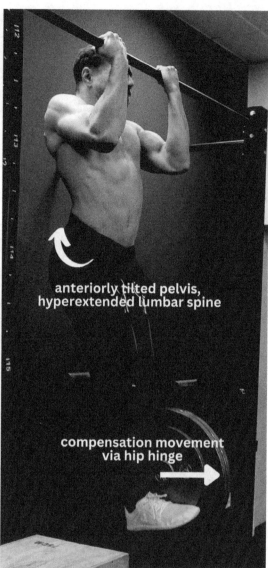

neutral/posteriorly tilted pelvis, neutral lumbar spine

anteriorly tilted pelvis, hyperextended lumbar spine

compensation movement via hip hinge

Chin up with stable hips (left) and with a stronger hollow back (right). To compensate for the hollow back, you can push your legs slightly forward.

shortening can lead to an unfavorable force-length ratio of the muscle. To prevent these issues, it is important for your abdominal muscles, particularly, to contract and prevent rotation in the hips and extension in the spine. If the rotation cannot be prevented, a slight hip flexion, within the competition rules, can be used to shift the additional weight slightly forward, assisting the latissimus in maintaining some length.

Before proceeding to the closing phase of the movement, which occurs after approximately 90° of elbow flexion and involves pulling yourself closer to the bar, let's review the sequence of movements thus far. You start by assuming an elevated entry point, gripping the bar from above, and locking your wrists into a semi false grip. Then, you position yourself in the hang under the bar, lifting your thoracic spine, depressing your shoulders, and stabilizing your hips and lumbar spine by engaging your abdominal mus-

cles. The pull is initiated with a hyperextended thoracic spine until reaching about 90° of elbow flexion or when the upper arm is parallel to the floor. From this point, you enter the closing phase, aiming to bring your chin over the bar or achieve a valid pull height. The efficiency of the closing phase depends greatly on how close you are to the bar after a technically clean lift-off.

At this stage, you have the option to bring your chin horizontally or vertically over the bar, depending on your chosen closing technique. For a horizontal chin position over the bar, you slightly release the stretched position of your spine and utilize a combination of arm extension and flexion, pushing your head forward. The degree of thoracic spine rounding during this movement depends on factors such as arm length and pulling technique. If your goal is a horizontal chin position, your closing technique should follow a horizontal path, known as horizontal closing.

In the case of a chin up, the required horizontal range of motion is minimal due to the supinated grip, and the differences between horizontal and vertical closing are relatively small. With the elbows positioned in front of the body and a firm grip on the bar, you can typically close a chin up in a more vertical manner. This means you can maintain the hyperextended position or deviate only slightly from it, primarily relying on the movement of the elbows and shoulders to pull yourself over the bar. This is also why chin ups in the top position often feel more manageable compared to pull ups. The forearms remain relatively stable, allowing for consistent force exertion in the pulling direction.

 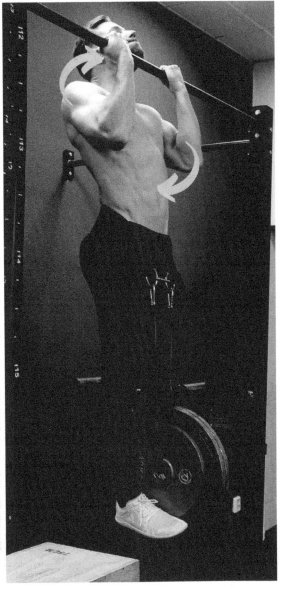

Horizontally closed pull up.

When it comes to pull ups, the approach to horizontal closing differs slightly. In order to bring your chin over the bar during a pull up, you need to retract your elbows and push your head forward. However, this movement compromises the optimal position of your forearms, making it more challenging to generate additional force in that position. As a result, pull ups generally become more difficult and less "grindable" at this stage. It's important to be aware that placing a strong emphasis on horizontal closing in pull ups increases the risk of injury. This is because achieving a sufficient horizontal range of motion may require sacrificing proper shoulder depression, putting your shoulder in an unstable position under load. It is advisable to avoid this in the long term for the sake of maintaining shoulder health.

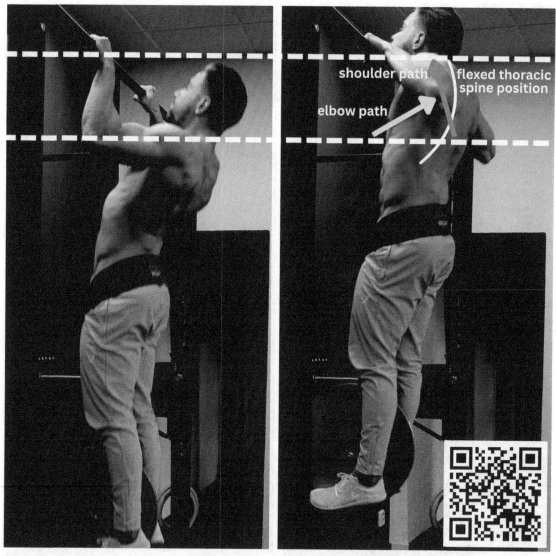

Horizontally closed pull up. The darker arrow marks the shoulder path and the lighter arrow the elbow path during the closing.

An alternative approach to closing pull ups is the vertical method, where you focus on lifting your chin in a purely vertical direction above the bar. While this technique allows you to achieve a valid pull up height, it can be more challenging to execute accurately. However, it's important to note that in competitive settings, this type of closing is rarely encountered. This is because a vertically closed pull up requires significantly more arm adduction compared to a horizontal close. Additionally, it places considerable demands on the muscles in your upper back to sustain the hyperextended position while being intensely contracted. When dealing with near-maximum loads, performing a purely vertical close becomes exceedingly difficult due to the substantial amount of force required. Nevertheless, incorporating vertical closing into your workout routine can be beneficial for targeting and strengthening the challenging upper portion of the pull up.

Vertical closed pull up.

To optimize your pull up closing technique, it is crucial to strike a balance between extremes. The goal is to minimize excessive elbow retraction and arm adduction while keeping your forearms relatively vertical under the bar. This positioning enables you to generate more power during the closing phase of the pull up. To bring your chin over the bar, you should release your hyperextended position slightly and apply a subtle compression. This gentle compression not only facilitates the closing movement but also creates a favorable force-length relationship for your latissimus muscle, as it accompanies a stretch. By implementing this technique, you can achieve an efficient closing motion without placing excessive strain on your shoulders.

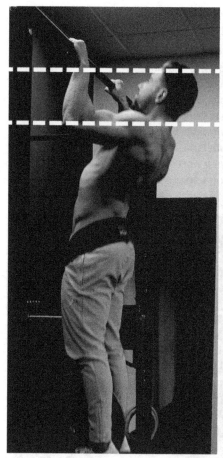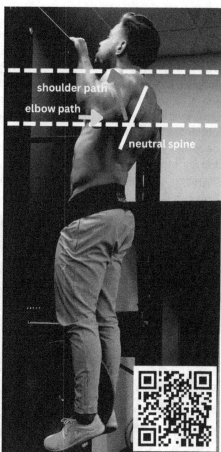

shoulder path
elbow path

neutral spine

Semi-vertical closing.

2.2.2.3   Breathing during chin/pull up

To prepare for the chin/pull-up, exhale while engaging your abdominal muscles to create tension and promote a posterior pelvic tilt (PPT). This action stabilizes your hips and prevents excessive hyperextension of the lumbar spine during the later phases of the pull-up. It is important to maintain this abdominal tension throughout the exercise. As you transition into the hang position, inhale and expand your chest, which allows for a more advantageous lifting position. Hold your breath as needed throughout one or more repetitions, and exhale during the passive hang phase.

2.2.2.4   Gaze direction

The direction of your gaze can have an impact on your body positioning and movement trajectory. During the lift-off phase, slightly lift your chin and focus your eyes on the bar. This will help facilitate the hyperextension of your thoracic

spine, creating a smoother and more natural movement. On the other hand, during the closing phase, lower your chin and look forward. This will make it more comfortable to transition into a compressed position and move forward. Being mindful of these subtle adjustments becomes increasingly important as you develop strength. However, even beginners can benefit from familiarizing themselves with these movement patterns to gain a better understanding of how to intentionally control and maintain proper body positioning.

Set Up   2.2.2.5

In order to optimize your performance in chin/pull-ups, there are several important settings and preparations to consider. Firstly, make sure that the height of the bar allows you to hang with your legs fully extended. A bar height of approximately 2.3m–2.5m is generally suitable for most athletes. Additionally, the bar should have a diameter that allows for a complete grip, and a textured surface to ensure a secure hold. Powder-coated bars with a diameter of around 30–35mm are recommended for optimal grip. Regardless of the type of bar grip, using chalk, preferably in liquid form, can greatly benefit in maintaining a secure and firm grip during your chin/pull-up exercises.

2.2.2.6   **Belt adjustment**

For beginners who are not using much additional weight, positioning the weight close to the hips may feel the most natural, as it minimally affects the body's center of gravity. Using a short chain or strap can also reduce the pendulum motion of the weight, making it easier to stabilize. Therefore, a high weight position is more suitable for beginners.
However, as you progress and start adding 15–20kg or more of additional weight, it is recommended to switch to a position between the feet. This allows you to brace against the weight and adjust your posture as described earlier. You can even push the weight slightly forward with your feet to achieve better compression and avoid the need for wide plates, which can make the pull more comfortable. The longer pendulum motion in this position also provides increased stability for a few repetitions, as it is harder to swing. However, once the weight starts swinging, it becomes more challenging to stabilize. Nevertheless, the low weight position is preferred for heavy loads and is worth considering. It's important to note that the difference in weight positioning is generally less significant in pull/chin-ups compared to dips.

2.2.2.7   **Entry**

To establish a solid starting point for your chin/pull-up, it is recommended to use an elevated surface, such as a box, to assist with positioning. Here is a guide to help you set up:

1. Place your weights on the box and secure them with a weightlifting belt, ensuring they are properly centered.

2. Step onto the box and put on the weightlifting belt, making sure everything is adjusted correctly.

3. Grip the bar with your desired grip.

4. Release the weight from the box while keeping one leg in contact with the box. Use the hanging leg to control the weight and minimize swinging or excessive movement.

5. Transition into the hang position, maintaining proper posture.

6. Finally, release the second leg from the box, allowing your body to support the full load. This ensures that your body position is optimized for the exercise.

By following these steps, you can establish a stable starting position and minimize unnecessary movements or swinging when performing the chin/pull-up.

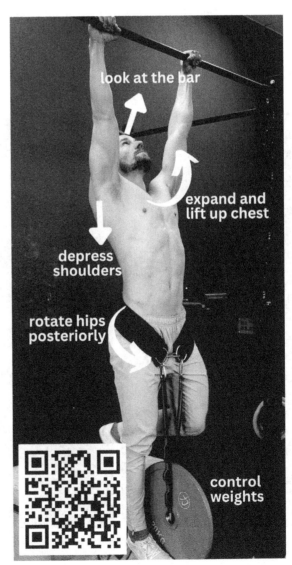

look at the bar

expand and lift up chest

depress shoulders

rotate hips posteriorly

control weights

Optimized entry into the pull/chin up

2.2.3

Common
weighted chin/
pull ups mistake

In the following section, I will discuss common errors or compensatory movements that it is important to avoid during your training sessions and in competition. By minimizing these compensations or keeping them within acceptable limits, you can decrease the risk of injury and optimize your long-term performance.

2.2.3.1

Depression without hyperextension of the thoracic spine

Initiating your chin/pull up by strongly depressing your shoulders without lifting your chest, which involves hyperextending your thoracic spine, places your shoulders in an unfavorable and weak position for the lift off. This action pulls your shoulder blades downward and narrows the subacromial space, potentially causing stabbing pain for some athletes. It is crucial to avoid this position, even if immediate issues are not present. To maintain the benefits of shoulder depression while preventing the constriction of the subacromial space, it is important to elevate your chest. This ensures that your arm is not directly overhead, reducing the degree of constriction. Alternatively, if you want to train the full range of motion of your shoulder blades without starting in a depressed position, you can initiate the movement without hyperextending your thoracic spine and gradually lift your chest as you begin the depression.

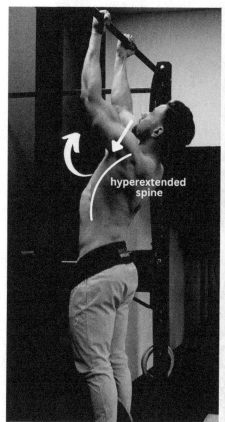 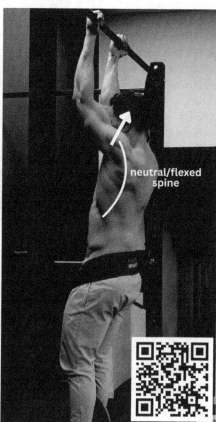

Lift-off with spine hyperextended (left) and spine straight/slightly curved (right). The hyperextended position allows for low-risk depression of the shoulder to optimize your range of motion.

Absence of shoulder depression

Regardless of whether you start with a shoulder depression or in a passive hang position, it is important to actively pull your shoulders into a depression during the upward movement of the chin/pull up. This active stabilization of the joint against external forces is crucial for minimizing the risk of injury during exercise. Allowing your shoulders to regularly elevate under load has been shown to increase the likelihood of shoulder injury. During pulling exercises, the shoulder undergoes 60° of abduction or 60° of flexion, both of which anatomically narrow the subacromial space (13). Therefore, it is important to avoid additional compression from external loads that are not actively stabilized. As mentioned earlier, maintaining a stable shoulder depression is also important for achieving a sufficient pull height.

Active depression of the shoulder (left) vs. elevation of the shoulder (right).

2.2.3.3

Unstable external rotation

Properly stabilizing external rotation, especially in the context of a pull/chin-up where the elbows are pushed inward, brings both health and performance advantages. On the other hand, insufficient external rotation stabilization has its drawbacks. In the case of a pull up, this is evident when there is significant internal rotation of the arms, causing the elbows to rotate backward and outward. As mentioned earlier, having the forearms approximately vertical under the bar is beneficial for generating force in the pulling direction. However, several muscles involved in the pull/chin up, such as the latissimus and teres major, exert torque that promotes internal rotation of the upper arm. If excessive internal rotation occurs during the pulling motion, the elbows move outward and backward.

As a result, the forearms deviate from the vertical position, leading to suboptimal force application in the pulling direction. Therefore, minimizing internal rotation is crucial for executing pull ups efficiently. From a health perspective, actively stabilizing external rotation offers additional benefits. By engaging the shoulder capsule in external rotation, specific mechanoreceptors in the shoulder are activated. This triggers muscle reflexes that counteract the tensile stresses experienced by the shoulders (18). As discussed in the previous section, during pulling exercises, there is a natural constriction of the subacromial space. This vulnerable position is further exacerbated by internal rotation and should be avoided under load whenever possible (13).

Comparison of the forearm position with stable external rotation (left) and abduction and extension of the upper arm resulting from strong internal rotation (right).

Lack of abdominal tension/hip control

2.2.3.4

As mentioned previously, during the pull/chin-up, the latissimus muscle has the potential to rotate your hip and hyperextend your lumbar spine if not actively stabilized. To prevent this compensatory movement, it is important to actively engage and brace your hips and lumbar spine by tightening your abdominal muscles during the pull/chin-up. By doing so, you can maintain proper alignment and minimize the risk of excessive movement in the hip and lumbar regions.

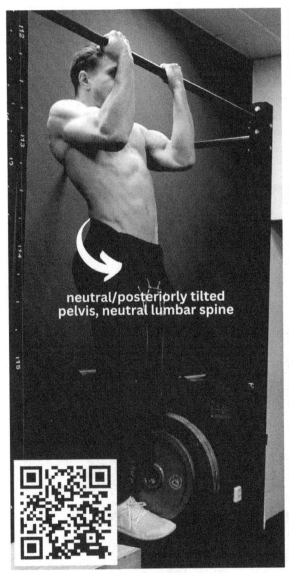

neutral/posteriorly tilted pelvis, neutral lumbar spine

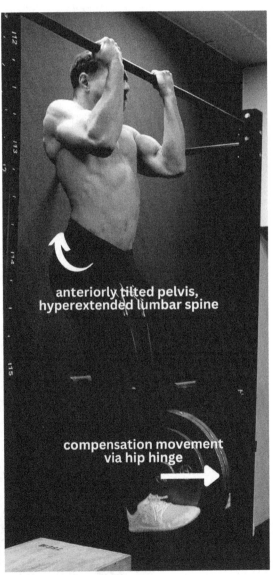

anteriorly tilted pelvis, hyperextended lumbar spine

compensation movement via hip hinge

Chin up with stable hips (left) and with a stronger hollow back (right). To compensate for the hollow back, you can push your legs slightly forward.

2.2.3.6

Curl & Shrug Closing

The 'error' referred to here is the combination of a lack of shoulder depression and unstable external rotation in the pull/chin-up exercise. Curl & shrug closing is a type of closing technique used in pull/chin-ups where you accelerate horizontally over the bar without additional arm adduction, using a curling movement of the arms and shrugging movement of the shoulders. This type of closing is commonly observed when performing pull-ups with near-maximal loads. However, this technique poses certain risks to the shoulders, particularly due to the absence of shoulder depression and external rotation, which can compromise joint stability. Additionally, there is an increased risk of elbow problems associated with this technique. The fast and forceful horizontal closing generates high peak forces in the elbow joint due to the strong contraction and flexion of the arms. Athletes who are susceptible to elbow in-juries or experience symptoms such as golfer's/tennis elbow may be particularly affected. In our coaching experience, we have found that many elbow and shoulder issues can be resolved by transitioning to a controlled pulling and closing technique in the pull/chin-up exercise.

Uncontrolled negatives

2.2.3.7

When performing multiple repetitions in pull/chin-ups, it's important to address the issue of swinging that can occur when executing the negative phase of the movement without control. As pull/chin-ups are an acyclic exercise, it's crucial to prepare for the subsequent repetition after completing each one. If the negative phase is performed in an uncontrolled manner, both you and any additional weight may start swinging in the sagittal plane, leading to difficulties in maintaining stability. To mitigate this, it's recommended to focus on controlling the negatives and slightly reducing the

A curl & shrug closing is created by an elevation (shrug) of the shoulders with a simultaneous flexion of the elbows (curl) to bring the chin over the bar.

speed of the movement to prevent excessive swinging. By doing so, you can ensure a better starting position for your next repetition. It's important to note that when aiming to perform multiple repetitions, it's essential to give equal attention to both the positive (lifting) and negative (lowering) phases of the exercise. By prioritizing control and minimizing swinging, you'll be better equipped to execute subsequent repetitions effectively.

2.2.4

Variations weighted pull/ chin ups

Having gained a thorough understanding of the optimal technique for chin-ups/pull-ups and the common mistakes to avoid, you are now ready to explore different exercises and exercise categories that can further enhance your performance in this movement. In the following steps, you will delve into various variations of the pull-up/chin-up and analyze which ones are most suitable for your training and why. By examining different exercise variations, you will be able to identify the ones that align with your specific needs and goals, enabling you to maximize your pull-up/chin-up performance. Furthermore, you will also explore assistance exercises that can complement your training, helping you identify and correct any technical errors that may arise during your pull-up/chin-up practice.

This comprehensive approach will equip you with the knowledge and tools necessary to continually refine and improve your pull-up/chin-up technique, ensuring long-term progress and minimizing the risk of errors in your training. Let's proceed to the next step, where we will explore the various pull-up/chin-up variations and their benefits.

2.2.4.1

Chin ups/pull ups

Execution: If your competition lift is the pull-up, incorporating the chin-up as a variation in your training can be highly beneficial (or vice versa). The key difference lies in the grip position, as the chin-up involves a supinated grip (underhand) instead of the pronated grip (overhand) used in pull-ups.

Application: Although the activation of muscles is similar in chin-ups and pull-ups, these two movements differ in terms of the planes they operate on, resulting in slight variations in the stress placed on your muscles and passive structures. To ensure holistic back muscle development, it is recommended to include exercises that involve both shoulder adduction and extension in your training. By incorporating the pull-up as a varia-

tion when the chin-up is your competition exercise, you can address these nuances and add the necessary accents to your training. Additionally, the chin-up and pull-up can serve as substitutes for each other in case of injury or limitations. If you are unable to perform one variation due to, for example, wrist problems preventing supination, you can rely on the other variation to maintain your performance. The similarity in movement patterns allows for a seamless transition between the two exercises. By considering these factors and incorporating both chin-ups and pull-ups into your training routine, you can optimize your back muscle development and adapt to any limitations or injuries that may arise. This ensures a well-rounded approach to your pull-up training.

2.2.4.2   **Neutral grip**

Execution: The neutral grip in pull-ups is achieved by using a parallel bar with a semi-pronated hand position, where the palms of your hands face each other.
Application: The neutral grip closely resembles the movement pattern of the chin-up. However, it offers the advantage of not placing as much stress on your shoulders and wrists, as it doesn't require complete supination of the hands as the chin-up does. This makes the neutral grip a suitable alternative for chin-ups if you experience any difficulties or discomfort with the chin up variation.

During the off-season or periods of longer training, incorporating the neutral grip can be beneficial. Additionally, it can be used for overloading purposes. Depending on the setup of the parallel bars, you can pull straight up without having to maneuver around the bar, resulting in increased efficiency. The grip position behind the imaginary crossbar also reduces the distance to the bar, making it a potentially stronger grip variation for many athletes. If you don't have access to a parallel bar setup, the neutral grip can be effectively performed on rings, providing a versatile and adaptable option for incorporating this grip variation into your training routine.

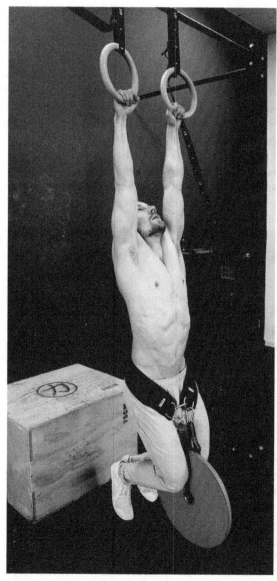

Chin up with a neutral grip on the gymnastic rings.

2.2.4.3

Tempo pull/chin ups

Tempo pulls/chin ups are all variations of execution that deviate from your normal movement speed in a planned manner. You manipulate the tempo of the individual movement phases with the intention of improving and strengthening these technically. In other words, you can use the tempo to control which part of the movement you want to pay particular attention to. In the following, we will present you with a 'best practice' of different tempos and explain when and why you should use them. From the tempos presented, many more combinations can be made that may be useful for your specific case. So don't be discouraged from testing other tempos for yourself just because they are not listed here.

2.2.4.4

Slow negatives 2-3/1/1/0

Execution: The negative movement of the pull/chin ups is slowed down to two to three seconds. The reversal points and the positive movement are performed at your normal pace.
Application: This variation is particularly useful when you experience stability or positioning issues with your shoulders. By incorporating controlled negatives, you can enhance your ability to maintain proper external rotation, which involves pushing your elbows inward and executing controlled movements of your shoulder blades from depression to elevation. This exercise can also improve your Mind-Muscle Connection, allowing you to focus more consciously on specific muscles during the movement. Developing this conscious targeting of movements and muscles is essential for implementing specific techniques that require precise activation and positioning.

2.2.4.5

Paused upper reversal point 1/1/1-3

Execution: The upper reversal point after the positive phase is held isometrically for one to three seconds.
Application: This variation holds significant importance for competitive athletes. Many athletes struggle to achieve the correct pulling height during competitions. By incorporating paused pull-ups at the upper reversal point, you can technically improve your positioning in this critical phase. This exercise allows you to better estimate the additional weight you can handle while still achieving the required pulling height in competition. With paused pull-ups, you can learn and reinforce healthy and effective positioning of your shoulders and elbows by emphasizing the depression of your shoulders and pushing your elbows inward under the bar. This helps to develop a solid and efficient technique.

Paused pull/chin ups at around 90° elbow flexion

2.2.4.6

Execution: In this tempo variation, you do not pause at one of the reversal points but instead pause before completing the closing phase of the pull/chin-up, typically at approximately 90° elbow flexion. From this paused position, you proceed to complete the repetition with a closing movement, focusing on specific closing techniques that are relevant to your training goals, such as horizontal or vertical closing.
Application: The point of approximately 90° elbow flexion is often a challenging sticking point for many athletes, as it represents the phase of the movement where you have the greatest distance from the bar. By incorporating an isometric hold in this position through the tempo variation, you can specifically target and strengthen this area, helping to overcome the sticking point. Additionally, this variation allows you to refine and improve your closing technique, providing an opportunity to enhance your overall pull/chin-up performance.

Explosive positive 1/1/X/0

2.2.4.7

Execution: The positive phase of the pull/chin-up is executed with maximum effort, aiming to generate as much acceleration and force as possible. While the actual speed may vary depending on the weight being used, the primary focus is on exerting maximum force per repetition, pushing yourself to the limit within your capabilities.
Application: This variation of the pull/chin-up is employed to enhance your strength capacity without necessarily

working with maximum or sub-maximum loads. By emphasizing strong acceleration in the positive phase, there is an expectation of improved strength development and potential carryover effects to exercises such as muscle-ups. The high recruitment and activation of relevant muscle fibers, similar to heavier loads, contribute to the desired training effect. However, it is crucial to maintain proper technique and ensure that the increased movement speed does not compromise your form or lead to a deterioration in your execution.

2.2.4.8

Slow positive 1/1/2-3/0

Execution: The positive phase of the pull/chin ups is performed with a reduced movement speed, intentionally slowing down the pace of the exercise.

Application: Slowing down the movement speed can have several benefits. Firstly, it allows for better control and stabilization of the shoulder blades and elbow position, reducing the likelihood of technique errors. This can be particularly helpful if you are working on improving your shoulder and elbow stability or if you are recovering from an injury. Additionally, by performing the exercise at a slower tempo, you can focus on learning new techniques or getting accustomed to certain exercises.

In all tempo variations, it is recommended to allocate one second to the lower reversal point. This pause allows for a moment of reorganization and ensures that you start each repetition from a perfect starting position. Incorporating this pause is especially beneficial during high-intensity sets, as it helps to maintain proper technique throughout the entire set. However, it's important to note that this approach is not mandatory for everyone and can be adjusted according to individual preferences and needs.

2.2.4.9

Extension biased pull ups/chest to bar pull ups

Execution: When performing the pull/chin up, there are two distinct pull phases that involve different positions of the thoracic spine: hyperextended (extension biased) and slightly rounded (flexion biased) due to compression on the front of the body. In this variation, the focus is on the hyperextended spine position. Instead of transitioning to compression as you close the movement, you maintain tension in your posterior muscle chain and strive to bring your chest to the bar from below. This keeps your forearms relatively vertical under the bar and allows for a fully vertical closing movement. The goal is to maintain an upward position of your sternum throughout the entire exercise, maximizing your range of motion and targeting end-degree positions.

Application: This variation is particularly beneficial for athletes who struggle to lift their ribcage under load during pulling exercises and have difficulty guiding and stabilizing their shoulder blades into retraction and slight depression. If you tend to round your thoracic spine and elevate your shoulders prematurely during pulling exercises, and find it challenging to maintain an upward position of your sternum, this variation can effectively address those issues. Additionally, it helps strengthen the top position of your pull/chin up by training a greater range of motion in a vertical closing movement.

Flexion biased pull ups   **2.2.4.10**

Execution: In this variation, the focus shifts from locking the thoracic spine in a hyperextended position and retracting the shoulders to adopting a protracted shoulder position and engaging the front muscle chain instead of the back. After the lift-off phase, where the thoracic spine is still lifted, you protract your shoulders, push your chest back, and engage your abdominal muscles to consciously lower your sternum.

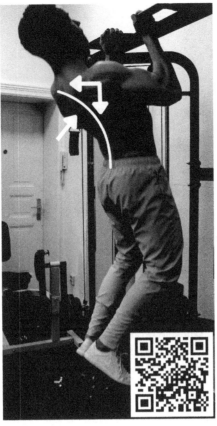

Extension biased pull ups   Flexion biased pull ups

Application: This variation of the pull up is beneficial for restoring full mobility to the shoulder blades and thoracic spine. If you struggle with pulling your shoulder blades apart and extending your arms forward, the flexion-biased pull up can help restore that range of motion. The more rounded posture during this variation provides a deeper stretch to the latissimus muscles and trains them over a larger range of motion. Consequently, many athletes consider this variation to be highly effective for targeting the latissimus muscles.

2.2.4.11

Partial repetitions

Execution: In this variation, the pull/chin up is performed over a reduced, partial range of motion, with the specific range determined by individual goals.

Application: Partial repetitions are utilized to target specific areas of the lift for technical improvement or overload. They can be used to address sticking points or unload certain positions by deliberately omitting them. Partial reps allow for the use of heavier weights, facilitating overload and strength development in the targeted range. Research suggests that partial reps can be slightly more effective for strength adaptations in the partial range of motion compared to full reps (20). However, for beginners and less advanced athletes, specialized training with partial reps may not be necessary, and they should focus on developing strength in the full range of motion.

For muscle building, training at longer muscle lengths is particularly important. If the full range of motion is already included in your training, the difference in muscle growth between partial and full reps may not be significant. Therefore, when incorporating partial repetitions, it is recommended to combine them with a full range of motion exercises in your training plan for optimal results and to ensure a well-rounded approach (20).

2.2.5

Assistance exercises weighted pull/chin ups

Similar to dips, weighted pull/chin ups as a primary exercise generally do not necessitate additional strength assistance exercises. The inclusion of additional weight allows for scaling the intensity of pull/chin ups across different ranges. Moreover, the versatility of pull/chin up variations enables training at higher frequencies without encountering significant challenges.

2.2.5.1

Hypertrophy assistance

When it comes to selecting hypertrophy assistance exercises for pull/chin ups, it's important to analyze your own execution and identify any weaknesses or limitations in specific muscle groups. Simply adding more sets or variations of the main exercise may not always be the most effective approach.

For example, if you notice that you're relying heavily on your arms during pull/chin ups and your legs start to move forward early in the set, indicating potential weakness in the latissimus muscles, adding another intense variation of pull/chin ups may not be the best solution. It could further fatigue the already loaded structures and hinder your recovery.

In such cases, incorporating a hypertrophy assistance exercise that specifically targets the latissimus while putting less systemic stress on your body can be beneficial. For instance, a latissimus dominant rowing exercise on a seated machine with a chest pad can be a good choice. The increased external stability allows you to focus more on the latissimus muscles, and the exercise involves fewer muscles for coordination and stabilization. As a result, it reduces overall fatigue and provides a targeted stimulus to develop the latissimus without overly taxing your system.

The key is to identify the specific muscle groups that need additional training and select assistance exercises that effectively target those areas while considering your overall training plan and recovery capacity.

Latissimus dominant pull assistance

2.2.5.2

While your latissimus is engaged in all pulling exercises, it's important to optimize the stimulus for maximum effectiveness during each repetition of your chosen assistance exercise. To achieve this, there are several factors to consider. Firstly, you should adjust your movement to establish a strong mind-muscle connection with the latissimus while minimizing the activation of other pulling muscles like the teres major, biceps, and trapezius. This can be achieved by positioning the fiber components of your latissimus in the optimal direction of the pull, based on your body position and setup. To accomplish this, keep the following points in mind.

1. **Avoid initiating the pull with retraction:** Initiating a pull movement with a retraction shortens the latissimus before the actual pull, limiting its potential for activation in the fully stretched position. It also activates the trapezius more, which can detract from the focus on the latissimus.

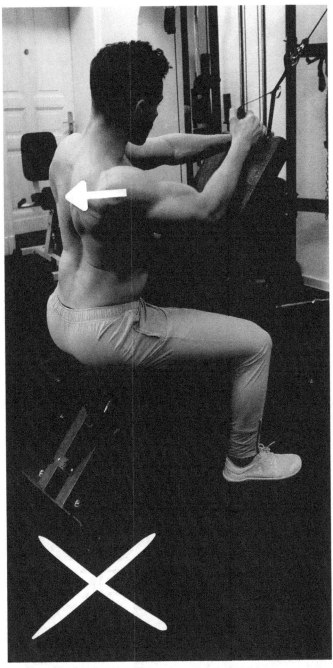 

Comparison lat pull with and without retraction

2. **Minimize strong elbow flexion (don't curl your rows!):** Consciously bending your elbow joint too much involves the arm flexors, taking emphasis away from the latissimus. Instead, focus on making the movement through your elbow and maintain forearm alignment with the cable. For dumbbell or barbell exercises, keep your forearms perpendicular to gravity. Pull the elbow close behind the body without excessive curling.

Comparison of cable rowing with strong and moderate elbow flexion.

3. **Work with different angles: Just like the chest, the latissimus has various fiber patterns. Training it in the same direction repeatedly may not stimulate all its fibers adequately. By integrating pulling exercises with different load angles into your training, you can target the latissimus from various perspectives. This can involve shoulder adduction movements and shoulder extension movements in different arm abduction positions.**

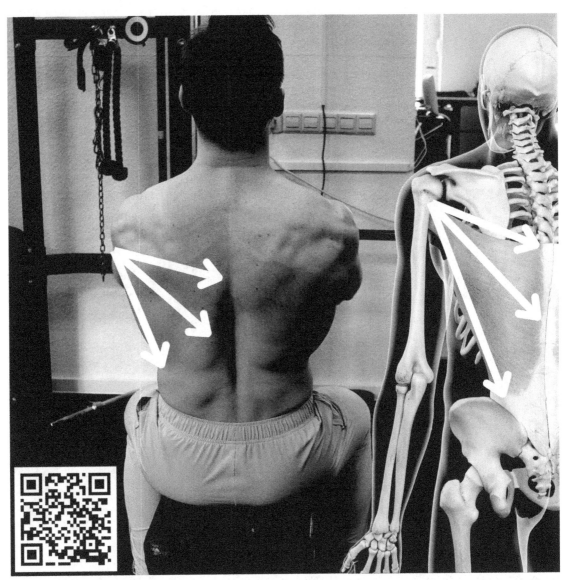

To train the latissimus holistically, you need to train different movements. These include shoulder adduction movements and shoulder extension movements in various abduction positions of the arm.

2.2.5.3

Upper back pull assistance

The upper back consists primarily of the trapezius, rhomboids, posterior shoulder, and latissimus fibers that run transversely. The trapezius is engaged in all pulling exercises as it plays a crucial role in shoulder blade movements and stability. Its different fiber sections contribute to shoulder blade retraction, depression, extension, and lateral flexion of the cervical spine. The upper portion of the trapezius is also involved in shoulder elevation through its connection to the clavicle and assists in the upward rotation of the scapula.

To emphasize the development of this area in your pulling exercises, as opposed to latissimus-dominant movements, consciously utilize the full range of motion of your scapulae from protraction to maximum retraction, including elevation. Initiate the rowing or pulling movement with a focus on retracting the shoulder blades. During the movement, try to maintain a slightly straightened and hyperextended thoracic spine. Instead of keeping your arms close to your body, you can slightly spread them apart to enhance muscle engagement and sensation in your upper back.

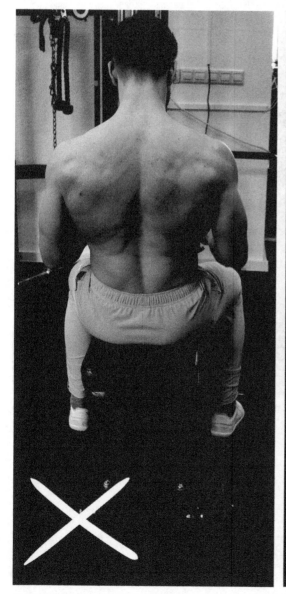

Contraction of the upper back by slightly spreading the arms, bringing the shoulder blades together, and hyperextending the thoracic spine.

Posterior shoulder dominant assistance

2.2.5.4

To specifically target your rear shoulder during rowing exercises, you can adjust your technique accordingly. Start by slightly spreading your arms away from your body as you perform the rowing movement. Allow the weight to pull your shoulders forward, maximizing the stretch in your rear shoulder muscles. For an even greater stretch, you can slightly rotate away from the cable or machine. When initiating the movement, focus solely on using your elbow and concentrate on pulling with your rear shoulder. Minimize tension on your arm flexors and instead generate force primarily

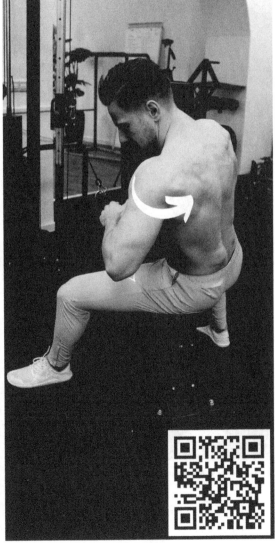

Rear delt row for a bias to the rear shoulder.

2.2.5.5   **Biceps curls**

While isolation exercises like biceps curls may not have a significant direct carryover to the main exercises, they still have their place in your training plan. Including isolated biceps training can be beneficial, particularly when combined with pull/chin up workouts. Performing curl variations with supination can be particularly effective.

During the chin/pull Up exercise, the shoulder extension places a stretch on the biceps brachii in the shoulder. This can limit the optimal stimulation of the biceps due to the decreased length change. By adding volume to your workout through isolated biceps training, you can compensate for this and provide additional stimulus to the biceps.

Training your biceps in different shoulder positions also contributes to shoulder stability. The long head of the biceps brachii serves as an important stabilizer of the shoulder joint. Additionally, this type of arms training, including biceps curls and triceps extensions, helps to strengthen and protect the scapular, elbow, and wrist joints. Therefore, apart from promoting hypertrophy of these muscle structures, including arm training exercises in your plan plays a crucial role in enhancing the resilience of your shoulder, elbow, and wrist to stress.

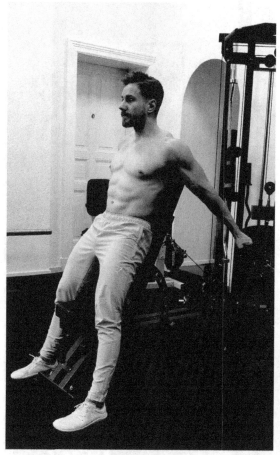
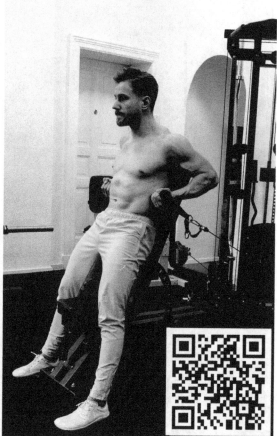

Behind the back curls (elbows behind the body).

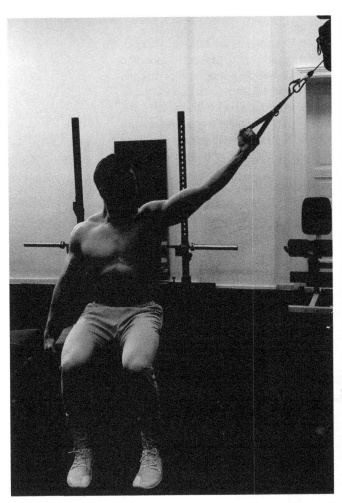 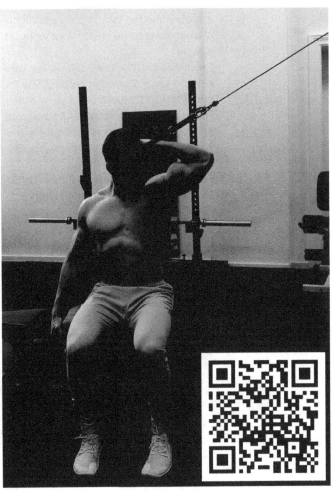

Front double biceps curls (elbows to the side of the body).

2.2.5.6

Core

To prevent hip rotation and maintain a stable core during chin ups and pull ups, it is important to have strong abdominal muscles. If you find yourself compensating with hip rotation or experiencing a hollow back during these exercises, it is recommended to incorporate additional abdominal training into your workout routine.

Exercises such as knee raises, leg raises, and toes to bar can be effective for strengthening your abdominal muscles. These exercises help engage your core and promote proper alignment by preventing both hip rotation and excessive spinal extension.

Ensure that as you perform these exercises, you focus not only on preventing hip rotation but also on maintaining a controlled flexion (curvature) of your spine. This will help you develop a stronger core and improve your stability during chin ups and pull ups.

Health assistance

2.2.5.7

Similar to dips, having mobile and stable shoulders with proper internal and external rotation is crucial for performing pull ups effectively. If you have limitations in any of these shoulder movements, it can negatively impact your pull up performance.

To address these limitations, I recommend referring to the corresponding section in the dips chapter that discusses shoulder health assistance exercises. These exercises can help improve the mobility and stability of your shoulders, which will have a positive impact on your pull up technique and overall performance.

By addressing any shoulder mobility and stability issues, you can enhance your ability to perform pull ups with proper form and reduce the risk of potential injuries.

Knee raises

Forearm training

Elbow injuries often stem from issues in the shoulder or wrist. By ensuring sufficient mobility and stability in the shoulder through the exercises mentioned earlier, you can minimize the risk of such injuries. However, it's important not to overlook the role of your forearm muscles in maintaining wrist and elbow health. In everyday life, if you place excessive and one-sided demands on your forearm muscles without providing compensatory movements and variety during training, you may be susceptible to overload injuries. These injuries often manifest as pain or inflammation in the tendonous attachment of the muscles on the elbow side, leading to conditions like golfers or tennis elbow. To prevent such injuries and promote wrist mobility and stability, incorporating additional forearm training into your routine can be beneficial alongside a well-rounded training plan and regular arm training. Here are some exercises you can incorporate:

Flexor Curls: Sit on the floor and place your forearm on a flat surface, such as a weight bench, with your palm facing up. Hold a dumbbell or small weight plate in your hand and slowly lower it down, allowing your hand to hang over the edge of the bench. Then, gradually bend your wrist upward, pulling the weight upward. Hold the tension for a few seconds and then slowly lower the weight back down to the starting position. This exercise targets the flexion of your wrist.

Extensor Curls: Place your forearm on the bench in the opposite direction, with the back of your hand facing up. Follow the same steps as the flexor curls, but this time focus on slowly bending your wrist downward, training extension.

Forearm flexor curls

Forearm extensor curls

Forearm twist (pronation & supination)

Brachioradialis curls

Forearm Twist (pronation and supination) - Sit on the floor and place your forearm on a flat surface, such as a weight bench. Take a unilaterally loaded dumbbell or curl bar in your hand and let it point upward perpendicular to the bench. Now slowly rotate your forearm to turn your palm down (pronation). Briefly hold the tension and then slowly rotate your palm upward (supination). Again, briefly hold the tension and then repeat the movement for several repetitions.

By incorporating these exercises, you can engage the muscles responsible for flexion, extension, and rotation of your wrist, thus improving its mobility and stability. Remember to start with lighter weights and gradually increase as you build strength and comfort with the movements.

Brachioradialis Curls - Supplemental training for the brachioradialis muscle can be highly beneficial in preventing elbow injuries associated with pull/chin-ups and muscle-ups. The brachioradialis muscle plays a key role in forearm flexion and wrist stabilization, as well as contributing to forearm supination and pronation.

Here's how you can effectively target this muscle with brachioradialis curls:
Hold a dumbbell in each hand, adopting an overhand grip with your palms facing down.
Stand with your feet hip-width apart, allowing your arms to hang down in front of your body in a fully extended position. Initiate the movement by bending your elbows, slowly lifting the dumbbells toward your shoulders. Focus on using primarily your elbow joint to drive the motion, minimizing involvement from your shoulder or wrist. As you lift the dumbbells, gradually rotate your palms so that they face upward at the end of the movement. This supination of the forearm helps further engage the brachioradialis muscle. Maintain control throughout the exercise, avoiding any swinging or excessive momentum. Slowly lower the dumbbells back to the starting position, fully extending your arms. Repeat the movement for the desired number of repetitions, ensuring proper form and engaging the brachioradialis muscle throughout the entire range of motion.

Athlete Michael Schulz, MMC competition 2021, Photo: Patrik Gossen and Nick Reisinger.

Weighted Muscle ups

2.3
Weighted
Muscle ups

The muscle up is a widely recognized and popular exercise in the field of calisthenics. In this book, we approach the muscle up from two perspectives: as a bodyweight exercise that can be learned as a skill, and as a competitive exercise in the realm of weighted calisthenics sport. The muscle up combines a pulling and pushing movement, aiming to transition from a hanging position to a support hold position above the bar, without relying on additional momentum from the body (unlike the kipping technique used in gymnastics). However, it's important to note that not all muscle ups are the same. Therefore, the first step is to establish the parameters of an ideal muscle up, allowing us to assess our current level and identify the necessary steps for achieving proper execution. In this book, we base our definition on the Final Rep rules used in 1RM weighted calisthenics competitions. It's worth mentioning that other sets of rules that permit different variations are not inherently inferior or incorrect. The underlying concept is to discourage the use of momentum and stretch-shortening cycles in order to make the muscle up more physically demanding and comparable across athletes. To achieve this, let's take a closer look at the guidelines outlined in the Final Rep rulebook.

"Once the first signal ("Platform ready!") is given, the athlete may step onto the platform. The athlete attaches the weight belt to his hip. Now the athlete moves to the start position on the box and grips the bar in a pronated grip. It is allowed to use a semi-false grip. The start position is considered to be taken as soon as the athlete has fully extended the elbows (180° joint angle). If it is necessary to achieve full elbow extension, the athlete is allowed to bend the knees slightly. The athlete waits for the start signal ("Go!") and may perform his attempt
after the given signal. It is allowed to swing forward and then directly initiate the pulling movement. As soon as the athlete finishes the Muscle Up with elbows fully extended (180° joint angle), he waits for the signal ("Box!") to finish the attempt. After the last signal is given, the athlete may swing back onto the box. The attempt is now finished. The judges then decide if the attempt was valid and the athlete is allowed to leave the platform.

Reasons for an invalid Bar Muscle Up:
The following list includes violations that result in a "No Rep".

1. Fail: the athlete is unable to pass the bar.

2. False grip: The athlete uses a false grip where at least one wrist or forearm touches the bar.

3. Bent Arms: The athlete starts the bar muscle up with bent arms. In certain cases of anatomically limited mobility (e.g. not being able to extend the elbows through 180˚), it is up to the athlete to tell and show this to the judges before entering the platform for the first attempt.

4. Kipping/kicking: The athlete generates momentum with an excessive tilting movement in the pelvis, an excessive hyperextension in the spine or with a kicking movement of the legs, which makes it easier for him/ her to overcome the bar. A minimal change in knee and hip angle that is not to the athlete's advantage is allowed.

5. Loss of control: the athlete loses control of the additional weight and the lower extremities, even after overcoming the bar.

6. Downward movement: the direction of the movement reverses before it is completed. A short pause on the bar is allowed. The chest may touch the bar.

7. Lockout: The direction of the movement reverses before full elbow extension is achieved after overcoming the bar.

8. Signal: the athlete misses or disregards a signal from the judges.

9. Chicken wing: The athlete performs a so-called "chicken wing" muscle up, in which the elbows overcome the bar one after the other. (1)"

To better understand the rationale behind the defined parameters for a clean muscle up in competitions, let's summarize some of the controversial points. It's important to note that this doesn't imply that other variations are inferior or less valuable. Context remains crucial in evaluating these factors.

1. **Initiation with extended arms: Starting the muscle up with extended arms eliminates the potential for generating momentum through the stretch-shortening cycle during arm flexion. By having all athletes begin with extended arms, no one gains an advantage in this aspect. The focus on extended arms mainly pertains to the initial swing phase of the exercise.**

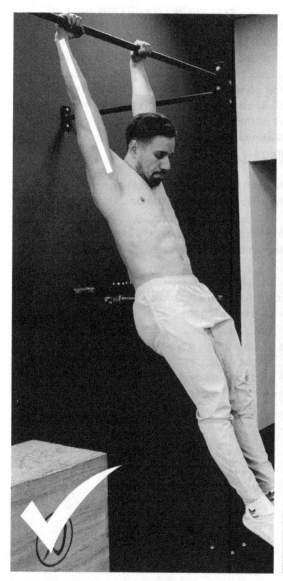
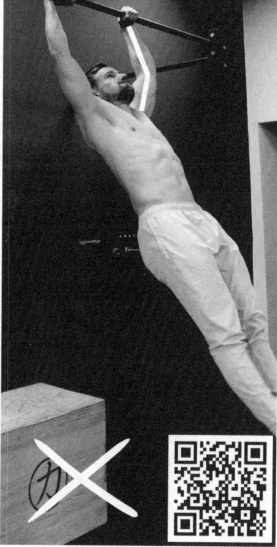

Prohibited movement initiation with bent arms

2. **Pulling phase initiated with extended hips and knees:** If an athlete strongly hyperextends their lower back and flexes their pelvis forward during the initiation of the muscle up, they create passive muscle tension along the front of their body, resembling an arch-like position. Pulling up from this hyperextended position and transitioning by rotating the pelvis into a C-shaped position can generate additional momentum to aid in pulling over the bar. To prioritize pure muscle power over momentum, it's essential to stabilize the pelvis and restrict excessive knee movements.

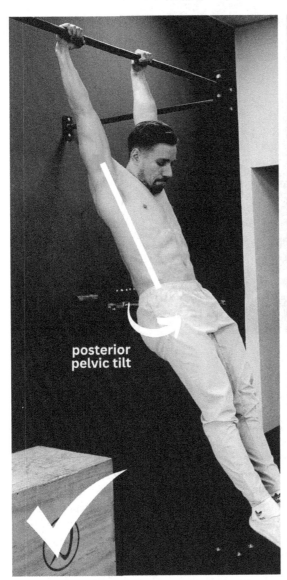
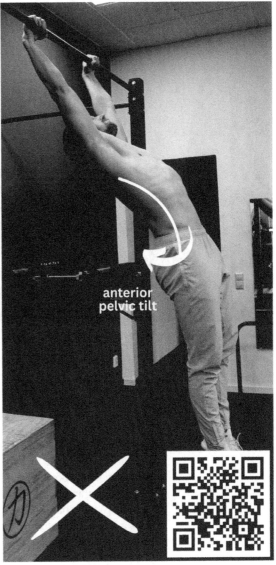

posterior pelvic tilt

anterior pelvic tilt

Prohibited movement initiation with a hyperextended spine.

3. **Transition from the pull to the push phase with even upward rotation of the elbows: The so-called 'chicken wing' muscle up involves the successive upward rotation of the elbows. This movement compensates for inadequate pulling height and, if not restricted in competitions, may lead athletes to modify the technique, resulting in a completely different movement where the goal becomes simply getting one shoulder and one elbow over the bar and then leveraging that position to move maximum weight. To preserve the essence of the muscle up, it is crucial to only consider repetitions where the upward rotation of the elbows occurs smoothly.**

Prohibited transition with one elbow before the other

This definition is not intended to discredit the various ways muscle ups are executed in other sports, but rather it serves as a specific definition and reference for the calisthenics sport.

After establishing the final form of the muscle up, this chapter on the exercise takes a different approach compared to the others. Instead of delving into the detailed execution, it begins with potential progressive training concepts aimed at learning the initial muscle ups. This sequencing is deliberately chosen to ensure that if you are still in the learning process, you do not fall into the misconception that the first muscle up has to be flawless and meet competition standards. The learning process requires some flexibility in execution. Particularly with an advanced element like this, each step towards success should be acknowledged and celebrated without prematurely comparing it to the end goal.

The following training system has been tested with a variety of athletes, and proven effective in practice. However, it does not claim to be the only or definitive approach for every athlete.

2.3.1

3-phase training system for muscle ups

The following training system for learning the first muscle ups is divided into three training phases. Depending on your performance level at the start of the muscle up training, you have already passed some phases consciously or unconsciously and have already managed the milestones to enter the next phase. The entry phase is therefore based on the milestones that you have already achieved.

2.3.1.1

Phase 1: Basic training

The muscle up requires the ability to accelerate your own body weight in such a way that you can pull yourself from the pull up position above the bar. This means you need a high, so-called relative strength in your pull. **Relative strength** is defined by the ratio of body weight to maximum strength. This means for muscle up training, the heavier you are, the more maximum strength you need, and the other way around.

So a heavier athlete will usually need to train longer for a first successful muscle up than a lighter athlete. **Maximum strength** is defined as the highest possible force you can exert with maximum voluntary contraction through your neuromuscular system. So, in order for you to be able to learn a muscle up, your goal for the basic training phase is to build up enough maximum strength in your pulling exercises, relative to your body weight, to create enough relative strength for the muscle up. To figure out how to implement this in your training, look at what maximum strength is made up of. It's made up of many different parameters. Many of them are genetically determined like your **anthropometry.** The individual length ratios and movement radii of the body's joints vary from person to person. This means that depending on your anthropometry and thus your mechanical advantage for an exercise, you can apply

more or less maximum strength. As discussed in the fundamentals chapter, the **moment arms of the muscular system** also determine your maximum strength ability. Depending on the point of the muscle's attachment, it can exert more or less torque with the same muscle strength. The more favorably a muscle attaches in order to have large lever arms for certain movements, the more power it can exert. Your **muscle fiber distribution** also has an impact on maximum strength. To generate large force impulses, you rely primarily on so-called fast-twitch muscle fibers. How pronounced the ratio of fast-twitch to slow-twitch muscle fibers is can only be influenced to a limited extent by training. So depending on how you were blessed by mom and dad, you naturally have a good or bad disposition for generating high maximum strength. In practice, this, along with a few other factors, also explains the wide variation in learning a muscle up. For some people the muscle up is a very easy skill, for others, it requires a training process of several years. So the decisive factors for you are the ones that can be actively influenced by your training. The following list is not complete, but covers the most relevant factors and is therefore sufficient as a basis for understanding your training and will allow you to derive a training plan in the next step.

The first factors you can influence through your training are **inter- and intramuscular coordination.** Without going too far into the theory here, **intermuscular coordination** is the time-optimized interaction of the various muscles in the different body segments that are responsible for movement. **Intramuscular coordination** defines how many muscle fibers of a single muscle can be recruited and also activated at the same time. In other words, the more muscle fibers of your single muscle are available to contract at the same time, the greater your potential strength output.

Another important factor that can be influenced by training is your muscle **size.** The strength potential of a muscle increases with its size, more precisely with the increase of its cross-section. (22) So if you have almost exhausted your strength potential through a high level of inter- and intramuscular coordination, your muscle must be stimulated to grow so that its strength potential can continue to increase.

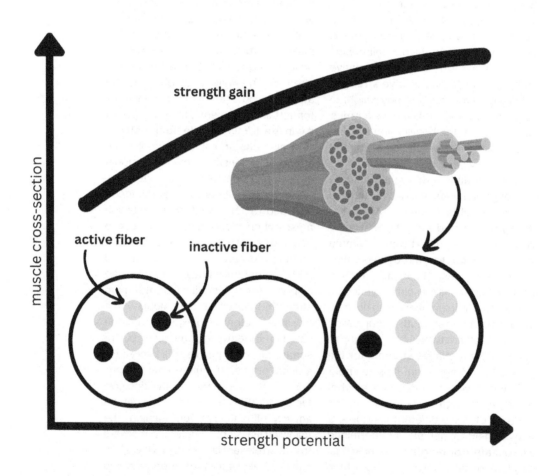

Mechanism of strength training: as the muscle cross-section increases, the strength potential of a muscle increases. To realize the potential, you need good inter- and intramuscular coordination

In addition to pure muscle strength, your **exercise technique and psychological** factors are also relevant. The more optimized your technique, the greater your potential strength output. With an improved technique and more experience, important psychological factors such as your self-confidence, your motivation and less fear of injury or pain usually improve as well. Of course, this is also subject to fluctuations.

In the basic training of the first phase, the aim is to develop the factors of maximum strength that you can influence in such a way that the transition to the muscle-up-specific training in phase 2 is possible, which requires a certain relative strength to be able to train the necessary exercises. To make the training phases quantifiable, milestones are defined for each phase, which marks the transition to the next training phase.

1. Milestone Phase 1: Weighted pull up 1RM with 40–60% of own body weight.

This value arises from a survey that we conducted internally at the beginning of 2022. Based on the values of 49 athletes, the correlation of the weighted 1RM value of pull/chin ups in percent of their body weight and the ability to perform a muscle up was examined. We found that the average of athletes who could achieve a muscle up with some momentum was approximately 50% of 1RM, and the average of athletes who could achieve a clean muscle up was approximately 57% of 1RM. The standard deviation was approximately 10% for both groups. The execution was checked with a video for each athlete to place them in one category or the other. On average, the lighter and smaller an athlete was, the lower the necessary 1RM relative to body weight. Following this, we tested these values with our coaching clients and were able to verify them. (23)

2. Milestone Phase 1: High pull ups with the forearms in the final position approximately parallel to the floor.

The ability to perform a muscle up is not solely determined by maximum strength in pull/chin ups. While there is a correlation between the two, it is important to note that correlation does not guarantee success. Therefore, it is beneficial to include an additional milestone to ensure progress. The high pull up has been recognized as an effective indicator of the required pulling height for training specific muscle up exercises without relying heavily on assistance systems. If you can perform a pull up with your forearms approximately parallel to the floor in the final position, you will have enough pulling height to initiate the transition and convert the pull up into a muscle up with minimal difficulty.

In the initial phase, the goal is to develop sufficient muscle mass and increase your strength potential to generate the necessary maximum strength in the pull/chin up, which in turn provides the required pulling height in the high pull up. Specific muscle up training is not essential at this stage. Instead, focus on increasing your repetition values in pull/chin ups initially, and then progress to adding additional weight in the subsequent steps. It is important to note that attempting specific muscle up training with strong elastic bands without being able to perform clean pull/chin ups for multiple sets will not contribute to your progress. Another important aspect of this phase is minimizing the risk of injury. Specific muscle up training involves explosive movements that can put significant stress on the shoulders, elbows, and wrists. By adequately preparing and strengthening these joints through training and developing supporting muscles, you can mitigate the risk of injury. If you rush into overly specific training too soon without proper preparation, the risk of injury increases.

The first step towards progress is to increase your work capacity in pull/chin ups to a higher level. As a beginner, a sample plan for building up your reps could be as follows. Keep in mind that the number of sets and assistance exercises should be adjusted based on your individual level, and this plan should serve as a starting point rather than a rigid prescription.

Exercises day 1	Exercises day 2	Reps	Sets	Intensity	Break
Pull ups	Dips	adapt to RIR	3	1–2 RIR, last set till failure	3–5min
Dips	Pull ups	adapt to RIR	3	1–2 RIR, last set till failure	3–5min
Vertical pull assistance	Horizontal push exercise	6–8	3	1–2 RIR, last set till failure	2–3min
Overhead press	Rowing exercise	6–8	2–3	1–2 RIR, last set till failure	2–3min
External rotation shoulder	Shoulder abduction	10–15+	2–3	1–2 RIR, last set till failure	2–3min
Triceps isolation	Biceps isolation	10–15+	2–3	1–2 RIR, last set till failure	2–3min

This is what an example upper body/lower body plan might look like with the two upper body workouts per week shown here. You can progress in the bodyweight exercises via a simple repetition progression. That means once you accomplish the planned reps with the intended reps in reserve on average, you plan for the next session with an additional rep.

You can train the last set until muscle failure. This way you can verify your reps in reserve and make sure to train neither too light nor too heavy, while still reducing fatigue and good technique, through the RIR in the first sets. In this way, you learn to evaluate yourself well and develop the ability to train autoregulative. A simple repetition progression scheme involving you training the last set to muscle failure or technique failure is then listed for you below. If you manage to do your sets of 1–2 reps in the tank, verified by the last set, this is recorded as a success and you can add one rep for the following week. If you don't manage that, you don't change your structure. It is important not to rush things. You will not be able to make progress every week. This is totally normal and not a reason to worry or change the system.

The following example shows a **repetition progression** of the pull ups exercise with a relative intensity of one to two reps in reserve in the first sets, followed by one set to muscle failure. The last set is used to verify the RIR.

Week 1
  Target: 3x6, 1–2 RIR
  Result; 2x6, 1x7 pull ups
  Action: The goal was reached, so one repetition is added for week 2.

Week 2
  Target: 3x7, 1–2 RIR
  Result: 2x7, 1x6 pull ups
  Action: The goal was not achieved, so no changes are planned for week 3.

Week 3
  Target: 3x7, 1–2 RIR
  Result: 2x7, 1x7 pull ups
  Action: The goal was not achieved, so no changes are planned for week 4.

Week 4
  Target: 3x7, 1–2 RIR
  Result: 2x7, 1x8 pull ups
  Action: The goal was reached, so one repetition is added for week 5.

In the exercises with additional weight, you can use a so-called **double progression.** Here you start by increasing the repetitions until you reach the end of the repetition range you set yourself with the given RIR average. Then, instead of continuing to increase reps, you increase the additional weight. Hence the name double progression. First, you progress the reps, then the weight. But always make sure to keep the quality high and to stick to your Reps In Reserve. The following example shows a double progression with a relative intensity of two to three reps in reserve. A set to muscle failure can be omitted if you already have enough experience with estimating your relative training intensities.

Week 1

Target: 3x6–8 with 20kg, 2–3 RIR
Result: 3x6x20kg, RIR: 3,3,2
Action: The repetition range has not been exhausted, therefore no action is required.

Week 2

Target: 3x6–8 with 20kg, 2–3 RIR
Result: 3x7x20kg, RIR: 2,2,2
Action: The repetition range has not been exhausted, therefore no action is required.

Week 3

Target: 3x6–8 with 20kg, 2–3 RIR
Result: 3x7x20kg, RIR: 3,3,2
Action: The repetition range has not been exhausted, therefore no action is required.

Week 4

Target: 3x6–8 with 20kg, 2–3 RIR
Result: 3x8x20kg, RIR: 2,2,2
Action: The repetition range has been exhausted while sticking to the RIR.
For the next training week, the weight will be increased by 1.25–2.5kg.

If you achieve 8–12 clean repetitions in the basic exercises of dips and pull/chin-ups, you can continue with the next plan example. Like the first example, this plan is a guide that you will have to adapt to yourself and your needs. So don't be afraid to customize the plan in terms of volume, exercise selection, splits, etc.!

Exercises Day 1	Exercises Day 2	Reps	Sets	Intensity	Break
Weighted pull ups	Weighted dips	1 x 3–5 2–3 x 6–8	3–4	2–3 RIR 1–2 RIR	3–5min
Weighted dips, tempo/technique variation	Weighted pull ups, tempo/technique variation	4–6	3–4	1–2 RIR	3–5min
Vertical pull assistance	Horizontal push exercise	6–8	3	1–2 RIR, last set till failure	2–3min
Overhead press	Rowing exercise	6–8	3	1–2 RIR, last set till failure	2–3min
External rotation shoulder	Shoulder abduction	10–15+	3	1–2 RIR, llast set till failure	2–3min
Triceps isolation	Biceps isolation	10–15+	3	1–2 RIR, last set till failure	2–3min

After you have achieved the repetitions in the basic exercises with your body weight of 8–12, you start to load them. To do this, it's best to work with **a top and back-off set system.** This way you integrate higher intensities into your training through the top-set to specifically train your maximum strength, and provide sufficient training volume for enough exercise and hypertrophy stimuli with more volume in the back-off sets.

You can use a **weight progression** in the top and back-off sets. So you stay in your rep ranges and steadily increase the additional weight as you complete your reps with the planned RIR. Every 4–6 weeks you can lower the rep range of your top-set by one repetition to get more and more specific to the one repetition maximum (1RM), meaning the maximum weight you can move for one repetition. After you get to one rep, start again at 3 or 4 reps with adjusted weights. For more specificity in terms of maximum strength training, you can also adjust the repetition range of the back-off sets downward over time. Be careful not to lower your overall volume too much. To regulate your fatigue and work progressively, you can start with your RIR a little higher and reduce it over time. This will give your body more time to adapt and allow you to increase in a planned way from week to week. How you can do this, you can see in the following example. Here you can also use many other combinations and progression schemes. The length of a training block is given only as an example with five weeks. You train for four weeks with increasing intensity and resulting from this with increasing volume, followed by a lowered week, also called deload.

Block 1
  W1: top set 1x5 RIR4, back off 3x8 RIR3
  W2: top set 1x5 RIR3, back off 3x8 RIR3
  W3: top set 1x5 RIR2, back off 3x8 RIR2–3
  W4: top set 1x5 RIR1, back off 3x8 RIR1–2
  Deload: top set 1x5 RIR4, back off 2x8 RIR3

Block 2
  W1: top set 1x4 RIR4, back off 3x7 RIR3
  W2: top set 1x4 RIR3, back off 3x7 RIR3
  W3: top set 1x4 RIR2, back off 3x7 RIR2–3
  W4: top set 1x4 RIR1, back off 3x7 RIR1–2
  Deload: top set 1x4 RIR4, back off 2x7 RIR3

Block 3
  W1: top set 1x3 RIR4, back off 4x6 RIR3
  W2: top set 1x3 RIR3, back off 4x6 RIR3
  W3: top set 1x3 RIR2, back off 4x6 RIR2–3
  W4: top set 1x3 RIR1, back off 4x6 RIR1–2
  Deload: top set 1x3 RIR4, back off 2x6 RIR3

The main exercises will continue to be trained twice a week in this plan. Once with a heavy top set and once with a tempo variation. Which tempo variation makes sense for you, is explained in the use cases in the respective chapters. If you reach the threshold of approx. 40–60% of your body weight for 1RM or e1RM, that means the 1RM calculated from your top set, you can move on to phase 3. If you are close to this threshold, it is already possible to integrate explosive high pull ups into the training 1–2 times a week to check how close you are to the second milestone and of course to train this ability. For each session, 2–5 sets of 1–3 reps per set of high pull ups is enough. Explosiveness and technique will be the main focus, so keep the reps low. You should always train explosive exercises, those performed with great acceleration, with as little pre-fatigue as possible at the beginning of your workout.

2.3.1.2

Phase 2: Explosive power conditioning and technique

In this training phase, you train the muscle up specifically and plan to achieve the first free muscle up. However, the milestone to exit the phase is more advanced.

Milestone Phase 2: 1–2 competition-valid muscle ups.

For this, you're mainly using two different exercises. These are high pull ups and muscle ups with a resistance band. In addition, you will continue training maximum strength specifically with pull/chin ups using a heavy top set, and generally continue to add weight to the basic weighted exercises in order to become stronger and more muscular.

High pull ups train your Explosive strength, which is important for muscle ups. Explosive strength is the ability of the neuromuscular system to give your body the highest possible strength impulse in the shortest possible time. (23) In addition, with the help of the resistance bands, you can go through the technically demanding and complex movement sequence of the muscle up several times, without too much effort, and thereby internalize and improve the technique. As mentioned earlier, you should integrate these new exercises with as little pre-fatigue as possible at the beginning of your workout. Here there are countless division and design possibilities to restructure and build up the plan. We will follow the example of Phase 1 and expand it with the new components.

Exercise day 1	Exercise day 2	Reps	Sets	Intensity	Break
/	High pull ups	2–3	3–5	2–3 RIR	2–3min
Muscle ups with resistance band	Muscle up with resistance band	3–5	2–3	2–3 RIR	2–3min
Weighted pull ups	Weighted dips	1x1–3 3–4x4–6	4–5	2–4 RIR 2–3 RIR	3–5min
Weighted dips, tempo/technique variation	Weighted pull ups, tempo/technique Variation	3–5	3–4	2–3 RIR	3–5min
Vertical pull assistance	Horizontal push exercise	6–8 / 8–12	3	1–2 RIR, last set till failure	2–3min
Overhead press	Rowing exercise	6–8 / 8–12	3	1–2 RIR, last set till failure	2–3min
External rotation shoulder	Shoulder abduction	10–15+	3–4	1–2 RIR, last set till failure	2–3min
Triceps isolation	Biceps isolation	10–15+	3–4	1–2 RIR, last set till failure	2–3min

You have now incorporated specific muscle up training into this plan. The repetition ranges and intensities on both days should be aligned with the assistance exercises. Divide them in a way that the different qualities required for the muscle up will be trained. For example, you can perform the 'Technique Weighted Pull Ups' at an increased tempo to further condition your explosive strength. On day 1 you should train the muscle up as specifically as possible by using the weakest possible elastic band that still allows you to do the reps and RIR. On Day 2, train them again, but with a stronger elastic band. This is on purpose because you are already pre-fatigued from the high pull ups and then the muscle ups with the band are only for technique adaptation. This allows you to accumulate less fatigue and still be able to fully train the movement twice a week. When you reach about 3 reps with the lightest resistance band, you can switch to muscle ups without the band. However, make sure that

quality over quantity continues to apply. You're progressing here with a technique progression. That means instead of trying more reps, you work on improving technique from session to session and using less momentum until you eventually reach the competition-valid form.

As you do this, you should naturally decrease the strength of the resistance band on Day 2.

Based on a week of four training days, including two upper body days, it is a good idea to change the second leg day to a full body day. For more exercise and less fatigue per session, many athletes prefer a frequency of three. Especially toward the end of phase two, you can accelerate your learning pace by increasing your frequency without taking an uncalculated overload risk. You are already used to the movement and your relative strength is at a high level. Under these circumstances, an increased frequency makes a lot of sense. This full body day could look like this:

Exercise day 4	Reps	Sets	Intensity	Break
High pull ups	1+1 cluster	3–5	2–3 RIR	2–3min
Barbell squat	1 x 1–3 3–4 x 4–6	4–5	2–4 RIR 2–3 RIR	3–5min
Romanian deadlift	6–8	3–4	2–3 RIR	3–5min
Hackenschmidt squat beltsquat/leg press	8–12	3	1–2 RIR, last set till failure	2–3min
Core/crunch exercise	10–15+	3–4	1–2 RIR, last set till failure	2–3min
Core rotation exercise	10–15+	3–4	1–2 RIR, last set till failure	2–3min

The high pull up is integrated before the leg workout. In this case with cluster reps. So you do two reps per set, but you do them separately with a small break between each rep.

This way the fatigue per rep is less and the technique is better. The squat assistance is best performed on a machine because you have already incorporated two exercises that axially load your spine. To keep the fatigue more localized in the legs, it's well suited to do exercises that give you a lot of external stability. At the end of the

day, perform some core exercises. If you train the extension of the spine a lot, you should not forget the flexion and rotation. Experience has shown that due to the many other exercises that require stability for the core, it is sufficient to integrate isolated abdominal training once a week in addition. If you achieve 1-2 muscle ups in competition form, you can pass to phase 3 and start to train the first weighted muscle ups or, depending on your goal, further expand the reps per set!

2.3.1.3

Phase 3: Increasing repetitions and additional weight

Phase 3 represents the final and ongoing stage of your training journey. The primary objective during this phase is to increase repetitions or, for competitive athletes, to progressively handle more additional weight.

Since you have the option to either increase repetitions or add more weight, there are no specific milestones within this phase. The training approach will largely depend on your individual goal-setting and priorities during this stage. The training protocols will vary based on these factors. Therefore, providing a generic example plan at this point wouldn't be meaningful without further knowledge about your specific needs.

Instead of presenting a plan, we can offer you some best practices that have proven effective in Phase 3 based on practical experience. These practices can serve as guidelines to help you navigate this phase and make progress toward your goals.

Microloading - When it comes to the muscle up exercise, the ability to add weight in small increments is important. If your smallest possible weight progression is 2.5kg, it may not be optimal for this exercise. For example, if your 1RM is 10kg, a 2.5kg increase represents a significant jump of 25% in additional weight. To ensure more manageable and meaningful weight progressions of around 2.5–5%, it is recommended to use microplates. These smaller weight plates allow for finer adjustments and enable you to increase the weight in smaller increments, which can be more appropriate for the muscle up exercise.

Low fatigue training - The muscle up exercise requires a high level of explosiveness and technical skill. Therefore, it is important to ensure that you have sufficient focus and energy reserves in your training plan when incorporating muscle ups. It is recommended to position them relatively early in your workout routine. Additionally, be mindful of any potential overlap with pull/chin ups. As you progress in your muscle ups and are able to handle more weight in this exercise, it can lead to increased fatigue. This increased fatigue may affect your performance in pull/chin ups more than desired. In such cases, it may be beneficial to reduce the volume of muscle ups per session and distribute the total volume across multiple sessions. This approach can help manage fatigue and optimize your training outcomes

High sets, low reps - As mentioned earlier, it is important to minimize pre-fatigue when training muscle ups. This principle also applies to muscle ups within your working sets. To achieve this, it is recommended to keep the number of reps per set low, typically ranging from 1 to 3 reps. To increase the overall volume of the exercise, you can simply increase the number of sets performed. If your training focuses on higher repetitions in the muscle up, a top and backoff set system can be employed. In the top set, you aim to perform as many reps as possible, pushing your limits. In the backoff sets, you leave 1-3 reps in reserve and prioritize maintaining quality form and, if needed, incorporating additional weight to enhance the challenge and progression. This approach allows for both volume and quality in your training.

Muscle up technique

2.3.1.4

To continuously enhance your muscle up technique during the latter part of phase 2 and throughout phase 3, a detailed analysis of the muscle up will be conducted, focusing on each phase of the movement. The objective is to identify the ideal technique that suits your individual needs. Due to variations in anthropometry, the technique may differ slightly among athletes. By understanding and adapting the technique to your specific body proportions, you can optimize your muscle up execution.

Phase 1: Entry (step-in technique)

2.3.1.5

To initiate the muscle up, you begin by gripping the bar. The semi-false grip can be used here, similar to the pull up, to reduce wrist rotation when transitioning from the pull to the dip phase. Just like in the pull up, you decrease the distance traveled and increase tension in your arm flexors with this grip.

161

However, it's important to note that the muscle up can still be performed effectively without it. It's worth noting that without the semi-false grip, more pulling strength is required as you will need to pull higher and apply more acceleration during the pulling phase. The entry and body position in the muscle up differs from the pull up. Instead of entering with a hyperextended thoracic spine, you enter with a slightly curved one. This is achieved by compressing your front side, and this compression should be maintained throughout the entire pulling phase. The compression creates a slight C-shape of the body during the muscle up, making it easier to pull around the bar. To execute the muscle up successfully, it's recommended to learn the step-in technique. To practice this technique, you will need a high enough bar that allows you to hang fully. Additionally, you will require a box that enables you to reach the bar with your arms extended, without the need to jump or stretch. Grip the bar using the semi-false grip (or neutral grip, depending on your preference). Place your feet on the box and connect your hands to the bar. Lift one foot off the box and position your body accordingly. Ensure that the box is not too far from the bar for this to work. The ^leg lifted off the box should be slightly stretched forward. Activate your

quadriceps to keep the knee extended and stabilize your hips in a posterior pelvic tilt by engaging your abdominal and gluteal muscles. By tightening your abs, your thoracic spine also assumes a slightly curved position. Your shoulders should be slightly protracted, and you can generate some preload in the depression by gently pulling down. To perform the muscle up, simply release your second foot from the box. Due to your slightly bent position and the raised entry from the box, you will naturally gain forward momentum. There's no need to jump or swing excessively as you might have to when starting from the floor. This facilitates maintaining your body position and better control of any additional weight, if applicable.

During the swing phase, it is crucial to maintain body tension. As you have learned in the pull up section, the latissimus requires a stabilized hip during hanging pulling exercises to develop its full strength. If you lose compression during the swing, the latissimus will not have optimal attachment. Sustaining constant body tension is also vital to achieving maximum pull height. When body tension is lost, strength is compromised, leading to unnecessary rotational movements in the body instead of being utilized for vertical pulling.

Step-in technique muscle up

To familiarize yourself with the position and the swing, you can practice two to three sets of the step-in technique before your actual muscle up training.

Now, the question arises: How much swing should you aim for? In practice, this may sound more complex than it actually is in theory. Firstly, you need to consider your goal with the swing. The primary purpose of the entry swing is to create a slightly inclined body position that aids in pulling around the bar. If your body is perpendicular to the ground, your pulling direction will also be mostly vertical. In this case, the bar becomes an obstacle, and repositioning becomes challenging due to the minimal distance to the bar and the limited horizontal strength component. It is not impossible, but it is inefficient.

By utilizing momentum, you generate a slight torque that aids in rotating around the bar more effectively. Without utilizing this momentum, achieving a smooth movement to position your center of gravity over the bar becomes significantly more challenging (though not impossible). In essence, the momentum is employed to initiate the movement of pulling yourself around the bar, rather than attempting to go directly through it.

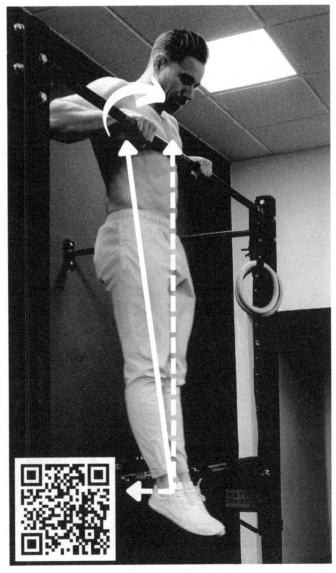

Resulting pulling direction with very vertical movement initiation

The optimal amount of swing required is highly individual and can vary depending on the athlete's technique, as well as the necessary horizontal strength component and body position during lift-off. The guiding principle here should be to aim for as little swing as possible while ensuring it is sufficient for the task at hand.

During the pulling phase, you have the ability to regulate the movement through the path of your arms, shoulders, and spine flexion. This allows you to fine-tune the motion according to your needs. When using additional weight, it is advisable to reduce the amount of momentum to minimize the strength impulses in the horizontal direction. This adjustment facilitates easier upward acceleration of the weight.

Due to the slight swing after entry, the body is at an angle to the ground. The body position during the pulling initiation decides in which direction the resulting pulling force is exerted.

2.3.1.6

Phase 2: Pull phase

The combination of swing and timing forms the foundation for an effective pulling phase. By executing this phase correctly, you can minimize potential issues during the transition. The initiation of the pull phase should occur when your hips are still slightly ahead of the bar during the backward swing. With a moderate swing, this moment typically occurs shortly after the swing's front reversal point. When executed accurately, most of your power is directed upwards, with only a small portion being utilized for the hori-

zontal movement needed to pull yourself around the bar. Initiating the pull too early or too late will result in a loss of valuable power for the upward motion. Your body position at the start of the pull should align with the desired direction of movement. If your body is too horizontal or too vertical, the movement will be inefficient.

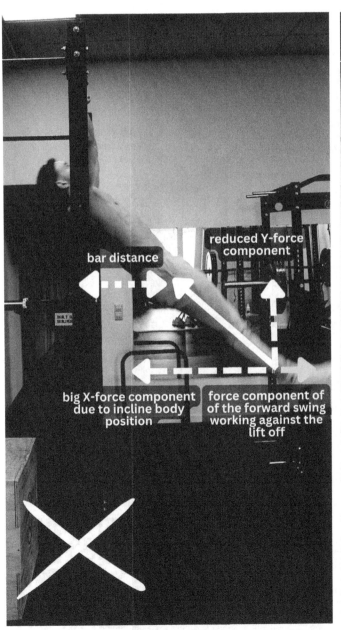

Resulting force & body position with too early pulling initiation and optimal pulling initiation.

This concept is evident in common mistakes made during the muscle up. Aside from timing, maintaining body tension at the moment of pulling is crucial. As described in Phase 1, your body is in a slight compression. As you initiate the pull, it's important for your body to move as a cohesive unit while maintaining compression. If body tension is lost during the initiation of the pull, power for the upward movement may be diminished as the energy is dispersed throughout your body. Once you've initiated the pull phase with optimal momentum and timing, the goal is to pull yourself up as close to the bar as possible. This minimizes the range of motion and allows you to utilize the upward acceleration for the transition. The closer

you are to the bar, the more efficiently you can execute the muscle up. You control the distance to the bar and the pull path in the initial part of the pulling phase by the timing and rhythm of your elbow bending while retracting your arms. Bending your arms too late may result in pulling away from the bar, while bending them excessively early can lead to pulling toward the bar too quickly, hindering your ability to transition around it. By optimizing this movement, the transition becomes smoother as your chest and center of gravity are already in close proximity to the bar.

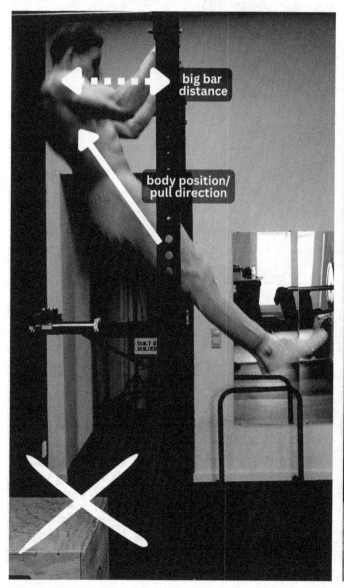
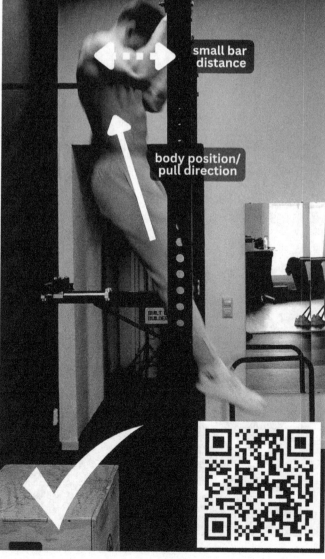

Pull path with little and much arm flexion (right) and the resulting distance to the bar.

2.3.1.7   Phase 3: Transition

The transition phase marks the shift from the pulling phase to the pushing phase. Its objective is to quickly and efficiently bring your chest and elbows over the bar in order to initiate the push-up movement. The necessary pulling height for a successful transition depends on several factors. The first determinant is the length of your arms. Longer arms require a greater distance for your elbows to pass around the bar. In other words, longer arms necessitate either a faster upward rotation of the elbows at the same pulling height or a higher pulling height within the same timeframe. Therefore, individuals with longer arms require either increased rotational speed or more pulling height to execute a successful transition.

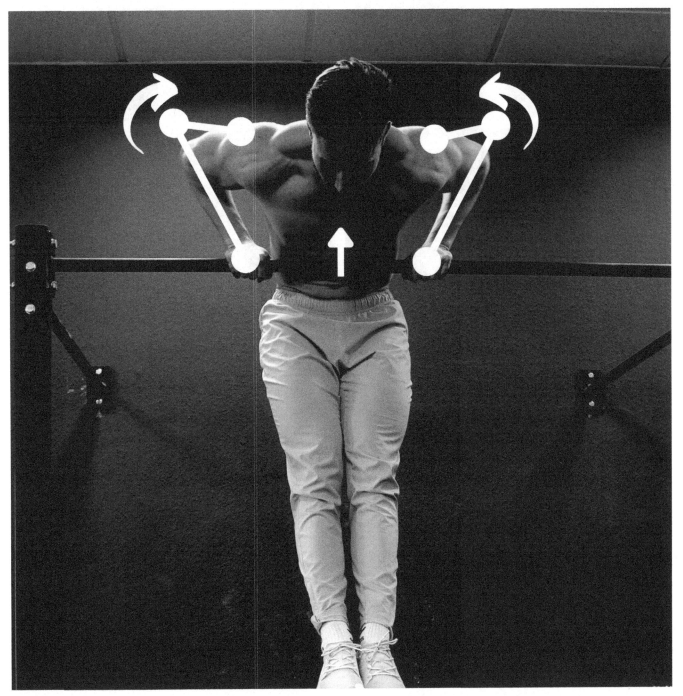

Upward rotation of the elbows for different arm lengths. If the arms are longer, more distance has to be covered during the upward rotation.

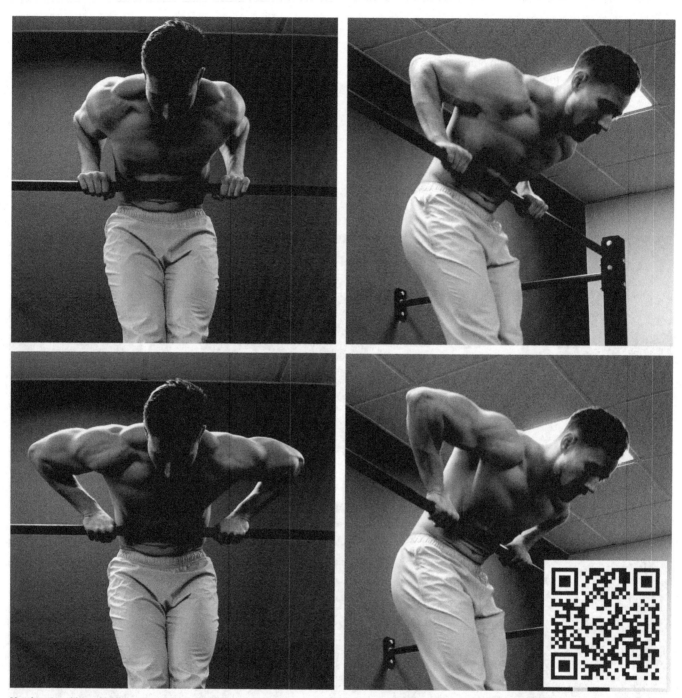

Muscle up transitions with elbows close to the body (above) usually require more pulling height during the transition because the distance to the bar is greater during the transition. If you extend the elbows by rotating the arms more internally, the distance to the bar and the required pull height will be slightly reduced.

Transitioning with a stable depression in the shoulder (left) and a stronger elevation (right).

The second crucial factor is your shoulder mobility, specifically the internal rotation and extension of your shoulders. The combination of internal rotation and extension determines the distance between your body and the bar during the movement and thus influences the required pulling height. To achieve close proximity to the bar during the transition, you need to bring your arms to the sides and back.

For individuals with longer arms, more internal rotation and/or extension are required to minimize the distance. Internal rotation decreases the effective arm length both sagittally and frontally. While it may seem that more internal rotation is always beneficial, in practice, it can pose risks. Performing a muscle up with strong internal rotation and arm abduction is a precarious position for many individuals. The explosive and coordination-intensive nature of the movement, coupled with the challenge of stabilization, increases the risk of shoulder injuries. Additionally, to facilitate an efficient transition, many athletes sacrifice stable shoulder depression for elevation, allowing for more extension and internal rotation.

However, adopting this technique may lead to short- to medium-term issues in the shoulder or elbows due to the high loads experienced during the transition. Only a few athletes can withstand such extreme shoulder loads. Consequently, in order to prevent injury in the long run, it may be necessary to compromise some efficiency and prioritize strengthening. Therefore, avoid excessive internal rotation or extension while compromising shoulder depression.

Next, consider the impact of grip width on the transition. The width of your grip determines the amount of elbow flexion required for the transition. Consequently, it also influences the load on your elbows to some extent. An appropriate grip width is approximately shoulder-width, allowing for a reasonable transition. A narrower grip may cause your hands to obstruct your chest during the transition, while a wider grip necessitates more abduction with the same amount of internal rotation. Additionally, a wider grip requires more extension to avoid excessive internal rotation, which often results in reduced internal rotation due to the backward movement of the elbows. Reducing rotation and abduction makes it easier to maintain scapular depression. Therefore, a narrower grip is generally less risky for the shoulders but may increase the load on the elbows to some degree.

Transition with different grip widths, shoulder-width on the left and slightly wider on the right.

Another reason to consider a closer grip as a starting point is the theoretical improvement in latissimus control. When performing explosive shoulder extension, it is typically more effective to engage the latissimus by keeping the arms close to the body. This makes a closer grip more powerful for most athletes, despite requiring a greater upward range of motion. However, it is important to remember that this recommendation should serve as a guide to finding your own optimal grip width.

The final factor in controlling the transition is the mobility of your thoracic spine. If you have good control over your thoracic spine and can arch it over the bar at the appropriate time during the transition, you can initiate the dip earlier and transition into the pushing phase more rapidly. Additionally, this minimizes the risk of falling behind the bar due to a loss of balance with minimal acceleration.

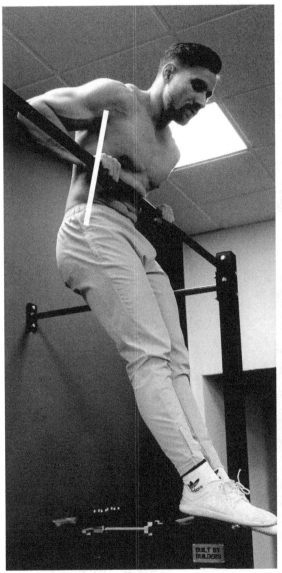 

Better balance due to the flexion of the thoracic spine (right) compared to a straight thoracic position on the left side, where the center of gravity is further behind the bar.

Phase 4: Dip

The dip, also known as the "push phase," is the part of the muscle up where you push yourself into the support position after successfully transitioning from the pull phase. The actual start of the dip can begin earlier than when your elbows are fully above the bar. As soon as your elbows are above the bar, initiating the dip by extending the elbows and bringing the arms closer to the body already contributes to the upward movement. Initiating the dip earlier has several benefits. It can compensate for the lack of acceleration from the pull phase, allowing you to continue the upward momentum. This is particularly important for competitive athletes who work with maximum weights, as it helps them achieve the last few centimeters of pulling height required for successful repositioning in competition. Initiating the dip earlier can also help compensate for a greater distance from the bar, as extending the arms reduces that distance.

By initiating the dip earlier and extending your arms, you generate upward strength while simultaneously shortening the distance to the bar. This effectively reduces the lever arm of the force pulling you downward. It also reduces the risk of not pushing your chest far enough over the bar after the repositioning phase, which could result in falling back down.

The dip phase concludes when you are in the support position above the bar with your arms fully extended. At this point, you have successfully completed the muscle up movement.

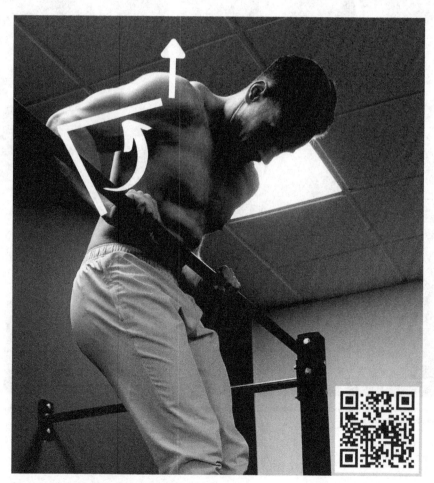

Compensation of low pull height with an early arm extension.

 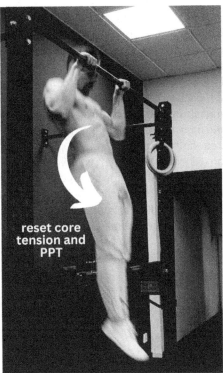 

Proper initiation of negative to generate sufficient momentum.

Phase 5: Negative movement/reset

2.3.1.9

During the reorganization phase of the second, third, and subsequent repetitions of your set, the objective is to restore the body tension and momentum to the same level as in the initial repetition. This can be achieved by effectively utilizing the negative portion of the movement. To accomplish this, it is crucial to release yourself from the dip at the appropriate angle and tempo, enabling you to restart phase 2 optimally.

To execute this effectively, it is recommended to lower yourself slightly into the negatives of the dip and then, in a controlled manner, guide the negatives forward and downward. By initiating the negatives in this manner, you can generate the necessary momentum for your specific technique. The angle at which you initiate the negatives will depend on the amount of momentum required for your technique. It is important to find the right angle to ensure sufficient momentum. As mentioned previously, maintaining a controlled tempo is essential. Instead of simply allowing yourself to fall downward, employing a deliberate and controlled tempo provides better control over the momentum and allows for more time to regain body tension.

2.3.2

Comment on the muscle up of the author

For competitive athletes in weighted calisthenics, the muscle up is a mandatory exercise. However, for many other athletes, possibly including yourself, the muscle up is a choice. It is important to consider whether the muscle up can provide added value to your training goals and whether it aligns with your overall training plan.

Assuming that you have already achieved proficiency in the muscle up and can perform it successfully, the decision to incorporate it into your training should be based on its compatibility with your goals. It's worth noting that the training modalities that are optimal for the muscle up may not be optimal for other goals such as strength or muscle building.

The muscle up is primarily a power exercise, where the aim is to accelerate weight to the maximum. Training for power exercises requires specific considerations, including low fatigue, low volume per session, low to medium absolute intensities, and ample rest. These variables, however, may conflict with the requirements of strength or hypertrophy training, which generally involve higher volumes, higher intensities, and consequently more fatigue.

While the muscle up is not necessarily unsuitable for strength and hypertrophy training, it may not be the most optimal choice. If your training goals primarily revolve around strength and muscle building, and you are not a competitive athlete with specific goals related to the muscle up, this exercise may not significantly contribute to your hypertrophy and strength training plan.

Ultimately, the decision to include the muscle up in your training should be based on whether the potential benefits outweigh the compromises you may have to make in terms of training modalities. If you believe that the muscle up is worth integrating into your plan despite the potential conflicts, there is nothing to prevent you from successfully incorporating it and enjoying its benefits.

2.3.3

Common muscle up mistakes

Below, I will outline typical errors or compensatory movements that you should strive to minimize during both training and competition. By avoiding these compensations or keeping them within acceptable limits, you can reduce the risk of injury and optimize your long-term performance.

2.3.3.1

Pulling too early

The objective of proper pull timing is to generate a resulting strength that is as vertical as possible while enabling you to pull around the bar. Based on my experience as a coach, initiating the pull too late is quite uncommon, so we will focus on the implications of initiating the pull too early. This occurs when you begin the pull while your body is still moving forward during the swing phase. Consequently, an additional force acts against your pulling direction. In this scenario, you not only need to overcome your body's inertia to accelerate it, but you also have to decelerate it beforehand in order to change its direction. Moreover, initiating the pull too early often results in a more inclined posture during the pull phase, making it challenging to efficiently transition around the bar. To compensate for this, you may need to employ a knee kick or perform a forceful hip flexion to achieve successful repositioning. Thus, it is crucial to initiate the pull either at or shortly after the reversal point, depending on your swing, to generate the optimal resulting strength.

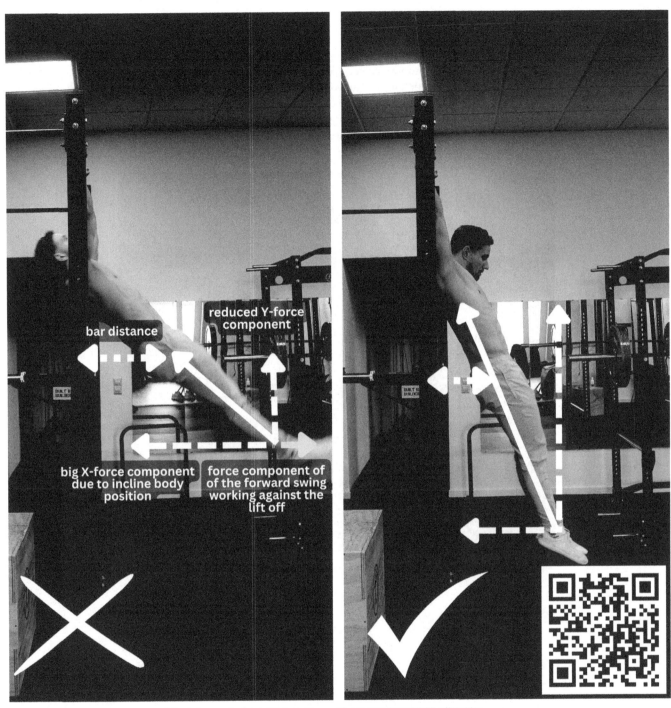

Initiating the pull of the muscle up too early leads to a very horizontal body position and thus to an unfavorable lift-off position.

When it comes to timing, the amount of swing you have affects how long you should wait before initiating the pull to ensure your body is at the correct angle again. If you have a minimal swing, you should start pulling at the reversal point once your body has come to a complete stop. However, if you have more swing, the ideal timing for the pull may be shortly after the reversal point. Therefore, your timing is directly influenced by the extent of your swing. The perfect pull timing is contingent upon your posture in relation to the bar, which should be predominantly upright with a slight inclination angle that facilitates pulling around the bar. By paying attention to this aspect, you can preemptively reduce the need for excessive knee and hip kicks.

Strong hip flexion during the transition as a result of too early pull initiation.

Loss of body tension

In the following scenarios, it is assumed that you are already proficient in performing a muscle up in a competitive manner. Therefore, any compensatory movements used to generate momentum can be considered as technique errors rather than a lack of strength.

If your primary issue is simply a lack of strength, the following information may not be relevant to you, as your momentum generation is likely due to insufficient pulling power rather than a lack of body tension. The human body is naturally inclined to utilize momentum for increased movement efficiency. For instance, when sprinting, we swing our arms forward; when jumping, we pull our arms upward; and when throwing, we generate momentum through body rotation. When aiming to perform an exercise explosively without relying on additional momentum, it may feel unnatural. The same applies to the muscle up. Attempting to solely rely on shoulder and arm strength while keeping your body rigid is highly inefficient. As a result, your brain instinctively resorts to its natural pattern of generating extra momentum for the intended movement. However, since this deviates from the prescribed rules, it distorts the exercise and renders it incomparable. Thus, it becomes necessary to unlearn and suppress these instinctual impulses. To aid you in this process, we will provide strategies for avoiding these common mistakes associated with the use of momentum.

Knee kick

A knee kick refers to the act of slightly pulling the knee towards the body, resulting in upward momentum. It is important to note that a knee kick is always accompanied by a hip kick, although the distinction is made for descriptive purposes.

If you notice a knee kick during your muscle up, it can typically be easily corrected by employing the Step-In technique correctly. During the step-in, ensure that you properly engage your knee extensor muscles. When your quadriceps are activated, it becomes difficult to bend your knee excessively. Another approach is to elongate your feet. By pointing your toes, you encourage a stretched and lengthened leg position, which helps reduce the occurrence of a knee kick.

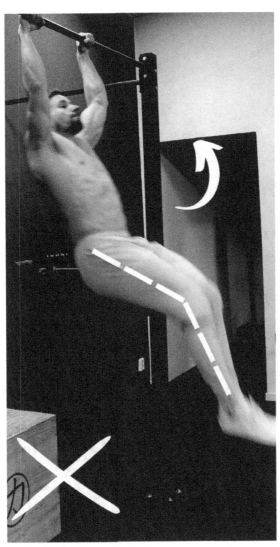
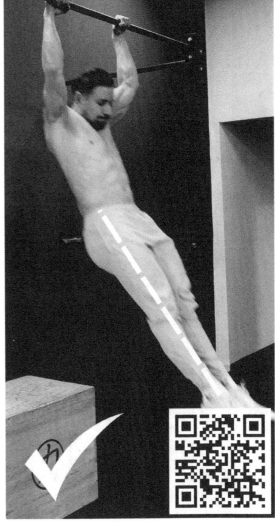

Muscle up with light knee kick

2.3.3.4   **Hip kick**

A hip kick in the context of a muscle up refers to the action of hip flexion without significant knee flexion. This type of swinging motion is quite common during the exercise. It is worth noting that a slight adjustment in hip angle may be necessary for maintaining balance during the transition and facilitating the pull around the bar. In this context, the hip kick mentioned as a 'mistake' refers specifically to the explosive hip flexion that occurs when initiating the pull phase.

To correct a hip kick, there are two possible actions you can take. Firstly, consciously engage your gluteal muscles by tightening your buttocks. This helps to keep your hips in an extended position. Additionally, a hip kick often occurs as a means of correcting the movement trajectory. In such cases, the hip kick is used to adjust a body position that is too horizontally oriented. To avoid this undesired hip kick, it is crucial to ensure proper timing during the lift-off phase, as discussed in the previous section.

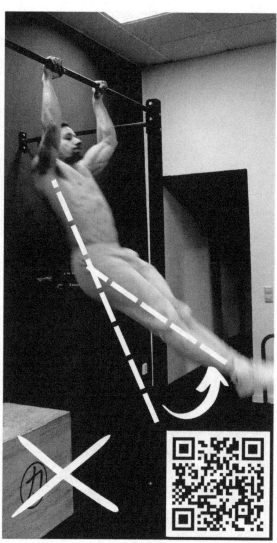

Muscle up with a slight hip kick/hip hinge before the transition to correct the pull path (left) and a hip kick directly after/during the lift-off (right).

Hyperextension of the spine

Another method of utilizing momentum in a muscle up is by generating it through pre-tension created by hyperextending your spine. This involves pushing your chest forward during the swing-in phase, creating a hollow back, and moving your hips into an anterior pelvic tilt.

This action stretches the front of your body significantly and generates passive mus-

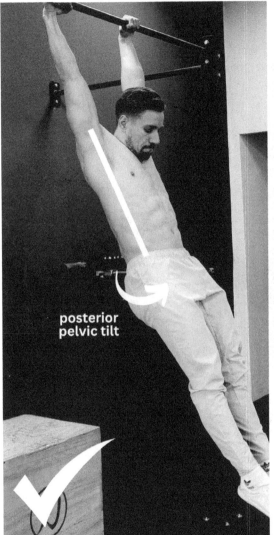
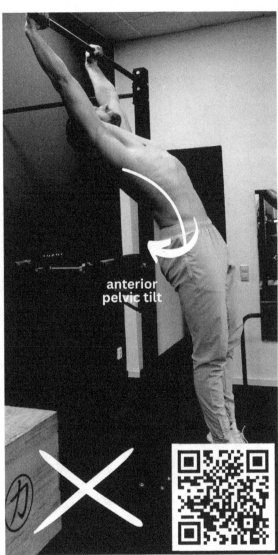

posterior pelvic tilt

anterior pelvic tilt

Muscle up with preload due to a hollow back

cle tension. When you initiate the pull phase, the change in the spine and hip position produces momentum that aids in your upward movement. However, it's important to note that in competition, this type of momentum is indirectly prohibited, as any change in pelvic position during the pull phase is considered invalid.

To prevent this compensation, it is crucial to master the correct walk-in technique. By swinging into the muscle up with a stable compression in your core, you can anchor your spine and pelvis in the appropriate position. As additional weight is added, such as in weighted muscle ups, maintaining this stability becomes increasingly challenging, as your core muscles need to exert greater force to stay engaged. In some cases, additional abdominal muscle training can be highly beneficial in achieving this stability.

2.3.3.6   Wrists blocking the transition

This particular mistake can greatly impact the success of a muscle up for many athletes. Failing to rotate your wrists upwards during the transition can result in difficulties finding balance above the bar and hinder your ability to initiate the dip. The position of your wrists increases the distance to the bar, impeding a successful transition even if the pull height is adequate.

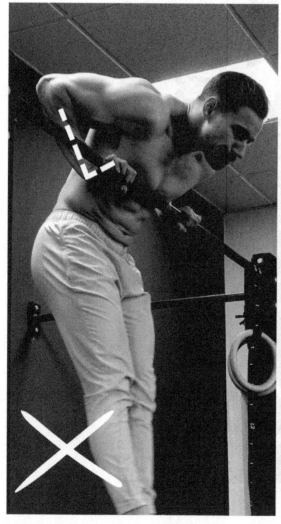 

Insufficient rotation in the wrist is blocking the transition

To avoid this mistake, there are various approaches and strategies you can employ. One effective solution is to slightly loosen your grip during the transition, allowing your wrists to rotate upwards along with your elbows, and then tighten your grip again at the appropriate moment.

Wrists properly rotating together with the elbow

However, it's worth noting that for athletes with long arms, this aspect of the muscle up requires a rapid transition and greater shoulder mobility. Consequently, this strategy may have limited effectiveness for such individuals. An alternative technique, known as the "Iron Wrist" transition, was popularized by Ruslan Saibov. In this approach, instead of rotating your wrists, you maintain a strong grip with your wrists anchored in a semi-false grip position. During the transition, you initiate the dip as early as possible by extending your arms while still moving upward. Although this places significant stress on your wrists, a successful transition is still achievable because the constant upward movement reduces the dependence on balance over the bar.

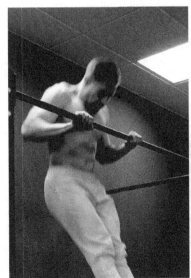  

Iron wrist transition: The wrist is not rotated evenly with the elbow.

2.3.4

Variations of the muscle up

Now that you have a clear understanding of what the perfect form of the muscle up should look like for you and the mistakes to avoid, it's time to guide you through selecting the right exercises and exercise categories to further enhance your muscle up performance. We will explore different variations of the muscle up and determine which ones are suitable for incorporation into your workout and the reasons behind it. Additionally, we will discuss a selection of assistance exercises that can help you identify technique mistakes in your muscle ups and correct them through changes in your training. It's important to note that this list represents only a sample of exercises that have been tested and proven effective in the King Of Weighted Coaching program.

2.3.4.1

Muscle ups with resistance band

Execution: Wrap the resistance band around the bar and position yourself in a way that the band runs through the middle of your body. Step into the band with one (or both) feet. The band assists you very strongly in the lower phase of the pull and the support then decreases towards the top. Depending on the strength of the band, the assisting effect differs.

Application: Banded muscle ups are primarily used for technique training. In addition, it can help you to accumulate more training volume if unassisted muscle ups cannot yet be trained with sufficient volume due to your strength level. You use the band as an intensity regulator to control the training volume.

Muscle ups with in-between swings

2.3.4.1

Execution: Instead of pulling yourself straight back up after the negative of the muscle up, you wait for another swinging movement of the body backward and forwards.

This means you lower yourself from the muscle up, commute back, and pull back up again with the right timing.

Application: This variation can be helpful for you if you have trouble with timing.

The longer pendulum phase gives you more time to get the right timing for the pull. However, the longer time in the hang causes faster fatigue and therefore must be taken into account when programming. In general, this variation offers you advantages if you are not yet confident with the technique, but strong enough for several repetitions.

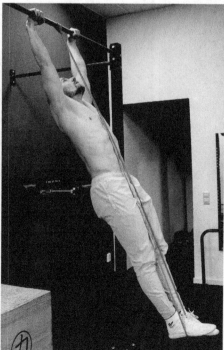

Muscle Ups with resistance band

Muscle ups without dip   2.3.4.3

Execution: You perform a muscle up with transition, but deliberately skip the dip. So you're trying to accelerate yourself out of the pull into the lower position of the dip without pushing yourself up into the dip.

Application: As described in Phase 4 of the muscle ups, by initiating the dip early you can compensate for the pull up and transition technique.

So to train the transition, especially the rotation of the wrists and the positioning of the center of gravity above the bar, this variation is excellent because it does not allow any compensations using the dip.

High pull ups with focus on a high pull

High pull ups   2.3.4.4

Execution: During high pull ups you only perform the pulling phase of the muscle up as explosively as possible. Instead of pulling yourself around the bar, you pull up past the bar.

Application: You can use high pull ups as a regression of the muscle ups. The high pull up can help you condition your explosive strength and learn the pull with proper technique.

Additionally, you can use it as an alternative to muscle ups if you are temporarily unable to perform the transition due to shoulder/wrist problems. You can additionally program the high pull up if you have difficulties with timing and body tension.

Similar to the muscle up without the dip, the reduced complexity of the exercise makes it easier to focus on the technique. If you are a bit more experienced, you can also use the high pull up to overload. This means you train the high pull ups with more than 100% of your muscle up weight for the selected repetition range. Especially for you as a competitive athlete, this is a very proven way to get your body used to heavy loads for the muscle up without accumulating too much fatigue and exposing yourself to a higher risk of injury due to possible technical errors during the transition.

2.3.4.5

Modified high pull ups, transition bias

Execution: The modified high pull ups with transition bias are the intersection between muscle ups and high pull ups. In this variation of the high pull up you reduce the momentum to the absolute minimum and try to pull yourself up as close to the bar as possible. Due to the reduced momentum, your center of gravity is still behind the bar, which is why you don't move into transition. You focus on getting your center of gravity close to the bar and rotating your elbows upward as much as possible.

Application: This variation is designed to help you get your pulling technique perfect. The low momentum forces an up-right posture. The small distance to the bar will force you to perform a clean 'transition' with a rotation of your elbows and wrists. This variation is very suitable as a substitution for muscle up training with higher frequencies and overloading the movement due to the low ROM, but still high specificity to the muscle up. Especially for weighted calisthenics athletes this variation offers the possibility to train muscle ups very specific with progressive loading without being dependent on a successful transition.

Modified high pull ups focusing on a movement close to the bar with an indicated transition by bringing the elbows back and curving the thoracic spine.

2.3.5

Assistance exercises
for muscle ups

The muscle up is a combination exercise of an explosive pull up and a dip movement. As already discussed, the most important assistance exercise for strength is the weighted pull/chin up. The hypertrophy and health assistance do not deviate from those you already know from the pull/chin up chapter due to the very similar movement patterns. So at this point go back to the pull/chin up chapter to find additional exercises from these areas.

! Has the book helped you this far?
Show it to me! It costs you 60s to leave a review on our site. It costs you another 60s to write an Instagram story about the book and tag us @kingofweighted and @micha_bln_!
Thank you so much for your support!

@kingofweighted

@micha_bln_

3.

Lever
Skills

3.
Lever Skills

Lever skills are isometric elements performed vertically against the force of gravity. These include the front lever, back lever, dragon flags, human flags, victorians, planches, maltese, and more. In order to establish training methods and a comparable standard for assessing the form and execution of calisthenics lever skills, specific form standards have been defined in this book. When your exercise execution aligns with these form standards, it is referred to as 'perfect form'. It's important to note that these form standards serve as a foundation for analysis in this book and may not be infallible or universally agreed upon.

If new and recognized associations establish a uniform definition in the future, these will be acknowledged in a subsequent edition of this book. Until then, the existing conventions will be considered as the accepted standard. In the following sections, I will provide a detailed explanation of the approach to standardizing lever skills and establishing form conventions. The first fundamental aspect of these conventions is rooted in the beauty of movement, which is a significant attribute in calisthenics.

The significance of movement aesthetics is evident in the origin of the word itself, with the Greek roots καλός (kalos) meaning "beautiful" or "good," and σθένος (sthenos) meaning "strength." (37) Within the realm of movement aesthetics, lever skills possess two key characteristics. The first is the ability to resist gravity. However, simply resisting gravity while maintaining a sagging posture like a banana does not fulfill the aesthetic ideal. The second characteristic, which truly enhances the visual impact of lever skills, is body tension. It is through maximal body tension that athletes achieve the illusion of floating perpendicular to gravity, effortlessly aligning their joints in a straight line in the air. From this idealized perspective of lever skills, universal conventions can be derived that apply to all lever skills, even those not specifically covered in this book.

These conventions allow for the definition of a theoretical perfect form for each lever skill, enabling a standardized assessment of their difficulty level, programmable training, and the ability to analyze mistakes for improvement. Without a theoretical optimum, there would be no errors or possibilities for optimization. By adhering to these conventions, you can establish a uniform standard for your own training, progressively working towards your goals. Any deviations from the theoretical optimum can be recognized as compensatory movements, prompting appropriate corrective actions in your training regimen. For the first form convention, the following is defined:

1. The body is stabilized in a line as perpendicular to gravity as possible.

Explanation: The level of difficulty in performing a lever skill is directly related to the distance between the body's center of gravity and the axis of rotation of the joint that is under the highest load, typically the shoulder joint. The greater this distance, the more challenging the lever skill becomes. The maximum distance is achieved when the lever skill is stabilized in a straight line and held parallel to the ground, which is considered the ideal position (perpendicular to gravity). Therefore, this position should be the target for lever skills. However, certain skills, like the dragon flag, naturally involve performing the skill at a slight angle to gravity. As a result, the convention of being "as perpendicular as possible" has been adjusted to accommodate these specific lever skills.

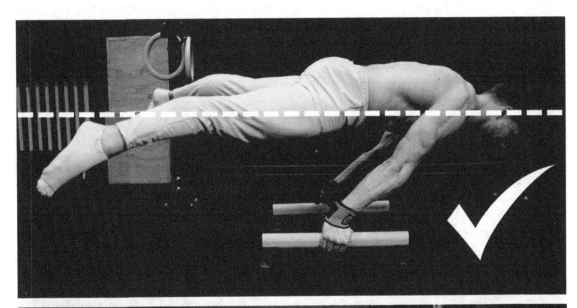

Application lever skill convention 1: A deviation from the horizontal alignment represents a simplification and is therefore considered compensation. In the example, the compensation arises from the flexed hip

2. All joints, that are perpendicular to gravity, are aligned in such a way that they can be muscularly stabilized as actively as possible against gravity.

Explanation: To achieve maximum body tension in lever skills, each joint needs to be stabilized individually against the pull of gravity. This involves aligning the body as parallel to the ground (horizontal) as possible. The goal is to anchor the joints in a way that counters the natural rotational or pulling forces exerted by gravity. By achieving this optimal alignment, you can maximize the leverage and maintain the highest level of body tension during the execution of lever skills.

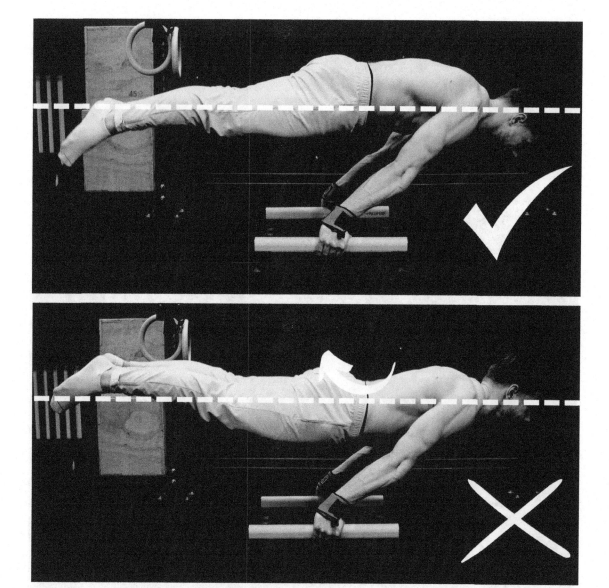

Application lever skill convention 2: If joints are not stabilized against the pulling direction of gravity, the difficulty of the element is reduced. These movements are therefore considered compensations. Thus, although both planches are relatively in line, in the example below, compensation is made via a hollow back and thus the spine is not sufficiently stabilized against gravity.

3. All (relevant*) joints are kept in an extended position, depending on the selected regression.

Explanation: It is important to consider the convention for both full lever skills and their regressions, which are simplified versions with reduced difficulty by adjusting the lever length. This convention ensures completeness and applicability to all lever skills. *The term "relevant" refers to the joints that need to be extended based on the specific skill. There is a distinction between bent-arm lever skills (arms bent) and straight-arm lever skills (arms extended), but since only straight-arm lever skills are discussed in this book, further considerations will focus on them. Depending on the chosen regression, the spine, hips, and/or knees can be kept extended or bent at an angle, and this will be discussed in detail later in the book.

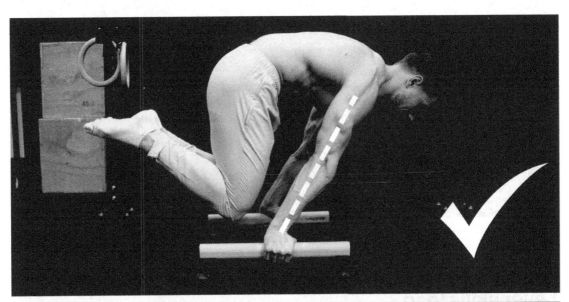

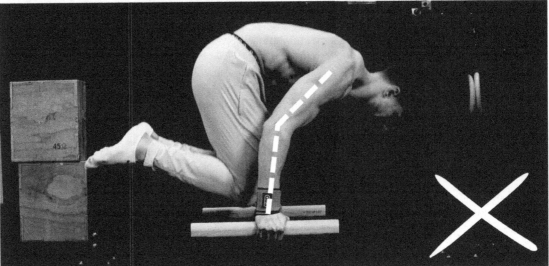

Application lever skill convention 3: If joints relevant to the selected progression are not fully extended, the difficulty of the element is reduced. These movements are therefore considered compensations. In this example, the compensation arises from bending the elbows, which should be kept extended.

By applying these three conventions, you can analyze the execution of lever skills, identify weak points, and recognize compensatory movements that deviate from perfect form. This analysis will help you develop strategies to address these compensations. In other words, when examining your lever skills, ensure that all three conventions are followed and adapted to your progression. If any deviations are identified, you can adjust your execution accordingly. If you are not yet capable of doing so, you can modify your training to learn the necessary skills as efficiently as possible.

Wording: In this book, the term "progression" is used when referring to the easiest form of a skill, and the exercise described for that form is considered a progression. Conversely, the term "regression" is used when referencing the final form of the skill as a reference point in the context of the explanation, and the exercise described is considered a regression.

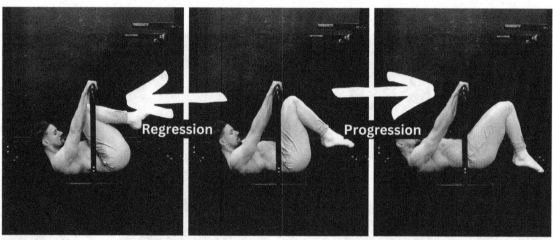

Definition progression and regression of a skill

3.0.1

Lever skills load variables

You can already determine whether a lever skill is being performed correctly based on the established form conventions. However, before delving into the training planning for lever skills, it is important to familiarize yourself with the various load variables that are essential to know and understand. This will provide you with an overview of the factors that influence the training of lever skills.

3.0.1.1

Intensity

In isometric contractions, the intensity is typically expressed as a percentage of MVC (maximal voluntary contraction) in the literature. However, this measurement is not applicable in lever skills training due to its impracticality. Instead, the intensity in practice is determined by the choice of progression and the duration of the hold.

The intensity is categorized into absolute and relative intensity. **Absolute intensity** refers to the difficulty or "heaviness" of the lever skill progression. It is influenced by the load arm, which is the normal distance between the body's center of gravity and the shoulder joint. Increasing the load arm can be achieved through various methods.

The first method is **extending the spine.** In a full tuck position, the spine is slightly rounded. By extending it, the normal distance between the body's center of gravity and the shoulder joint increases, resulting in a greater load arm and higher intensity.

The second method is **extending the hip**, typically following the extension of the spine. Increasing the angle of the hip further intensifies the skill by increasing the load arm on the shoulder. Additionally, when the hip is extended beyond 90°, the load arm on the abdominal muscles becomes relevant, as they experience increased load.

The third method, which follows the extension of the hip, involves **extending one or both knees.** This extension further increases the load arms and conse-quently intensifies the skill. Another way to adjust the intensity is by modifying the **angle of hip spread.** Spreading the legs decreases the load arms while bringing the legs together increases the load arm. This allows for fine-tuning the progressions according to individual needs. It is important to note that these four methods can be combined to further adjust the intensity as desired.

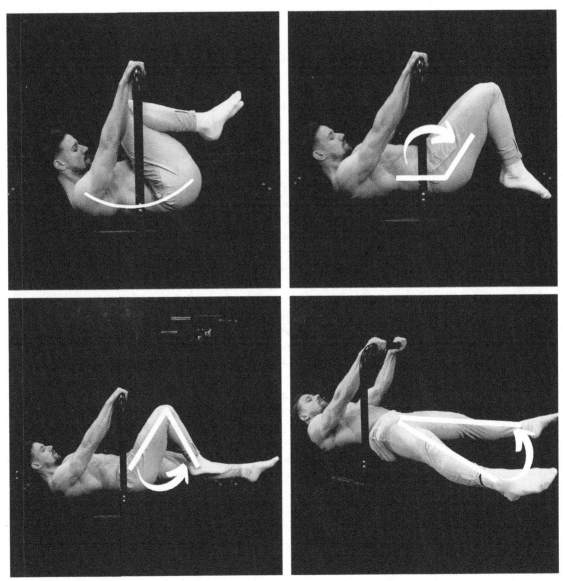

Lever skills intensification sequence

In training practice, it's crucial to monitor your progress in terms of absolute intensity. To effectively track this, it is advisable to regulate the intensity using only one method, especially in the beginning. For example, you can start with a full tuck progression and focus on extending your spine until you can maintain that position. Once you can consistently keep your spine extended, you can then work on adjusting the hip angle while keeping the knee angle constant. By focusing on one method at a time, you can better assess whether the resulting load arm is truly increasing and if you are progressing effectively.

However, as you advance and for individual reasons, you may choose to combine multiple methods, such as in a half-lay straddle lever skill (hips extended, legs spread, knees bent). In such cases, it's important to be cautious and use only one method of scaling intensity within that combination. Otherwise, it can become challenging to track your progression objectively.

Apart from absolute intensity, there is also **relative intensity** to consider. Relative intensity refers to how close you are training to the maximum possible holding time for your chosen progression. The closer you train to failure, which is when you can no longer maintain the progression with adequate form, the higher the relative intensity. It is recommended to train until technical failure, where the form no longer meets your desired standards, rather than pushing to the point of complete inability to hold the position. This approach reduces the risk of injury, maintains high training quality, and allows for angle-specific training (more on this later). Typically, training until technical failure corresponds to stopping the hold around 1–3 seconds before reaching the maximum possible holding time, allowing for slight drops in form

Volume

This point is very difficult to define for lever skills because there are only few references on it and volume always interacts with intensity. In addition, it is difficult to define fixed values due to the mixture of isometric holding times and dynamic assistance exercises. Therefore, the following values should only be considered as guidelines that you can use as an orientation. The individual deviations can therefore be very large.

Holdtime per hold
The relevant range of hold times for you are derived from the sensible MVC ranges. If your muscle contracts with too low intensity, no adaptation will take place in the long run. To stimulate muscle hypertrophy, the MVC should be at least 70%, and for strength adaptations 80–100%. This leads to hold times for hypertrophy of approximately 3–30s and for strength of approximately 1–5s. (24) These data were never collected specifically for isometric lever skills and should therefore be taken as a guide and not as absolute truth. What you can learn from this, however, is to be careful when choosing hold times. Pick a hold time that allows you to train intensely enough to trigger the desired adaptation. In our King Of Weighted Coaching, the following holdtimes have proven to be very effective in their specific context.

Ballistic holds - 1–3s
Ballistic holds can be defined as any exercise where you accelerate into a progression of an isometric hold. An example of this is L-Sit to planches, front lever raises, planche lean to holds or various lever change holds. These ballistic holds are used to increase strength in a specific progression. You work with several suc-

cessive short but very intense holds. In this way, you accumulate higher total hold times with a very high MVC despite very short holds in order to achieve a strength adaptation in this position. They are suitable for advancing to a new progression when longer holds are not yet possible with sufficient quality. However, they are challenging and demanding, requiring coordination and strength. Beginners should approach ballistic holds with caution. In the section 'Lever skill specific assistance', you will find more information on the use of ballistic holds.

High intensity holds - 2–5s

These short but intense holds are primarily used to build strength in a specific progression. The high intensity limits the hold time per hold and the total hold time per session due to resulting fatigue. These holds are more suitable for advanced athletes who are technically experienced and have the necessary strength capacity for short intense holds.

Medium intensity holds - 5–8s

This range provides a good compromise for accumulating enough volume while maintaining a high enough intensity for strength adaptation. The risk of injury is relatively lower compared to high-intensity holds, making it more likely to maintain a high-quality lever skill performance.

Low intensity/conditioning holds - 8–10s+

Longer holds at low intensity are suitable for developing coordination, positioning, control, and balance in lever skills. They also help beginners practice the correct technique and prepare their joints, tendons, and ligaments for future, more intensive stresses associated with lever skills.

Holdtime per session

Assuming you would train exclusively isometric, recommendations can be found in the range of 80–150s holdtime per session for hypertrophy and 30–90s holdtime per session for strength. Logically,

these holdtimes must be performed at the appropriate absolute intensity. (24) Again, unfortunately, this data has not been collected in the context of calisthenics lever skills and therefore must be taken with a lot of caution. Since you are usually not only training lever skills but also doing other exercises to stimulate your strength/hypertrophy, you can use the lower ranges of hold times per session as a guide to having a starting point. Hopefully, there will be better and more specific data in the future.

Holdtime per week

The hold time per week is the product of the selected frequency and the hold time per session.

Assistance volume

As mentioned earlier, it is very unusual for an athlete to train only lever skills. So when talking about volume, all exercises that train the same muscles as the lever skill must be taken into consideration. Here you can roughly base yourself on 10–20 sets per movement or muscle group. (25)

The **total volume** is therefore composed of the hold time per week (seconds per session x frequency) plus the specific assistance volume of 10–20 sets per week. As the specificity of the assist decreases, the carryover to the lever skill also decreases. So a dip has less carryover to a planche than a planche push up. So the goal should be to make the volume as specific as possible while respecting all other training goals and individual circumstances.

3.0.1.3   **Frequency**

The frequency indicates how often per week a lever skill is trained.
The choice of frequency is based on a number of factors that you should consider in order to train a lever skill at low risk.

1. Training experience

If you have little to no training experience with a lever skill, it is recommended that you start with a frequency of 1 to a maximum of 2. Give your joints, ligaments, tendons and muscles time to get used to the sometimes very extreme and unfamiliar positions. The more experience you have, the higher the frequency is that you can choose.

Very experienced, highly specialized athletes can train lever skills almost daily. However, the norm is 2–3x per week for advanced athletes.

2. Body weight and height

The bigger and heavier you are, the greater the workload (absolute weight x hold time) for a lever skill. In other words, for a full tuck progression, a heavier athlete needs more strength than a lighter one. The same is true for body size. There are detailed explanations of this in the 'influencing factors' section. Intensity and frequency are interdependent. The more intense you train, the less often you can do it, because the load on your body is very high. So the bigger and heavier you are, the lower you should initially choose the frequency because your lever skill training is automatically a bit more intense due to the larger workload. A frequency of 1 to a maximum of 2 is recommended here. With increasing relative strength, the intensity of an element logically decreases over time, even for heavy athletes, which means that the frequency can be increased again.

3. Interference with other exercises

There are only a few athletes who exclusively train a lever skill and have little to no other training content. Therefore, overlap with exercises that train the same muscle groups must be considered. If you also train skills such as the handstand push up and heavy dips, you will have to cut back in one area. Depending on your priorities you have to adjust the frequency to avoid overload.

4. Priority

As already mentioned in point three, the prioritization of the lever skills in training also determines the frequency. To maintain your level, one workout per week is usually sufficient, as long as you maintain your body weight. If you want to make progress, you have to invest more time and train the skill more frequently in consideration of points one to three.

Influencing factors

As stated in the volume and frequency section, several significant factors influence your training in lever skills. It is essential to understand these factors in order to adjust your training accordingly. Furthermore, comprehending these factors will provide insight into why certain skills may be more or less challenging for you.

Firstly, consider your **height and weight** as influential factors. Higher body weight corresponds to lower relative strength. This is due to the fact that an athlete's strength is proportional to the muscle's cross-sectional area rather than its volume. Consequently, smaller and lighter athletes have a more favorable ratio of muscle cross-sectional area to body weight (28). This explains why most professional gymnasts tend to be small and light. Hence, if you have a larger and heavier build, lever skills will likely be more difficult for you. Nevertheless, it is important to note that size and weight alone do not determine your ability to learn lever skills.

Similarly, a small and lightweight road bike rider with a significant proportion of muscle mass in their thighs will encounter similar difficulties as taller athletes, despite their smaller size and weight. This is because the **distribution of weight** in your body also plays a role. For example, an athlete with a well-developed upper body and lighter legs, despite having the same body weight as someone with heavier legs and a lighter upper body, will possess advantages in relation to lever skills. Another factor worth mentioning is **body fat percentage (BF%)**. Even if two athletes have the same body weight but different BF%, the athlete with a lower BF% will have an advantage. Likewise, **body proportions** are significant. Individuals with long legs and short torsos tend to face disadvantages, whereas those with short legs and long torsos have certain advantages. This is because having more weight close to the axis of rotation in lever skills reduces the effective load arm.

Shift in center of gravity with different body proportions. The longer and/or heavier the lower body becomes in relation to the upper body, the more force the athlete must apply. If the body's center of gravity is lower (further to the right in the picture) the athlete must apply more force to remain in balance.

Moreover, **internal torques** play a crucial role in determining your aptitude for a specific lever skill. The **force arm of a muscle** relies significantly on its attachment points. When a muscle has a larger force arm in a specific position, it can exert more power. For instance, in the case of the front lever, the attachments of the latissimus dorsi and teres major on the upper arm are key factors that determine the level of difficulty for the skill. Having favorable muscle attachments in the latissimus and teres major provides a decisive advantage in performing the element.

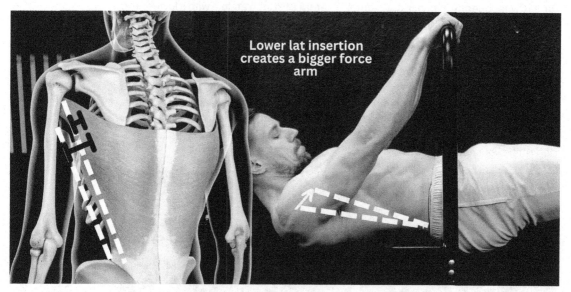

Example of long and short force arm of latissimus during front lever. The larger the force arm (longer line), the more torque the latissimus can apply with the same muscle strength.

The same principle applies to other muscles involved in various lever skills. Another factor that is often overlooked is your **maximum strength capability**. If you have limited training in developing this aspect, it will be less prominent. Lever skills, as mentioned earlier, demand a high level of relative strength, which combines maximum strength and body weight. Therefore, if you predominantly train with light weights and higher repetition ranges while lacking strength development, you will be at a disadvantage compared to an athlete with similar muscle mass, size, and body weight but a higher maximum strength level.

To illustrate this, let's consider the e1RM (estimated one-rep max) results of a client from the King Of Weighted Coaching. Two graphs display the athlete's e1RM for weighted dips and weighted chin ups. Despite having advanced training experience, this athlete faced significant difficulties in progressing with the front lever and handstand push-ups (HSPU) skills. However, within a span of fewer than four months, the athlete managed to advance from an advanced tucked position to a full front lever and from pike push-ups to HSPU, all without increasing the volume of skill-specific training. This remarkable progress was mainly achieved through maximal strength-specific training. It is essential to note that this is an extraordinary example and may not represent the typical progression for most individuals. Nonetheless, it demonstrates the substantial influence that maximum strength ability can have on skill training.

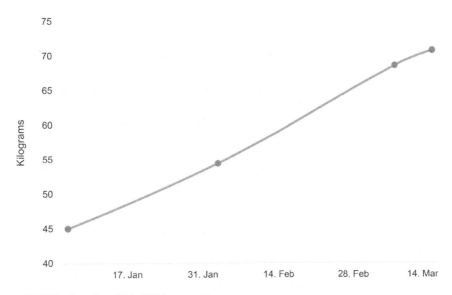

King Of Weighted coaching client e1RM dip progress.

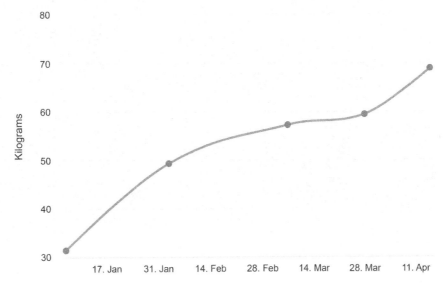

King Of Weighted coaching client e1RM chin up progress.

Gender also indirectly affects lever skill training. On average, women tend to have a higher body fat percentage (BF%), a smaller proportion of muscle mass in relation to total body weight, and a higher percentage of type 1 muscle fibers, which can adversely impact relative strength. However, these factors primarily affect the starting point rather than overall potential. Evaluations by Greg Nuckols indicate that women can actually expect higher relative strength gains throughout their training journeys compared to men. Therefore, women should not be discouraged by the potential initial disadvantages (29). Similar considerations apply to different **age groups.** Greg Knuckols published an article suggesting that relative strength gains do not significantly diminish with age. The observations made by the King Of Weighted Coaching, based on over 300 clients to date, align with this finding, as they have not observed substantial differences in relative strength gains among various age groups. Nevertheless, it can be assumed that younger athletes may anticipate greater long-term relative strength gains, providing them with an advantage (30).

3.0.2

Progression

Allow me to begin this section with a personal anecdote. When I was learning the straddle planche, I dedicated 2–3 sessions per week for several months to practice it. I persisted, continuously pushing myself into the position until, after almost a year, I finally achieved success. Why do I share this story? It is to emphasize that, despite the various methods, techniques, and systems discussed in the following section that have proven effective for our clients and myself in coaching, the fundamental principle remains exposing yourself to the position over the long term to compel your body to adapt. This can be approached strategically, as outlined in the subsequent section, or straightforwardly, much like how I pursued it nearly eight years ago.

Lever skills can be progressed in four different areas that can be combined with each other. Progressions must be used to provoke an adaptation in the body over time by progressively increasing different load variables. This is the only way to get stronger in the long run.

1st full planche by me in 2016, find all compensations ;)

3.0.2.1

Technique/conditioning - progression

One of the most commonly overlooked and underestimated methods of making progress is by improving your technique within the current progression. Even if you are holding the same lever position for the same duration, doing so with better technique constitutes progress. Improved technique typically involves achieving a more stable and controlled position of the joints. This can only be accomplished once you have become stronger and adapted to the demands of the position (conditioning). Consequently, this development should be acknowledged as a form of progression. If you find yourself feeling stagnant in your progress, it is advisable to assess the quality of your execution over time.

3.0.2.2

Holdtimes - progression

Hold time progression refers to the ability to maintain a specific progression, with the same absolute intensity, for an extended duration. In lever skills, hold time progression is analogous to repetition progression in dynamic exercises. It does not involve lifting heavier weights or utilizing additional levers, but rather the capacity to perform the hold more frequently or for a longer period. Another approach to progress hold times is by increasing the number of sets per session. If you can successfully complete more sets during a session, it is considered a sign of progression.

3.0.2.3

Frequency - progression

To enhance the total hold time over the course of a week, you can also progress through frequency. This entails increasing the number of times you train the lever skill within a week. However, this progression should be approached with caution and only considered by athletes who initially train lever skills at a low frequency of 1 to a maximum of 2 sessions per week. It is advisable to increase the frequency after a conditioning phase to ensure that your body is adequately prepared for the higher training load. Once again, highly specialized athletes may be an exception to this guideline.

Lever - progression

3.0.2.4

You use the lever progression to increase the absolute intensity of your lever skills. You can compare this with the weight progression in weighted exercises. So if you increase the leverage of a progression with the same hold time, you have made progress.

Resistance bands/assistance systems progression

3.0.2.5

In calisthenics, resistance bands and other assistance systems using straps and counterweights are utilized to regulate the absolute intensity of lever skills. By incorporating resistance bands, for example, you can effectively decrease your body weight, enabling you to perform heavier progressions or prolong your hold times in current progressions. A valid method of progression when using bands or assistance systems is to gradually reduce the assistance over time. However, it is crucial to exercise caution and avoid exclusively training with assistance. When relying too heavily on assistance, especially if the assistance is initially set at a high level, it not only reduces your body weight but also externally stabilizes you. Consequently, you may fail to adequately integrate the coordination aspect, which includes maintaining proper balance, body tension, and muscle control, into your training. It is important to ensure that you sufficiently address these components in your training alongside the use of assistance systems.

3.0.3

Training methods

In this section, we will explore training methods that facilitate long-term progress in lever skills and assist you in developing and adjusting your personalized training plan over time. Before delving into the theoretical training methods, it is important to address a crucial aspect of lever skill training: **angle-specific adaptation**. In isometric training, the strength adaptation primarily occurs in the **specific angle of contraction** that is trained. The carryover to the full range of motion is generally limited. This has several implications for your training with lever skills. Firstly, it is essential to employ an optimal and highly specific technique to ensure that you target the appropriate joint angles and promote adaptation in those specific positions. This emphasizes the significance of precise positioning and execution. Secondly, relying solely on isometric training is usually insufficient to achieve long-term progress throughout the entire range of motion of a joint. It is crucial to incorporate complementary training methods to address the complete range of motion effectively. (24) (26)

3.0.3.1

Triple progression

The first method you can use to plan your lever skills is the triple progression. It is a very simple and therefore user-friendly system to achieve sustainable progress in your lever skill training. The system is called triple progression because you use three different progressions step by step in a predefined order. You define a fixed scheme of sets and hold times and the corresponding progression.

Progression 1: Technique progression
You train a fixed scheme and try to improve the technique and thus the quality of the hold from session to session. If you continue to improve your technique, you do not change your system. If you achieve a sufficiently high quality of execution in all sets, you move on to progression 2.

Example: You start your front lever training with 4x6s holds in a tucked front lever. You focus on implementing all conventions and improving your technique from session to session.

Session 1:
Target: 4x6s
Result: 4x6s, medium to strong technique breakdowns towards the end of sets.
Action: No action required

Session 2:
Target: 4x6s
Result: 4x6s, slight to moderate technique breakdowns towards the end of sets.
Action: No action required

Session 3:
Target: 4x6s
Result: 4x6s, no to just slight technique breakdowns towards the end of sets.
Action: Transition to progression 2

Progression 2: Holdtime progression
You continue to train your fixed scheme but increase the hold times per set. Give yourself a range of about 2s in which you have to progress per set. If your hold times do not increase for two sessions in a row, you increase the number of sets by one. This will increase your total hold time per session and allow you to achieve more adaptation to accelerate the hold time progression per set. When you reach the upper end of the holdtime range on average, you move to progression 3.
Example: After achieving 4x6s with a solid technique, increase the range to 6–8s. The goal is 8s holdtime to move on to the next progression. Whether these 8s work well for you or you can move to the new progression sooner or later is something you simply test. This can vary for you and also change over time.

Session 1:
  Target: 4x8s
  Result: 6s, 6s, 6s, 6s
  Action: No action required

Session 2:
  Target: 4x8s
  Result: 7s, 7s, 6s, 6s
  Action: No action required

Session 3 & 4:
  Target: 4x8s
  Result: 7s, 7s, 7s, 6s
  Action: increase by one set due to stagnant hold times

Session 5:
  Target: 4x8s
  Result: 7s, 7s, 7s, 7s, 6s
  Action: No action required

  .
  .
  .

Session 10:
  Target: 4x8s
  Result: 10s, 9s, 7s, 7s, 6s
  Action: At this point, you have reached your planned 8s average for four sets and you are moving into a new, more intense progression.

Progression 3: Lever progression (absolute intensity progression)

To advance your training in lever skills, there are two primary methods: increasing the lever in your current progression or raising the absolute intensity by decreasing the assistance (such as resistance bands or counterweights) you utilize. Once you have reached the limit of your current progression, you can transition to a new and more challenging progression. The process then restarts as you focus on improving the technique, followed by increasing the hold time and finally advancing the lever position. This cycle allows for continuous progression in your training.

Example: You change your progression from a tucked to an adv. tucked 90° progression and work your way back up from about 6 to about 8s.

When transitioning to more intense progressions, it is common to experience an adjustment period of one to two weeks as your body adapts to the new position. It is normal for your hold times to decrease slightly during this period due to the increased intensity. In such cases, you can automatically combine progression 1 and progression 2. Longer phases of technique adaptation are typically encountered when introducing completely new progressions, such as transitioning from advanced tuck to straddle or one leg progressions.

It is **important to note** that any stagnation, regardless of which step of the triple progression it occurs in, with increasing body weight should still be considered as progress. No immediate action is required in such cases, as an increase in body weight over time inherently represents an escalation in absolute intensity and signifies progression.

Variables for the system:

To begin, it is recommended to aim for approximately 30 seconds of total hold time per session and gradually increase your hold times from there. However, this 30-second target is not mandatory, as you can compensate for shorter hold times by using additional assistance without any issues.

If you are working with full tuck progressions, focus on light to medium intensity holds. If you have progressed to the advanced tuck progression or beyond, aim for medium to high intensity holds. The number of sets can be determined by dividing the total hold time by the desired hold time per set. Choose the frequency of your sessions based on the guidelines provided in the frequency section. As you increase the intensity of your training, reduce the total hold time accordingly, and consider accumulating additional volume through the use of assistance.

When is this system suitable?

The triple progression system is suitable for training within a progression that offers ample opportunities for scaling. This refers to the phase of your training where you progressively improve your technique, hold time, and leverage within a specific lever progression that you can already hold for approximately 4–6 seconds. Examples of suitable progressions

Scaling from an adv. tuck front lever with approx. 60° hip flexion to approx. 120° hip flexion.

include the advanced tuck, one leg, and straddle progressions, which can be scaled over several weeks without difficulties. As long as you foresee no immediate progression changes, you can effectively utilize the triple progression method to achieve consistent progress without extensive planning.

Example: Linear increase of adv .tucked front lever from adv. tucked 60° to adv. tucked 120°.

3.0.3.2   **Top and back-off set systems/division of intensities**

During your lever skill training with the triple progression system, it is common to encounter a plateau at some point. As you continue using the same system and hold time range for an extended period, the adaptations that your body undergoes become less pronounced, resulting in a stagnation of progress. To overcome this plateau, it becomes necessary to introduce additional strategies to the system. One situation where the triple progression alone may be insufficient is during a transition between two progressions that require a significant increase in intensity. For instance, moving

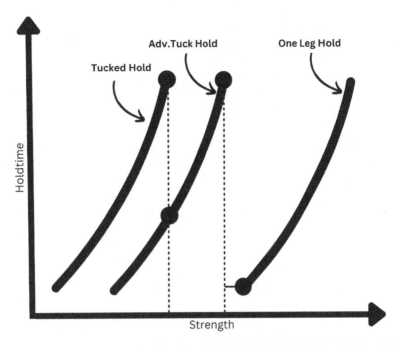

Holdtimes do not behave proportionally to force adaptation. The higher the holdtimes, the lower the force adaptation and the lower the transfer of the training to more intensive holds. The progressions in the graph represent only a random example.

from an advanced tuck to a one leg front lever or from an advanced tuck planche to a straddle planche can present challenges when relying solely on the triple progression.

In such cases, it is advisable to consider incorporating complementary training methods or techniques to facilitate the transition. This could involve implementing specialized exercises, varying intensity, or incorporating assistance exercises to target specific weaknesses or prepare your body for the more advanced progression. By supplementing the triple progression system with appropriate strategies tailored to your specific needs, you can effectively navigate through challenging progressions and continue making consistent gains in your lever skill training.

When transitioning from one progression to a more intense progression in lever skills, it is common to face challenges due to the low specificity of your training for the new progression. Simply increasing hold times in a lighter progression does not guarantee success in holding shorter times in a more intense progression. After a certain point, higher hold times do not automatically lead to greater strength adaptation. When hold times become excessively long, your maximum voluntary contraction (MVC) decreases, and force adaptation is limited. The exact threshold for each individual during the progression transition varies. To bridge this gap between progressions, it is necessary to implement a strategy that addresses the issue. One effective approach is to incorporate a split in intensities within your training. This allows you to adjust your total workout time more sensibly to different intensity ranges, providing sufficient stimulus for force adaptations while maintaining an adequate total hold time, avoid injury and excessive fatigue. This can be achieved by using **top sets and back-off sets.**

Top sets are used for more intense holds, where you focus on challenging yourself with higher intensity and shorter hold times. These sets target the specific demands of the advanced progression. On the other hand, back-off sets are used for less intense holds, where you work on maintaining technique, and endurance, and accumulate more total hold time. These sets help bridge the gap and provide a smoother progression.

To assist you in understanding how to split your training, here are some examples of different use cases that can serve as a guide.

Transition to a more intensive progression

Example 1: For the top sets, use a light resistance band that allows you to keep the new more intense progression in the high intensity range. For the back-off sets, use your current main progression in a moderate intensity range.

Application note: This split works very well for you if you want to work on both expanding the hold times of your main progression and in parallel developing the next, more intense progression.

top sets	progression + light band	high intensity holds
back off sets	regression	medium intensitys hold

Example 2: In this split, you work exclusively with the new, more intense progression. You use different resistance bands to split the intensities.

Application note: This split is very suitable for you if you want to accumulate as much practice as possible in the new, more intense progression. Especially for progressions that are technically difficult for you, you can benefit from this division.

top sets	progression + light band	high intensity holds
back off sets	progression + medium band	medium intensity holds

Example 3: This split is very similar to example 1. Instead of a resistance band, you use ballistic holds to accumulate holdtime in the new, more intense progression to make them accessible. You fill up the back off-sets with holdtime from your main progression.

Application note: Just like in example 1, you use this split if you want to work on both expanding the hold times of your main progression and in parallel developing the next, more intense progression. So depending on the skill, individual preference, and available equipment, you can use either resistance bands or ballistic holds for this split.

top sets	progression	ballistic holds
back off sets	regression	medium intensity holds

Example 4: In this split, as in example 2, you work exclusively with the new, more intense progression. You use resistance bands in combination with ballistic holds to divide the intensities.

Application note: This split is therefore again very suitable for you if you want to accumulate as much practice as possible in the new, more intensive progression. Especially with technically difficult progressions of a lever skill you can profit from this division.

top sets	progression	ballistic holds
back off sets	progression + medium band	medium intensity holds

Variables for the system:
Base the total hold time on the value you previously obtained using the triple progression system. You can start a little lower because the average intensity at which you will train is a little higher. The higher it is, the lower your total hold time needs to be. Start with two to three top sets and fill up the remaining total hold time with the back-off sets. Continue to progress within the system using the triple progression. Progress the top sets first and the back-off sets second. If you reach a level with your top sets that allows you to skip the back-off sets in order to reach your total hold time approximately (slightly reduced as you work with more intensity), you can go back to the normal triple progression. Another possibility would be to make the progression of the top sets the regression of the back-off sets and choose the next, more intensive progression for the top sets.

3.0.3.3   **Progress backup**

Lever skills require relatively high relative strength. Therefore, to become stronger in a lever skill in the long run, you need to build muscle and increase your maximum strength. You can't optimally build both qualities with isometric hold exercises alone. Exercises that train the relevant muscles over a wide range of motion and can be scaled in intensity using additional weight work better here. So to get better at a lever skill in a sustainable and plateau-free way, you can combine it with at least one exercise I call ‚progress-backup'.

What is a Progress Backup?

Using progress back-ups can be an effective strategy to complement your lever skill training. A progress backup is a multi-joint exercise that targets the same muscle groups and movement patterns as the lever skill you are training. By incorporating basic exercises as progress backups, you can make long-term progress through weight progression. Here are a couple of examples:

Planche as a lever skill with weighted dips as a progress backup: The planche primarily targets the shoulder flexors. Weighted dips also engage these muscle groups. By progressively increasing the weight in your dips, you can stimulate further strength gains that support your progress in the planche.

Front lever with weighted chin-ups as a progress backup: The front lever requires significant strength in your shoulder extensors. Weighted chin-ups involve similar muscle groups. By progressively increasing the weight in your chin-ups, you can enhance the strength needed for the front lever.

These examples demonstrate how progress backups can provide an additional stimulus to the targeted muscle groups and contribute to overall strength development. It's important to choose progress backups that closely align with the lever skills you are working on and ensure proper form and technique in both exercises. Additionally, gradually increasing the weight in the progress back-ups over time will help promote continuous progress and support your lever skill training.

The tasks of the progress backups

Incorporating progress backups into your training plan requires careful consideration of two important tasks: generating sufficient training volume for muscle stimulation and improving maximum strength specific to the lever skill.

The primary goal of a progress backup is to provide enough training volume to effectively stimulate the muscles involved in the lever skill. The recommended range is 10–20 sets per week per muscle group or movement (25). If you are incorporating multiple exercises that target the same muscle group or movement, the total volume will be divided among them. As a beginner, it is advisable to start with a lower volume and gradually increase it as you gain experience.

The second task of a progress backup is to directly train your maximum strength for the specific lever skill. While this is indirectly achieved through muscle growth, it is also important to focus on training maximum strength directly. This can be accomplished by performing the progress backups at high intensity ranges, specifically targeting the relevant muscles.

When programming progress backups, it is crucial to align them with the lever skill you are training. Consider whether you are training within a progression or transitioning to a more intense progression. Beginners may follow a slightly different approach. Dr. Eric Helms' recommendations for dividing repetition ranges and associated intensities for strength and hypertrophy-oriented training phases can serve as a guide (see table). It's important to note that strength and hypertrophy phases should never be programmed exclusively, as strength phases still require sufficient volume to maintain muscle mass, and hypertrophy phases should cover high enough intensities to preserve maximum strength ability.

By utilizing progress backups effectively and following appropriate programming guidelines, you can enhance muscle stimulation, promote maximum strength development, and optimize your progress in lever skills.

| Intensity | Strength | ⅔–¾ of volume in the 1–6 rep range, remaining volume in the 6–15 rep range, at a RPE 5–10 |
| | Hypertrophy | ⅔–¾ of volume in the 6–12 rep range, remaining volume in the 1–6 and 12–20 rep range, at a RPE 5–10 |

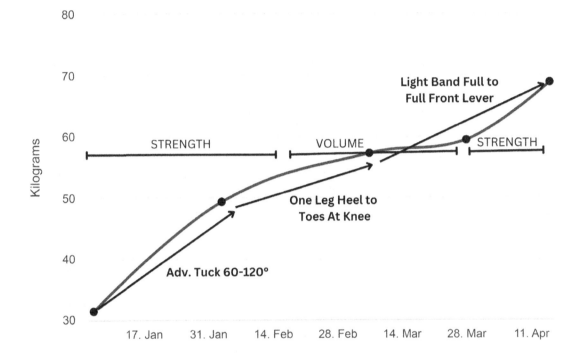

Real-life example of an athlete in King Of Weighted Coaching. The graph shows the correlation of the e1RM in the weighted chin up and the primary used progression of the Front Lever in training.

Case 1: Training within a progression

This phase in your lever skill training is best combined with a hypertrophy/volume training phase of the progress back-up. This means you should perform the 10–20 sets of your progress back up and the associated assistance to approx. ⅔ to the repetition range of 6–12 and divide the rest between repetition ranges 1–6 and, if necessary, 12–20 depending on the exercise.

Case 2: Transition to a new progression

In this phase, an increase in maximum strength is very helpful to ease the transition to the new, more intense progression. Therefore, it makes sense to also enter a strength-oriented phase with the progress back up at this point. To do this, you should divide the 10–20 sets of your progress back-up and the associated assistance to approx. ⅔ of the repetition range 1–6 and the rest to the repetition ranges 6–15. If your priority is your progress backup, plan your lever skills programming based on the training phases of your progress backup and not vice versa. The approach remains the same.

Intensity

As a beginner, it is recommended to avoid training above 80% of your maximum strength (Fmax) when incorporating progress backups into your routine, even during a strength phase. This is because beginners typically lack experience and may have limited exercise techniques, increasing the risk of injury. Moreover, high intensities are not necessary for beginners to increase their maximum strength, as they can make significant progress with lower intensities. In the context of strength training, 100% Fmax corresponds to the maximum weight you can lift for a single repetition. Advanced athletes, with more experience and developed technique, can perform the strength-oriented sets in the 80–95% Fmax range. This range provides an appropriate level of intensity to stimulate further strength gains. Very experienced athletes may even work in the 85–100% Fmax range during strength phases to further enhance their maximum strength capabilities. It's important to prioritize safety and gradually increase the intensity of your progress backups as you gain experience and improve your technique. Working with appropriate intensities helps minimize the risk of injury while still providing an effective stimulus for strength development (27).

Frequency

When incorporating progress backups into your training routine, it is generally recommended to train them 2–3 times a week. Starting with twice a week is a good initial frequency, and if needed, you can increase it to three times a week. However, it's important to avoid concentrating all the high-intensity work on a single training day. To distribute the workload effectively and minimize the risk of overloading specific muscle groups, it's advisable not to include more than one heavy basic exercise per muscle group within each training session. By focusing on a single heavy exercise, you can prioritize proper technique and sufficient recovery for that particular movement pattern. For the remaining basic exercises targeting the same muscle group, it's recommended to keep their intensity at a moderate level. This approach helps balance the overall training stress and allows for adequate recovery between sessions, reducing the risk of excessive fatigue or overuse injuries.

Overlaps

It is important to avoid overlaps in your training plan, especially with exercises that have similar movement patterns. Be cautious when assigning high intensities to multiple exercises targeting the same muscle groups simultaneously. Prioritize and allocate the appropriate intensity and volume to different exercises within the same category. Focus on one or two main exercises at a time while keeping others at a lower intensity or as complementary exercises. Rotate or cycle exercises strategically and seek guidance from a knowledgeable coach or trainer to create a balanced training plan.

Stimulus to fatigue ratio

It is important to ensure that your progress backup exercise has a good stimulus to fatigue ratio. This means that the exercise should effectively stimulate your target muscles without causing excessive overall body fatigue. If your progress backup exercise has a poor stimulus to fatigue ratio, it may lead to increased fatigue and the need for longer recovery periods or more frequent deloading. This can hinder your long-term training progress, as it may require more frequent breaks or adjustments to manage fatigue levels effectively.

3.0.4

Lever skill specific assistance

In addition to the training methods presented, you will be introduced to other assistance exercises that you can incorporate into your training whenever needed to help you overcome plateaus and make faster progress.

Ballistic holds

Ballistic holds in the context of lever skills encompass different exercise categories where you accelerate into an isometric hold. These holds are used to progress to more challenging positions that cannot be achieved in a controlled manner without prior acceleration. The main purpose of ballistic holds is to familiarize the body with the new position and develop strength in that specific position through repeated, short, and intense holds.

There are two common categories of ballistic holds that can be applied to almost all lever skills: **raises and negatives.** Raises involve accelerating into the skil position against gravity with a concentric muscle contraction. The level of momen-tum or acceleration you choose during the raise will determine the difficulty. It is possible to perform raises without any momentum, but that would deviate from the purpose of a ballistic hold in this context. Examples of raises include planche raises from a support hold and front lever raises on the high bar. On the other hand, negatives involve using gravity to accelerate yourself into the skill position using an eccentric muscle contraction. In the negatives, you slow yourself down against gravity to assume the position. Examples of negatives include front lever negatives, backlever negatives on the rings, or planche negatives from the handstand.

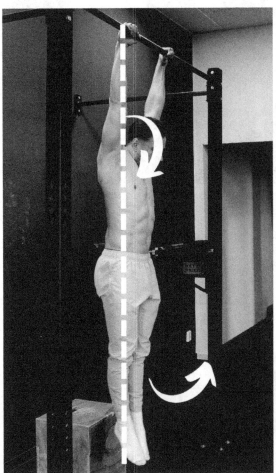

Example of a ballistic hold: front lever raise on the high bar

3.0.4.2

Full ROM assistance

Not all athletes are able or willing to incorporate weighted calisthenics or systems like the progress back-up into their training. However, there are alternative ways to accumulate specific volume and train with adjustable intensity in calisthenics. One approach is to incorporate dynamic variations of your lever skills that involve a greater range of motion in the skill-specific position. Good examples of these variations are planche push ups and front lever pull ups. Similar to a progress back-up, you can scale the intensity of these exercises using resistance bands or, if you are highly advanced, by regressing your lever skill. This allows you to include these exercises in your workout at moderate or even high intensities, depending on your training phase. For more information on planche push ups and front lever pull ups, refer to the dynamic lever skills section.

Additionally, performing full range of motion assistance exercises for your lever skills, regardless of your training system, provides an opportunity for relatively specific skill training without excessively fatiguing the hold position itself. For instance, if you reach a point where you can no longer perform high-quality holds in the lever skill position due to fatigue, incorporating additional full ROM assistance exercises can offer further high-quality lever skill training. This is because the lever skill position itself is only held in a regression for a short duration during these exercises.

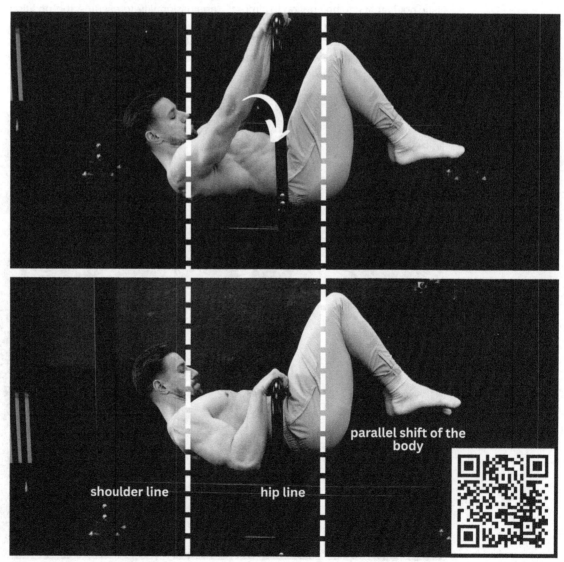

parallel shift of the body

shoulder line   hip line

Full ROM assistance example: front lever pull up.

Intensity techniques

To manage the relative intensity within a set during your lever skill training, you can employ different intensity techniques. One such technique is called **lever change holds**. Lever change holds involve performing variations of a lever skill where you adjust the lever position during the set. This allows you to create **drop sets**, starting with a lever position that provides a greater amount of leverage and gradually reducing it as fatigue sets in. This enables you to achieve longer hold times while maintaining a higher relative intensity. Lever change holds are particularly useful for backoff sets, especially if you need to perform them with higher pre-fatigue. By reducing the absolute intensity through lever changes, you can still complete your holds effectively.

Alternatively, you can also utilize this technique to progressively increase the intensity throughout the set. In this case, you would adjust the lever position to make the exercise more challenging as you go along. This variant of lever change holds functions similarly to ballistic holds, allowing you to benefit from the effects of acceleration into the skill position.

The second intensity technique you can incorporate into your lever skill training is **cluster sets**. A cluster set involves performing two to three individual holds, with each hold separated by a short pause of 10–30 seconds. Instead of doing a single hold for 4–5 seconds, you split it into smaller clusters, such as two holds of 2–3 seconds each. Cluster sets can be beneficial when working with progressions that significantly fatigue your muscles. By splitting the hold into clusters, you can maintain the quality of each hold while still achieving the same total hold time. This technique is particularly useful for integration into your top sets, where you aim to work with higher intensities.

Example of lever change holds: tucked to adv. tuck front lever

3.0.5

Program Design

You have already been provided with various training methods and variables. In this section, you will learn an example of how to incorporate these methods into a training plan. Additionally, you will discover a division of training days that will help you schedule your training more effectively. To do this, you will divide the lever skill sessions into primary, secondary, and tertiary sessions. Each session will be assigned specific training methods and variables, and a sample plan will be created. A slightly modified version of this approach, tailored to weighted calisthenics, can also be found in our programs and programming courses.

3.0.5.1

Primary session

The primary session should be the most intense and focused training session of the week. It is important to structure the rest of your sessions in a manner that allows for optimal recovery and preparedness for the primary session.

Load variables
Intensity, absolute: 75–95%
Intensity, relative: 1–3s in reserve, RPE6–9
Volume: moderate-high as measured by your individual training volume
Exercises: isometric holds, ballistic holds and full ROM assistance, progress backup

3.0.5.2

Secondary session

The secondary session is slightly less intense than the primary session, but still focuses on specificity. It is an opportunity to accumulate additional volume, address sticking points, or work on technique. The content of this session should complement the primary session and help prepare you for it without causing excessive fatigue. Some pre-fatigue is normal, inevitable, and even beneficial for making progress.

Load variables
Intensity, absolute: 65–85%
Intensity, relative: 2–3s in reserve, RPE5–8
Volume: moderate-high as measured by your individual workout volume
Exercises: isometric holds, conditioning holds, progress backup (variation)

3.0.5.3

Tertiary session

The tertiary session is the least intense and least specific session. Its purpose is to accumulate assistance volume without placing excessive stress on your already pre-fatigued structures. It serves as a supplemental session to support your primary and secondary sessions.

Load variables
Intensity, absolute: 60–80%
Intensity, relative: 2–4s in reserve, RPE5–8
Volume: low-moderate as measured by your individual training volume
Exercises: conditioning holds, more non-specific assistance exercises

Depending on the frequency of your training, you can divide your lever skill training into different sessions. If you train with a frequency of one, focus on the primary sessions. When training with a frequency of two, you can add an additional primary session. It's important to maintain high specificity in all sessions when training at low frequencies to promote maximum adaptation. With 1–2 primary sessions per week, recovery and interference between the sessions are usually manageable and not a major concern.

At a frequency of three, you can introduce a secondary session. For a frequency of four or more, you can incorporate tertiary sessions. It's crucial to adjust the total volume and intensity per session to ensure sufficient recovery before the next session. There's no benefit in training with a frequency of 4 if it leads to a decline in performance after just 2 weeks due to excessive training. Therefore, start with conservative volume and frequency and gradually increase them over time. For more information on regeneration, fatigue management, and training plan creation, you can refer to our programming courses and coaching resources.

Sample plan for weighted & skills

To demonstrate the principle in action, let's create a step-by-step training plan using the following example parameters.

Your assumed goals are:

1. Improve front lever and planche holds

---

2. Improve 1RM in chin ups and dips

---

3. Integrate leg training, but low priority

General conditions: 4 training days, session length 90–120min
Classification: Experienced athlete > 2 years of training, starting point is a strength-oriented phase.

You begin with your leg workout, which can be divided over multiple days if you prefer not to have a dedicated leg day. However, in this case, you choose to have a separate leg day. This leg day offers the advantage of providing more rest time between your upper body sessions, allowing for better recovery of your upper body structures. Additionally, full body days can be time-consuming, especially when incorporating exercises like squats or deadlifts, as they require longer warm-up and rest periods due to the higher weights involved. Since leg training is not your top priority, one primary leg day is sufficient. In terms of volume, you aim for the lower end of the recommended range of 10–20 sets per movement. This serves as your minimum effective volume (MEV), meaning you're aiming to do the minimum amount of leg training necessary to make progress. This approach helps minimize fatigue from intense leg training while still incorporating leg exercises. It's a good compromise if your main focus is on developing your upper body while maintaining a holistic training approach.

Your primary leg day might look like this:

Focus	Legs	Reps	Sets	RPE
A	Squat, top set	4	1	6–7
A	Squat, backoffs	6	3–4	7–8
B	Hip hinge exercise	6–8	3–4	7–8
C	Squat assistance	10–12	2–3	7–8
D	Hip hinge assistance	12–15	2–3	7–8
E1	Biceps exercise	10–12	3–4	8–9
E2	Triceps exercise	10–12	3–4	8–9

The exercises are numbered on the left side. Exercises with the same letter indicate that they are the same exercise but divided into different intensities or rep ranges. Consecutive numbers with the same letter indicate that those exercises can be performed as a superset. In a superset, you start with a set of exercise A1, take a short break of 1–2 minutes, and then perform a set of exercise A2, followed by a longer rest period.

For the leg day, it is recommended to choose moderate relative intensities to avoid excessive fatigue. However, the intensity should still be sufficient to provide an effective stimulus. In this plan, a top set of four reps is combined with backoff sets of six reps. Both sets are intense enough to stimulate strength adaptations while allowing for enough volume accumulation to promote muscle growth.

As you only have one leg day per week, it is somewhat of a compromise. Along with a squat exercise, your leg day should also include a hip hinge movement, which involves hip flexion and extension. This can be achieved through exercises like deadlifts, romanian deadlifts, hip thrusts, or back extensions. To ensure enough volume to reach your assumed minimum effective volume (MEV), incorporate a higher volume squat assistance exercise such as hacksquats, leg presses, lunges, or similar movements. Using a guided machine movement may be more beneficial in this context, as it reduces loading on the spine and helps minimize fatigue accumulation in the legs.

The arm workout at the end of the leg day is included to distribute the volume more effectively and regulate the length of your workouts. It's put in here as there was simply some additional room in the training plan. The training weight, including the percentage of 1RM, is determined individually based on the RPE (Rate of Perceived Exertion) values combined with the desired number of repetitions.

Moving on to the next day, it's an upper body day where you combine a primary pull and a primary push session. This arrangement makes the most sense when you have three upper body days, allowing for the distribution of fatigue between the pull and push sessions. It's often beneficial to schedule one of the intense primary sessions on the weekend when you are likely to be better recovered and have less time pressure.

Focus	Primary Push, Primary Pull	Reps	Sets	RPE
A1	Planche isometric holds	4–6s	3–4	8–9
A2	Front lever isometric holds	4–6s	3–4	8–9
B1	Front lever full ROM-assistance	3–5	2–3	7–8
B2	Planche full ROM-assistance	3–5	2–3	7–8
C	Dips, top set	3	1	6–7
C	Dips, backoffs	5	3–4	6–7
D	Chin ups, top set	3	1	6–7
D	Chin ups, backoffs	5	3–4	6–7

The combination of pull and push exercises provides an opportunity to incorporate antagonistic supersets into your training. These supersets involve pairing two exercises that have minimal influence on each other as they don't pre-fatigue the muscles involved in the antagonistic set. The session begins with intense holds of the planche and front levers. Following that, you perform full range of motion (ROM) assistance exercises since the lever positions themselves will be fatigued after multiple sets of intense holds. Using a dynamic assistance exercise may be more suitable and provide higher quality volume compared to additional holds.

Next, you move on to the progress back-ups for your selected lever skills. For the progress back-ups, you choose weighted dips and chin-ups based on your goals. In this strength phase, you aim for top sets of triples and backoff sets of five repetitions to ensure sufficient strength

adaptation. This places you on the threshold in terms of the intensity distribution in the training plan, which will be discussed further.

Since you are training your upper body with a frequency of three sessions per week, it is important not to select RPEs that are too high. This is to ensure adequate recovery between sessions. With lower frequencies, you can afford to set higher RPEs.

To accommodate two primary sessions within a four-day training week and allow for sufficient rest between two consecutive primary sessions (48–72 hours), another primary push session is combined with a secondary pull session, and vice versa. This approach reduces the overall intensity of the sessions compared to creating an additional double primary session.

Focus	Primary Push, Secondary Pull	Reps	Sets	RPE
A	Planche, ballistic hold	3x1–3s	3	8–9
A	Planche, backoff sets	4–6s	3–4	7–8
B	Front lever, conditioning holds	8–10s	3–4	6–7
C	Dips variation	5	3–4	6–7
D	Overhead press	6–8	2–3	7–8
E1	Upper back dominant-assistance	12–15	2–3	7–8
E2	Chest dominant -assistance	10–12	2–3	7–8

The session begins as a primary push session focusing on planche training. This includes ballistic holds and backoff sets. While repeating the same scheme as in the first primary session is possible, incorporating variation can make the training more exciting and enjoyable in the long run. For dips, a technical variation can be added, but if it's not necessary, performing normal weighted dips is perfectly fine. The absolute and relative intensity should be chosen based on the strength phase, but it's important not to go too high as planche holds are already very intense. Five repetitions can be a good compromise, although four or six repetitions are also viable options.

As for assistance exercises, the overhead press is chosen to add a missing component to the range of motion of shoulder flexion in the training plan. Additionally, another chest-dominant assistance exercise is included to complement the shoulder-dominant push exercises. Moving on to the secondary pull portion, conditioning holds for the front lever are utilized. These holds have a low intensity, which means they don't cause much fatigue but still accumulate exercise and hold time, leading to improved technique. To balance out the latissimus and flexion-biased exercises in the first session (such as chin-ups and front lever holds), it's recommended to include upper back and extension-biased assistance exercises. These assistance exercises should be programmed with higher repetition ranges, reducing the absolute weight and systemic fatigue, and allowing for faster recovery for the next session.

Focus	Primary Pull, Secondary Push	Reps	Sets	RPE
A	Front lever top sets	4–6s	3	8–9
A	Front lever backoff sets	6–8s	3–4	7–8
B	Planche, conditioning holds	8–10s	3–4	6–7
C	Chin up variation	5	3–4	7
D	Health-assistance, chin ups	12–15	2–3	8–9
E	Health-assistance, dips	12–15	2–3	8–9
F	Core	12–15	3–4	8–9

Based on the same principle, you create the final session and add further components that are often beneficial. This includes potential health assistance exercises such as face pulls for shoulder external rotation and side raises for shoulder abduction. Additionally, incorporating core exercises can ensure that your core strength doesn't become a limiting factor for your progress.

When you consider the total volume and analyze the distribution of intensities, you're very close to the recommended ranges and have established a solid starting point. From here, you can further customize the plan based on your individual needs. This involves periodizing the plan over time by adjusting the load variables according to the training stimuli that will be most beneficial for your goals.

Exercise/Volume	Sets	Effective assistance	Total	Rep Range 1–6	Rep Range 6-15
Planche	11–13	2–3	13–15	75%	25%
Front lever	11–13	2–3	13–15	75%	25%
Dips	7–9	2–3	9–11	66%	33%
Chin ups	7–9	2–3	9–11	66%	33%
Squat	4–5	2–3	6–9	55%	45%
Hip hinge	3–4	2–3	5–7	0%	100%

Non-specific assistance exercises such as isolated arm training and health assistance are not included in this consideration. In practice, however, these exercises are also relevant and must be well-regulated so as not to overload these structures or pre-fatigue them too much, which can lead to a loss of performance. To provide enough rest between sessions, choose the following setup for your training week.

Monday	Off
Tuesday	Primary Push, Secondary Pull
Wednesday	Off
Thursday	Primary Pull, Secondary Push
Friday	Primary Legs
Saturday	Off
Sunday	Primary Pull, Primary Push

! **As always, this plan serves as an example and can be customized to suit your specific needs. It was important for me to provide a practical application example using the theory we discussed. Now, armed with this example and the knowledge you've gained, you can create your own lever-skill plan for a training week. Remember to adapt it on a weekly basis to ensure continuous progress and optimal results.**

KING OF WEIGHTED

Level up your training.

KOW Coaching

We help you to unlock your full potential injury-free.
Stop wasting your time with unprogressive training.
Learn how to do it right and become stronger!

Our Service

- 1 RM Competition Preperation

- Calisthenics Skill Coaching

- Rehab Coaching for injured athletes

- Mastermind for calisthenics coaches

Front Lever at the Hackerbridge in Munich, 2019

Front
Lever

3.1
Front Lever

The front lever is a calisthenics lever skill from the pull category. This means the front lever is also classified as a pull exercise when it comes to workout planning. To understand how a front lever works, which movements you have to perform isometrically during the exercise, and which muscles are working, apply all defined lever skill conventions to this skill one after the other and work out the correct execution step by step.

3.1.1

Execution and anatomy

To gain a deeper understanding of the front lever, begin by analyzing the starting point of the exercise, which is the passive hang position on a pull-up bar. From this position, let's revisit lever skill convention 1 and apply it step by step.

The body is stabilized in a line as perpendicular to gravity as possible.

To transition from a passive hang to a position perpendicular to gravity in the front lever, several joints must either be stabilized or adjusted. Let's begin the analysis by focusing on the shoulder joint, as it bears the greatest load during the exercise. In order to achieve a horizontal position perpendicular to gravity, you need to raise your body until it becomes parallel to the ground. Conversely, to return to the hanging position, you must lower your arms by pushing them down. This movement is known as shoulder extension, where you bring your arms closer to your torso until you reach a horizontal position. The primary muscle responsible for performing this movement is the latissimus, making it the key player in executing the front lever.

**! **Has the book helped you this far?
Show it to me! It costs you 60s to leave a review on our site. It costs you another 60s to write an Instagramstory about the book and tag us @kingofweighted and @micha_bln_!
Thank you so much for your support!

@kingofweighted

@micha_bln_

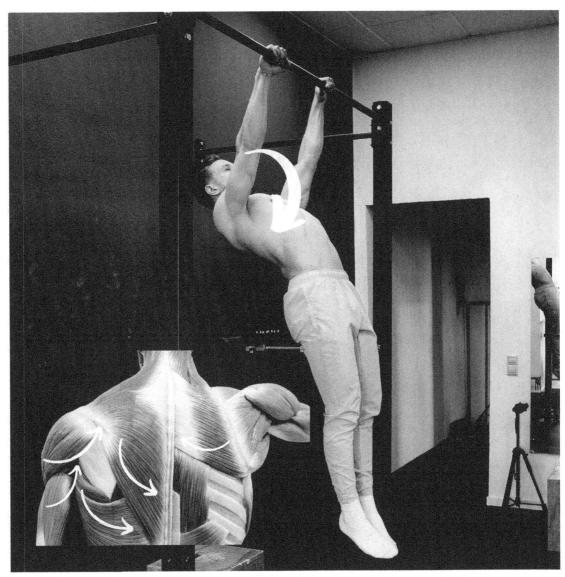

Shoulder extension from the passive hang.

In addition to the latissimus, the rear part of the deltoid muscle also plays a significant role in the execution of the front lever. This becomes especially important in variations such as touch front lever or front lever pull ups, where the elbow moves behind the body. In these variations, the latissimus loses its optimal position for pulling, and the rear shoulder takes over as the primary contributor to shoulder extension. The extension movement is further assisted by the long head of the triceps, which can help move the arm backward due to its attachment to the shoulder blade. Therefore, if you have experienced muscle soreness or encountered triceps-related issues during front lever training, it can be attributed to the involvement of the triceps in shoulder extension. For a comprehensive list of muscles that assist in this extension, refer to the table provided in the fundamentals chapter.

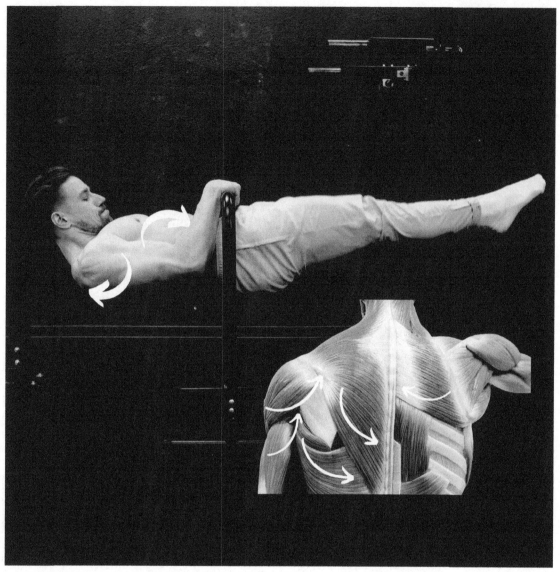

Touch front lever with heavy load on the rear shoulder and long triceps head.

If you were to attempt to hold the front lever solely by performing shoulder extension, your rib cage would align horizontally, but your lumbar spine would be pushed into hyperextension, resulting in a hollow back due to the force of gravity without any additional stabilization. To execute the front lever correctly according to convention 1, it is crucial to maintain alignment in your spine. Given that gravity causes hyperextension in your lumbar spine, your abdominal muscles, particularly the rectus abdominis and oblique muscles, are essential for this movement as they need to engage in flexion to stabilize your lumbar spine and keep it in line.

In addition to your spine, you also need to ensure that your pelvis is anchored in a neutral position. As you activate your abdominal muscles, be mindful not to tilt your pelvis excessively backward. It's important to establish an appropriate tension balance between your abdominal muscles and back extensors, allowing for stabilization of your body's center from both sides and maintaining a neutral position for your pelvis and spine.

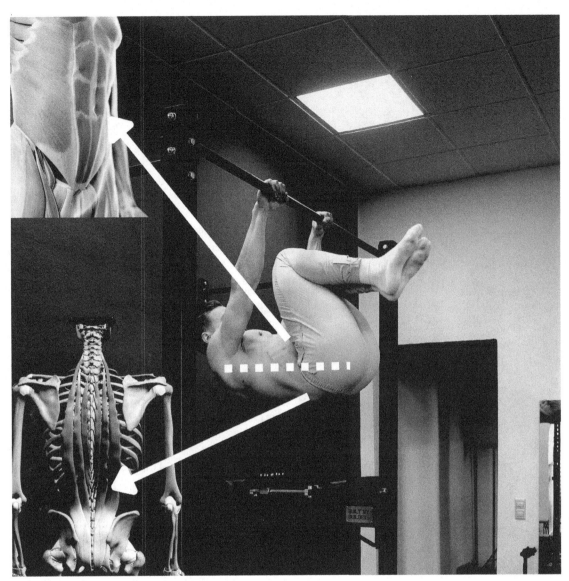

The shoulder and spine are stabilized perpendicular to gravity.

To ensure that your legs are aligned with your upper body, you need to extend your hips and knees. However, these two movements require relatively less strength from the hip and knee extensor muscles and are therefore less emphasized in the training process. Nevertheless, the ability to move your hips independently of your pelvis and spine is crucial for mastering lever skills and will be addressed in more detail during the progressions.

It's worth noting that individuals who spend a significant amount of time sitting in their daily lives often encounter difficulties fully extending their hips while maintaining a neutral position of the pelvis and spine. Once you have achieved a straight alignment, your body will be perpendicular to the force of gravity. This alignment is essential for executing the front lever properly according to convention 1.

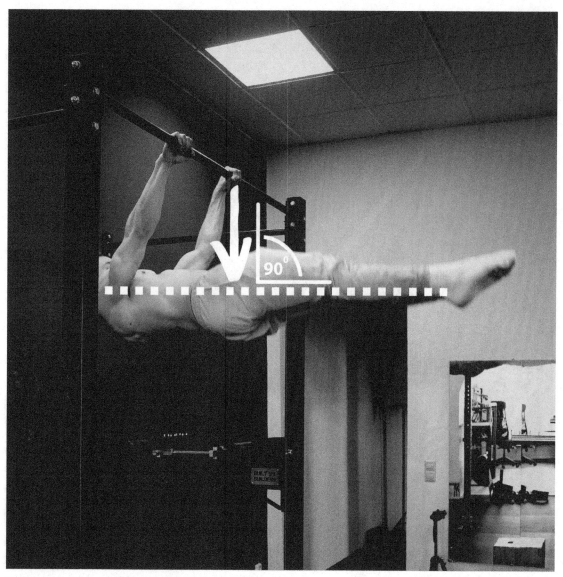

Shoulder, spine, hip, and knee are stabilized perpendicular to gravity

At this point, to further optimize your front lever, look at lever skill convention 2.

All joints, that are perpendicular to gravity, are aligned in such a way that they can be muscularly stabilized as actively as possible against gravity.

Due to the force of gravity, your body is pulled downward during the front lever. As your arms are fixed to the bar, gravity causes your shoulder blades to abduct and your thoracic spine to flex. These two movements are closely interconnected in the front lever, as the muscles responsible for stabilizing the shoulder blades also contribute to extension the thoracic spine when the arms are locked.

Furthermore, the angle at which your arms are positioned causes gravity to exert a slight upward force on your shoulders, elevating them towards your ears. To actively stabilize this area against gravity, you need to straighten your thoracic spine and pull your shoulder blades down and slightly back. The key muscles involved in this stabilization are the lower and middle trapezius, rhomboids, and, of course, the latissimus.

It is crucial to find the right balance in this position. Excessive compression of the upper back by excessively adducting the shoulder blades and hyperextending the thoracic spine can be detrimental to your strength and ability to hold the front lever. This excessive compression can shorten the latissimus, reducing its strength potential, and causing the attachment of the latissimus to the upper arm to move more towards the body's midline when strongly retracted. This can lead to a decrease in the effective torque that the latissimus can generate for shoulder extension. Additionally, excessive retraction may prevent proper depression of the shoulder blades due to the strong contraction of the rhomboids. Therefore, it is important to maintain a slightly retracted position of the shoulder blades for stability without going to the point where it compromises your performance.

Whether you stretch your feet or not has little influence on your front lever and should rather be put in the category "individual style". Finally, take a look at the lever skill convention 3 to optimize your front lever further.

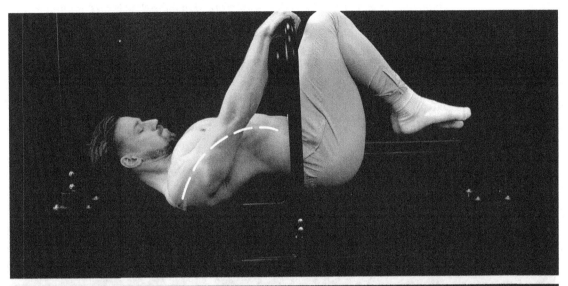

Strong retraction of the scapulae and hyperextension of the thoracic spine with unfavorable latissimus lever ratios (top) vs. slight retraction of the scapulae and neutral thoracic spine with favorable latissimus lever ratios (bottom).

All (relevant) joints are kept in an extended position, depending on the selected regression.

When you achieve the full lever position using this derivation, it is important to actively extend your elbows. The ease or difficulty of doing so will depend on how much false grip you are using. Using a false grip requires overcoming the challenge posed by the active insufficiency of your wrist flexors. This is because maintaining a false grip makes it harder to extend your elbows due to the limited flexibility of your wrist extensors. To address this issue, you can perform a basic stretch: Make a fist and place it on the ground, ensuring your arms are fully extended and your shoulders are directly above your wrists. Position the knuckles of both fists to face each other. Gradually flex your wrists without bending your elbows and open your fists. Increase the pressure gradually whenever you feel the stretch diminishing slightly. By practicing this stretch, known as the semi false grip stretch, you can improve wrist flexibility and facilitate elbow extension while maintaining a false grip. For more details on this stretch, refer to the pull up chapter.

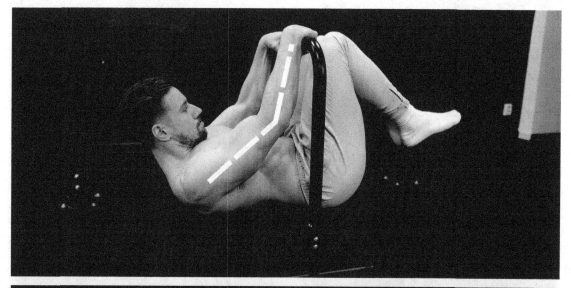

Slightly flexed arms due to active insufficiency of the wrist flexors (top) vs. extended arms with sufficient flexibility in the forearm (bottom).

Progressions

In the previous chapter on lever skills, we explored how the lever and intensity of a lever skill can be adjusted in numerous ways. By manipulating the angles of various joints, you can position the center of gravity in a way that aligns with your strength level. There are six commonly used progressions that we will delve into further. Understanding the form and execution of these progressions will enable you to derive and customize variations according to your needs.

It's important to note that each progression of the front lever offers different levels of difficulty. The intensity increase may not follow a linear progression, as it depends on your execution and individual body proportions. The sequence presented here is based on the coordination demands of each progression relative to the lever size. However, it's perfectly normal if your training chronology differs from the sequence shown. There is no right or wrong order, and you have the flexibility to adapt it to your own preferences and capabilities.

Tucked front lever

Definition: Hip angle up to < 90°, knees flexed
Scaling: spine extension, hip angle
Recommended assistance/variation: Band assisted lever change holds, protraction to retraction front lever, progression holds with assistance, dragon flags

Full tucked front lever with round lumbar spine (left) and tucked front lever with straight lumbar spine and approx. 60° hip angle (right).

The full tucked front lever serves as the starting point for mastering the front lever skill. It is the progression with the smallest lever possible achieved by rounding the lumbar spine and bending the hips and knees to their maximum extent.

During lever training, it is recommended to begin with scaling a specific joint or body segment. This approach allows for comparative and progressive work throughout the training process. It also helps develop body awareness and control over the various joint angles.

In the first step, you scale the tucked front lever by extending the lumbar spine. This entails straightening the spine through the interaction of the back extensors and abdominal muscles, thereby increasing the hip angle via lumbar extension. Once the spine is straightened, you progress to scaling the hip angle by extending the hips. This control can be challenging as it requires the ability to move the hips independently of the spine in the front lever position. It takes practice and patience to master. Adjusting the hip angle affects the entire front lever position, necessitating changes in the shoulder flexion angle

to maintain balance and keep the center of gravity beneath the hands. This requires exerting more downward force through the shoulders. Failure to do so will cause the hips to drop and disrupt the alignment.

To develop the necessary activation and technique, additional training methods can be employed. Lever change holds are particularly effective for this purpose, and it's advisable to initially use assistance systems to keep the intensity low and focus on technique. Additionally, you can practice the movement pattern on the floor as a dry run. Lie on your back and assume a tucked front lever position with your arms beside your body. Gradually extend your hips while keeping your abdominals engaged to maintain a neutral to slightly rounded spine position. This exercise helps you gain control over your hips while stabilizing your spine. By mastering the full tucked front lever and gradually progressing through the scaling process, you can advance your front lever training effectively.

Hip control exercise - extension of the hip with the lumbar spine fixed.

The dragon flag, specifically, can serve as a beneficial assistance exercise for the front lever. As your front lever training progresses and you open your hips to a greater extent, the demand for your abdominal muscles increases. While the load on your core will never be as pronounced as on your shoulders during the front lever, it's important to address any potential strength deficits in the core that may become limiting factors.

To prevent such limitations, incorporating the dragon flag exercise into your training routine can provide the necessary conditioning for your core. The dragon flag involves maintaining control and stability while performing a straight-body lowering motion from a bench or elevated surface, using mainly your core muscles next to your shoulder extensors to resist gravity and control the movement. By including the dragon flag as an assistance exercise, you can specifically target and strengthen your core to ensure it is adequately prepared to support your front lever progression.

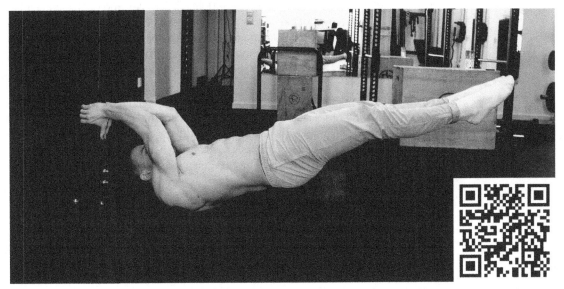

Full dragon flag

Advanced tucked front lever

3.1.2.2

Definition: extended spine, knees bent, hip angle 90°–120°.
Scaling: hip angle
Recommended assistance/variation: Progression holds with assistance, regression holds, lever change holds, dragon flags

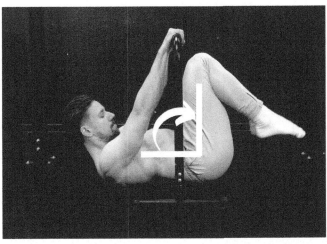 

Advanced tucked front lever with approx. 90° hip angle (left), advanced tucked front lever with approx. 120° hip angle (right).

The advanced tucked front lever is a highly adjustable progression that can be suitable for both beginners and experienced athletes. In this progression, the knee angle remains constant while you focus on extending your hips from approximately 90° to 120°. This allows for a progressive increase in intensity as you advance in your training. During the advanced tucked front lever, the load on your abdominal muscles significantly increases for the first time, particularly when the hip angle reaches around 90–120°. Previously, the abdominal muscles played a minor role due to the minimal torque exerted by the high center of gravity. However, with a larger hip angle and a greater load arm acting on the shoulders, maintaining the stability of the lever becomes more challenging.

Additionally, as you scale the advanced tucked front lever, you will encounter and need to master the simultaneous control of multiple joints. This involves coordinating your shoulders and thoracic spine to maintain position while extending your hips. Furthermore, you must coordinate your abdominal muscles and back extensors to ensure a neutral position of the lumbar spine and pelvis. It is important to note that in this progression, the focus should primarily be on adjusting the hip angle. If you find it extremely difficult to maintain proper form, it may indicate that you have progressed to this level too quickly and might benefit from light assistance or regression exercises.

It's normal to experience some form breakdowns with each transition between progressions, as you are still adapting to the new position. However, with consistent practice, these adjustments should improve over time. Devoting ample time to mastering the advanced tucked front lever is crucial, as it serves as an important foundation for your further front lever training. Building a solid technical understanding and body control in this progression will facilitate smoother transitions to subsequent progressions.

Based on experience, it is generally sufficient to advance the intensity of the advanced tucked front lever up to a hip angle of approximately 120° before gradually transitioning to the one leg front lever or the half lay. This allows for a more targeted focus on hip extension in the extended position at an earlier stage of your training progression.

3.1.2.3	**One leg front lever**

Definition: Spine extended, one hip extended, one knee extended, one hip flexed at angle < 180°, one knee flexed > 0°.
Scaling: hip angle, knee angle
Recommended assistance/variation: Progression holds with assistance, regression holds, (adv.) tucked front lever pull ups, ballistic holds in a progression, dragon flags.

By reaching the one leg front lever, you will realize that lever skills are not as complex as they may initially seem. You have already mastered the tucked front lever and the advanced tucked front lever. Now, you will progress to fully extending one hip and one knee while repeating the process you are familiar with from the tucked to advanced tucked positions.

In the one leg front lever, the scaling technique is slightly different. Instead of solely adjusting the hip angle of the non-stretched leg, you will also change the angle of the knee, ensuring that your foot remains at approximately the same height as the stretched leg. This feature provides a significant advantage in terms of scalability and measurability. The one leg front lever offers distinct and precisely definable progression levels, enabling you to program the scaling of this skill effectively. With the one leg front lever, you have clear milestones that allow you to track your progress and gradually advance in difficulty. This structured approach enhances your ability to scale the skill appropriately and continue your training with precision. In our King Of Weighted-Calisthenics-Coaching we work with the following:

One leg full tuck front lever

In this progression, you combine the one leg front lever with the full tuck position. This allows you to train the one leg variation even with a very small lever. Make sure to maintain a fully extended spine during this progression, despite being in the full tuck position. This progression is particularly helpful for taller athletes who may experience a greater intensity jump when transitioning from the advanced tucked front lever to the one leg variation due to their longer legs in proportion to their body size. Most athletes who have successfully scaled the advanced tucked front lever can directly move to the one leg - toes at the knee - and skip this progression.

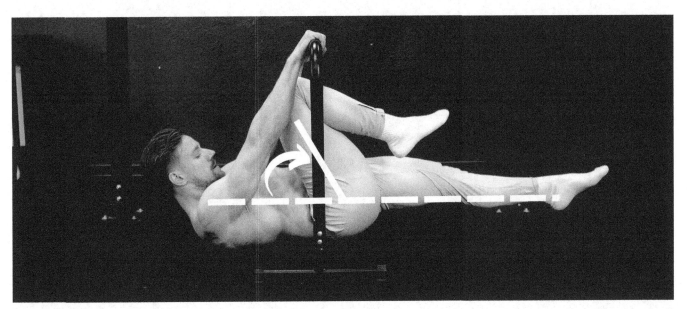

One leg full tuck front lever

One leg toes at knee front lever

At this intensity level of the one leg front lever, it's important to use a consistent measuring point to ensure consistent intensity in each training session. The knee of your extended leg can serve as a reliable guide. Keep the toes of the extended leg at approximately the same level as your knee throughout the exercise. This will help maintain a standardized position and ensure consistent progression.

One leg heel at knee front lever

Once you have achieved your desired hold time with the toes at the knee position, you can progress further by extending the lever. In this progression, you will be working with the heels at the knee instead of keeping the toes at the knee. This can be referred to as the advanced tuck one leg front lever. By reaching this stage, you are getting closer to achieving the full front lever. Keep up the progress!

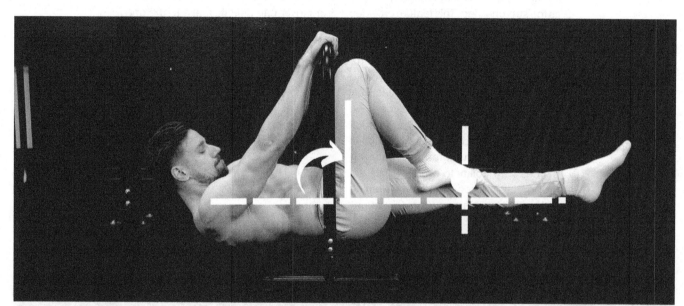

One leg toes at knee front lever

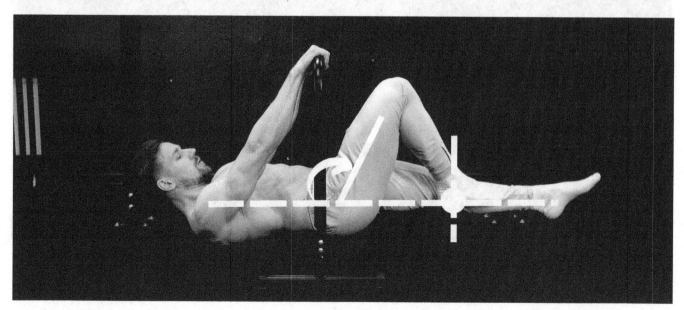

One leg heel at knee front lever

One leg toes at heel front lever

This progression is often the final step before working on the full front lever. In this stage, you will keep the non-extended leg almost fully extended, using the heel as a reference point for positioning the toes of the tucked leg. It is worth noting that at this point, some athletes may also choose to work on the full front Lever with minimal assistance from resistance bands. However, this progression is less commonly used, as most athletes prefer to focus on training in the final position of the full front lever.

One leg toes at heel front lever

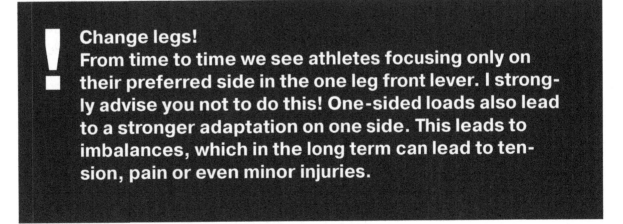

Change legs!
From time to time we see athletes focusing only on their preferred side in the one leg front lever. I strongly advise you not to do this! One-sided loads also lead to a stronger adaptation on one side. This leads to imbalances, which in the long term can lead to tension, pain or even minor injuries.

3.1.2.4   **Half lay front lever**

Definition: Spine extended, hip angle > 120°, knee angle >= 90°.
Scaling: hip angle, knee angle, hip spread
Recommended assistance/variation: Progression holds with assistance, regression holds, (adv.) tucked front lever pull ups, ballistic holds in a progression, dragon flags.

Half lay front lever

The half lay front lever can be chosen as a progression similar to the one leg front lever after mastering the adv. tucked front lever. While the one leg front lever provides a more precise way to adjust intensity through fixed measuring points on the leg, making it easier to program, the half lay front lever offers a good alternative for athletes who struggle with stabilizing their hips in the one leg position. By equally stretching both hips, some athletes find it easier or more natural to stabilize in the half lay position.

During the initial intensification phase, it is important to fully extend your hips. However, many athletes either struggle to achieve full hip extension or compensate by arching their back excessively. This compensation is particularly common in athletes with sedentary jobs, as prolonged sitting shortens the hip flexor muscles, making hip extension difficult when the knee is bent. If you face this issue, I recommend stretching your hip flexors before your front lever workout to ensure a proper half lay technique.

Once you have increased the intensity to the point where you can work with extended hips, further scaling is traditionally achieved by adjusting the knee angle. However, in addition to hip and knee extension, the half lay offers several options for adjustment to help you find the right intensity for your training. Keep experimenting and finding the best approach for your progression.

Straddle half lay front lever
The straddle half lay is frequently used in practice. The light straddle position makes it easier for you to target the glutes through the slight abduction and external rotation in the hips, which in turn help to actively extend the hips and thus stabilize this position. Depending on how far you straddle, the intensity difference from the half lay is greater or lesser. The further you straddle, the less intense the hold becomes.

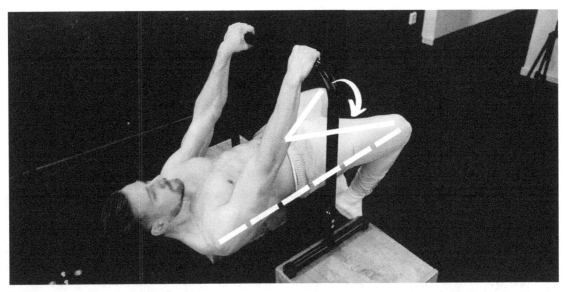

Straddle half lay front lever

One leg half lay front lever

You can also combine the one leg front lever with the half lay front lever for creating a very advanced position. This progression is hardly distinguishable from a full lever in terms of intensity and is therefore hardly relevant in practice. One possible application would be to use this progression in a drop set from a full front lever.

Straddle one leg half lay front lever

As already mentioned, you can combine any progression with each other. For example, you can combine the staddle half lay with a one leg to create a completely new hybrid form. However, when training and experimenting with such hybrid forms, make sure that you continue to work progressively.

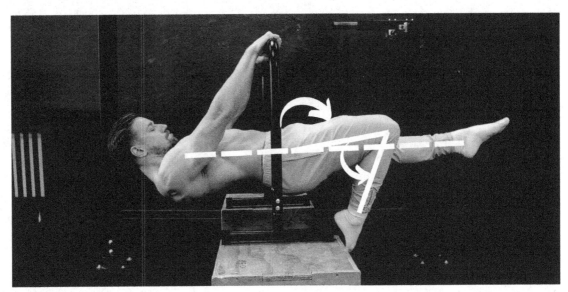

One leg half lay front lever

3.1.2.5   **Straddle front lever**

Definition: spine extended, hips extended, knees extended, legs spead
Scaling: hip spread
Recommended assistance/variation: Progression holds with assistance, regression holds, (adv.) tucked front lever pull ups, ballistic dolds in a progression, dragon flags.

Straddle front lever

A straddle front lever with hip flexion is an indicator of entering this position too early

The intensity of the straddle front lever is adjusted based on the angle at which you spread your hips. Therefore, if you choose to train the straddle front lever, it is important to do so only when you can hold it at the maximum spread angle with your hips fully extended. It's crucial to avoid working with a flexed hip in this progression as it reduces the ability to plan a progressive angle change. Since the straddle front lever does not have specific measuring points like the previous progressions, it may be slightly more challenging to plan and track your progress. Therefore, it's recommended to use the straddle front lever only when you have full control over it and can execute it with proper form.

> **!**
>
> **In our King Of Weighted Coaching, we prioritize the use of the one leg front lever instead of wide straddle angles. However, as you approach the full front lever, the straddle front lever can become interesting again. At this stage, you can often train with very specific and light spread angles, which allows you to closely target the full front lever position. By working with controlled and precise spread angles in the straddle front lever, you can fine-tune your strength and technique in preparation for achieving the full front lever.**

Every exercise requires the right setup and entry technique, and the front lever is no different. To optimize your performance and ensure safety, it's crucial to understand the key considerations and points of attention for finding the best start and setup for you. Let's explore these factors in detail.

3.1.3

Entry

Especially during the learning phase of the front lever, it is important to position your-self optimally when entering the hold. Once you are in the hold, making corrections becomes more challenging and requires greater effort. A good entry technique can significantly impact your hold time and overall progress in the front lever. There are primarily three different ways to enter the hold.

To achieve the best form and minimize pre-fatigue, the horizontal entry is highly rec-ommended. This involves using a bar or rings that are not higher than your maximum shoulder height. With a horizontal entry, you can efficiently build tension in your shoul-ders and core, position one leg and the hips, and then lift yourself the last few cen-timeters into the final hold. It's crucial to ensure that your hips are approximately under your wrists before entering the hold to avoid creating momentum that requires excessive strength to compensate for.

Athletes who haven't yet achieved a solid full front lever should avoid the vertical entry. This entry occurs when using a high bar and requires lifting yourself from a hang into the front lever position. It demands significant strength and can result in reduced hold time and less optimal technique compared to the horizontal entry.

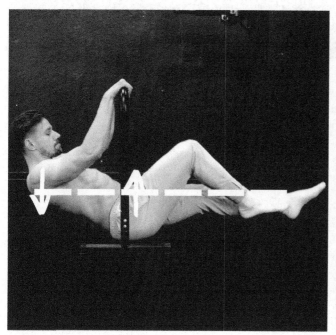 

Tension buildup before horizontal entry

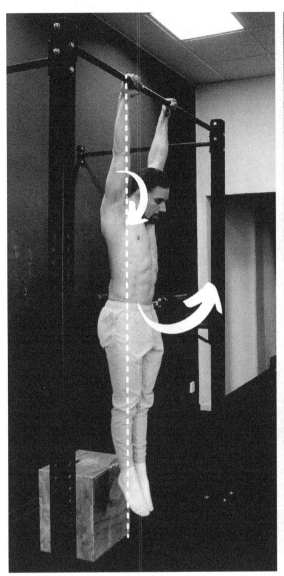

Vertical entry via a raise into the front lever

If you train in a standard gym that lacks a low bar, the smith machine can be a suitable alternative. The bar on these machines is typically non-rotating and adjustable in height. Another option is to use your own gymnastic rings, although balancing becomes more challenging in this case. The last method is the entry with preloading, which involves lowering yourself into the desired progression through a negative movement or transitioning from a regression.

Preloading entry from the inverted hang

This entry represents the midway between the previous ones. It offers you, compared to the vertical entry, the advantage that you have hardly any load in the inverted hang or a slight regression and can position yourself correctly here to then go into the final hold. This also requires strength and therefore maybe reduces your hold times, but can still be the better way for some athletes. By using the initial tension from the negative movement/regression, you can get better control of your body if necessary. So you should try the different methods and then decide for yourself which one offers the most added value for you.

Assistance systems

As several training methods discussed in this book involve the use of assistance systems, it is important to understand how to use them effectively. In this book, we will focus on resistance bands, as they are the most commonly used system. While there is no right or wrong way to use them, there are variations in the positions of use, each with its own advantages and disadvantages.

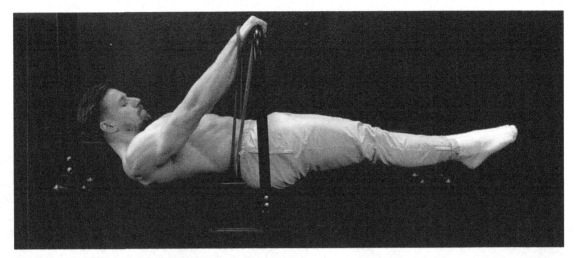

Assisted front lever with a band on the lumbar spine.

Band on the lumbar spine

This method minimally interferes with the front lever. The band is positioned close to the body's center of gravity and pulls upward, reducing the body weight and making the front lever easier. Since the band is in front of the hips, you have to stabilize them primarily on your own. This allows for a high level of specificity and smooth technique transition to holds without a band.

Band on the lumbar spine and thigh

For athletes struggling with hip alignment and stabilization, this band application can be useful as a temporary method until stability is achieved. The band is divided into two pairs of loops, with one positioned at the lumbar spine and the other below the hip. This provides better support to the hip without significantly altering the natural front lever position. However, in the long term, it is recommended to switch to the method with the band at the lumbar spine.

Assisted front lever with a band on the lumbar spine and thigh.

Band on the foot

If you have used bands primarily in muscle up or pull up workouts, you may be more familiar with this method. Here, the band is attached to the bar, and you step into it with your feet. The advantage is that you don't have to hold the band with your hands. However, using stronger bands will significantly alter the control of the front levers. As your legs are in the loop of the band, you are in more of a plank position rather than a front lever position. Therefore, beginners should start with light progressions rather than strong bands in the full progression. The carryover to free holds is not as significant compared to the other methods due to the change in load distribution. When using very light bands, the influence is likely negligible, and all methods work similarly efficiently. By working without a band alongside training with band support, you can further minimize the differences and make them negligible.

Remember to choose the method that suits your needs and goals, and gradually progress towards performing front levers without assistance to ensure overall development and proficiency.

Assisted front lever with a band around the feet

3.1.5

Grip

During your front lever training, you have the option to use different grip techniques and widths. In theory, a shoulder-width grip is considered optimal because it allows for efficient utilization of the latissimus muscles. As the grip widens, holding the front lever typically becomes more challenging. With a wider grip, it becomes harder to target the vertical fibers of the latissimus, which generate the most torque for shoulder extension.

While a semi false grip is not mandatory for the front lever, it can assist in generating more strength for shoulder extension. The semi false grip involves rotating your wrist around the bar, allowing for a more specific transfer of strength to the bar as the contact surface increases. By pushing down with your hands towards your body, you can apply strength in the desired direction through your hand position.

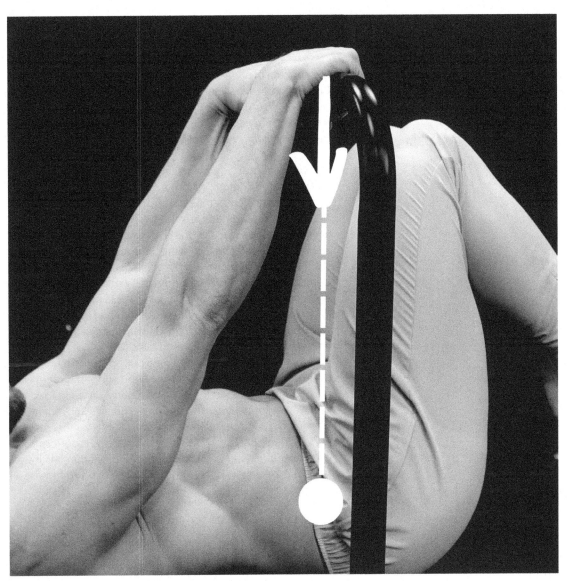

Front lever with semi false grip for better strength transfer to the bar.

The choice between a semi-false grip or a normal grip depends on your individual anthropometry and can vary in terms of balance. There is no general rule. The grip that enables you to position the center of gravity of each progression below your hands usually feels the strongest and most natural for you. The differences between the semi false grip and a normal strong grip are not significant. However, the semi false grip provides a greater advantage in exercises like front lever pull ups or touch front lever variations, as it shortens the forearm and offers a mechanical advantage. If you have previously experienced issues such as golfer's elbow or forearm overuse symptoms, it is advisable to use the false grip with caution.

3.1.6

Progress backup

The concept of progress backups was explained in detail in the chapter "Lever Skills". So you don't have to scroll back, here's a quick definition again.

"A progress backup is a multi-joint exercise that targets the same muscle groups and movement patterns as the lever skill you are training."

For the front lever, you are aiming for a multi-joint exercise that primarily targets the latissimus dorsi, trapezius, teres major, and rear deltoid. The exercise should involve shoulder extension as the primary movement.

In the realm of weighted calisthenics, two exercises stand out: the pull up and the chin up. Both exercises meet all the criteria for an effective progress backup exercise. They effectively engage the target muscles, can be scaled over time, offer different intensity levels, and have a favorable stimulus-to-fatigue ratio.

Comparatively, exercises such as bent-over barbell rows have a lower stimulus-to-fatigue ratio in relation to the front lever. While bent-over barbell rows do provide some carryover to the front lever, they also create significant fatigue along the entire posterior chain, potentially limiting long-term training capacity compared to pull ups or chin ups with similar carryover to the skill.

In theory, the chin up or neutral grip pull up is slightly superior as a progress-backup exercise compared to the pronated pull up grip. This is because the chin-up or neutral grip places the elbows in front of the body, allowing for pulling in the sagittal plane, which closely resembles the shoulder extension movement in the front lever. This high movement specificity likely results in a slightly better carryover compared to the pull up, which emphasizes shoulder adduction and is performed in the frontal plane. However, the magnitude of this difference and whether it is truly significant is not yet established. In our King Of Weighted Coaching, both lifts have yielded excellent results as progress backups.

3.1.7

Assistance exercises

Your chosen progress backup exercise serves as your primary assistance for strength and hypertrophy. It allows you to regulate the volume and intensity of your front lever training. By adjusting the strength and hypertrophy assistance provided by the progress backup, you can maintain a relatively intense front lever training with moderate to small total hold times throughout the week. If you decrease the strength and hypertrophy assistance from the progress backup, you will need to incorporate more holds and longer total hold times in your training.

In addition to the normal front lever holds, there are two other categories introduced in the lever skills chapter: ballistic holds and full range of motion (ROM) assistance. These variations offer different ways to train the front lever. For more detailed analysis and techniques for these exercises, refer to the chapter "Dynamic lever skills".

Ballistic Holds

Front lever negatives/negatives to hold

Execution: For front lever negatives, using rings is a suitable method. Start in a complete inverted hang on the rings, ensuring you are positioned optimally. Once you have transitioned into your desired progression, such as the one leg front lever, you should lower yourself in a controlled manner, adjusting the angle between your arms and torso while keeping the rest of your body stiff. Lower yourself either into a hold position or into a full range of motion, reaching a passive hang.

Application: Front lever ballistic holds in the form of negatives are highly favored due to their numerous advantages. Starting from the inverted hang allows you to prepare yourself technically and perform higher-quality progressions with more intensity. The negative phase provides a light pre-loading effect, enabling you to execute very intense progressions for shorter hold times. Combining negatives with holds is an effective approach, especially if you are training new and more intense progressions while still feeling somewhat uncertain about the technique. If you are unable to control the descent in the front lever position, it indicates that the progression you are currently working on is still too challenging for you.

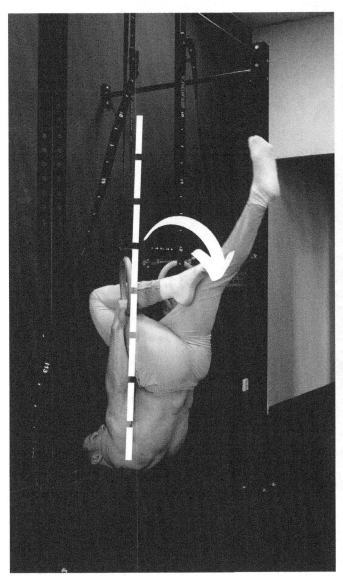 

Lowering from the inverted hang into the front lever.

Front lever raises

Execution: Front lever raises are best performed on a high bar that allows you to fully lock out your arms. Begin in a passive hang position, then tighten your body to the desired progression and initiate a shoulder extension. You can use a bit of momentum to position your latissimus muscles for a more powerful movement. Once you reach the front lever hold, focus on holding the position or slowing down the movement as much as possible.

Application: Front lever raises are effective for accumulating short hold times with more intense progressions by incorporating acceleration followed by a hold. They can also enhance your lat control and provide a strong contraction for your front lever holds. It is recommended to use raises with progressions that you are already proficient in from a technical standpoint. Otherwise, it can be challenging to achieve a high-quality hold due to the extensive range of motion and acceleration involved.

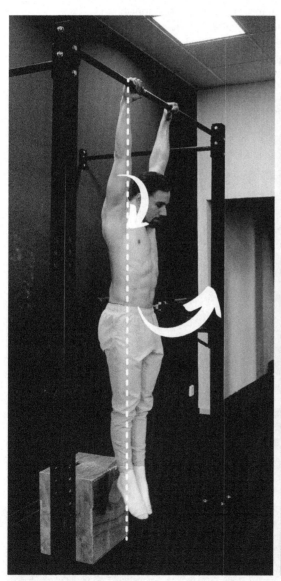

Front lever raises from passive hang

Front lever raises from hold
Execution:

This variation of ballistic holds combines the elements of negatives and raises into a single exercise. It is recommended to perform this exercise on rings. Start from an inverted hang and lower yourself into a hold position. Maintain the hold for your desired duration, and then return to the inverted hang by performing a raise.

Application: This exercise is particularly beneficial for advanced athletes as it allows them to combine multiple short holds in an intense progression without needing to rest between each hold. This enables you to accumulate more total hold time while reaping the technical advantages of negatives and the training effects of raises.

Front lever raises from hold

Ice-cream makers

Execution: To perform ice-cream makers, begin in the upper reversal point of a pull up with your chin above the bar. This exercise requires a high bar. From this position, extend your arms and lift your hips to transition into a front lever hold.

Application: Starting from the pull up position allows your elbows to be close to your body, creating an isometric contraction in your shoulders. The angle in your shoulders remains relatively stable throughout the exercise. By incorporating the tilting movement into front lever, you can accumulate multiple short holds efficiently. It is important to focus on performing controlled and brief holds during this exercise to achieve a meaningful training effect.

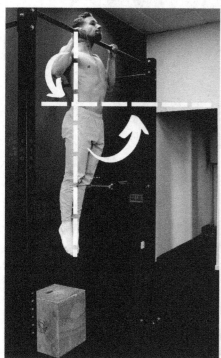  

Ice-cream makers

Full ROM assistance

Unlike the ballistic Holds, the following exercises are not performed with the goal of accumulating holdtimes in the front lever, but rather to train the muscles involved in the most specific way that is possible over a wide range of motion.

Front lever pull ups

Execution: Begin in your front lever regression position, and then pull yourself towards the bar without deviating from the horizontal front lever position parallel to the floor.

Application: Front lever pull ups can be incorporated alongside front lever hold training to accumulate additional volume that targets the specific muscles involved in the front lever. This exercise allows you to work on the pulling aspect of the movement without being limited by the hold position itself.

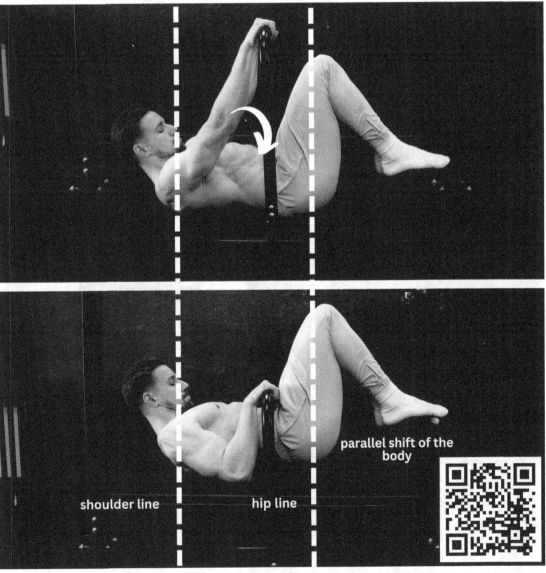

parallel shift of the body

shoulder line   hip line

Front lever pull ups

Full front lever raises

Execution: Begin in a passive hang position on the bar and pull yourself up and over into a front lever raise, reaching the inverted hang position. From there, perform a controlled negative descent.

Application: Full raises are highly demanding exercises that enable you to train shoulder extension throughout its entire range of motion. Due to the intensity involved, this exercise is best suited for advanced athletes who wish to add specific volume to their front lever training.

Full front lever raises

Winging in a lateral position of the shoulder blades

Many athletes who join our coaching program initially report experiencing sharp pain in the shoulder blade area towards the end or shortly after releasing the front lever hold. Our observations suggest that this pain often coincides with winging of the shoulder blades in the lateral position. This means that the scapulae do not maintain contact with the rib cage but lift off at their medial borders during protraction.

This positioning indicates a difficulty in effectively compressing the shoulder blades against the rib cage. This can be attributed to either limited mobility of the rib cage or weakness in the muscles surrounding the shoulder blades. Fortunately, this "misalignment" of the shoulder blades can be easily corrected in the short to medium term, unless it is caused by nerve damage or injury. If you struggle to actively compress your shoulder blades against the rib cage, the following exercises can be helpful.

Scapular winging in lateral position of the scapulae during a front lever hold.

Protraction to retraction front lever

In this exercise, you will utilize a regression that is very easy for you. The primary focus is on controlling and stabilizing your shoulder blades. Start in a front lever position and allow your shoulder blades to slide into protraction, pushing your chest downward. Then, retract your shoulder blades and push your chest upward, holding this position for a few seconds. Unlike your regular front lever holds, you can go into maximum retraction during this exercise. It's important to ensure that you are truly moving your shoulder blades and not just your thoracic spine. This exercise is beneficial for advanced athletes as a warm-up or pre-activation before your planned lever workout, and it can serve as the main exercise for beginners who are still struggling to properly stabilize their shoulder blades.

Protraction to retraction front lever

Chest supported rows

Chest supported rows refer to exercises in which you perform a rowing movement with your chest supported by a pad. Examples of such exercises include Chinese rows or T-Bar rows. The chest support provides stability and reduces the use of momentum from your hips or back extensors, allowing for more controlled movements. These setups are particularly effective for improving the retraction of your shoulder blades while accumulating training volume. When performing these rowing variations, it's important to focus on pulling your shoulder blades from a protracted position to a retracted position. Allow the weight to naturally separate your shoulder blades before pulling them back together and straightening your thoracic spine. You can also hold the final retracted position for a few seconds to enhance the training effect. By incorporating chest supported rows into your routine, you can target the muscles responsible for scapular retraction and promote better shoulder blade control. These exercises can be beneficial for improving your ability to stabilize your shoulder blades during front lever training.

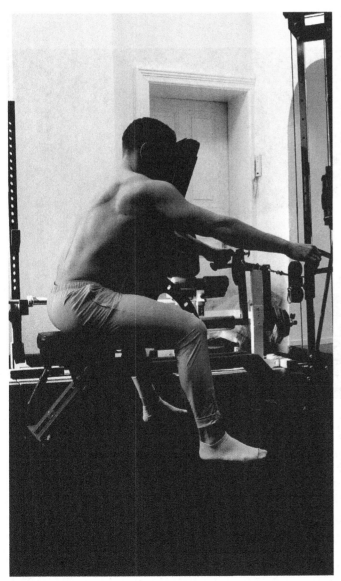
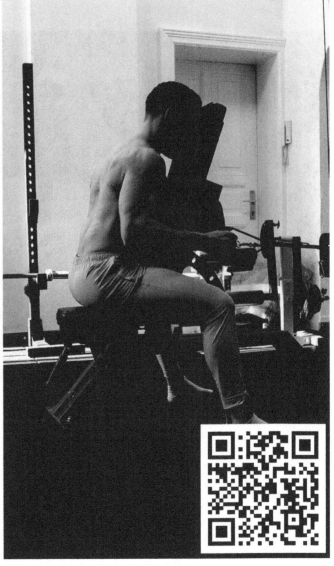

Example chest supported rows

3.1.7.4

Lowering of the hip/legs

The lowering of the hips/legs is a compensation that can be related to a strength deficit in the shoulder extension in most cases. The lowering of the hips reduces the load arm on your shoulder and the front lever hold becomes easier. This means there is not a technical deficit per se, but rather working at too high intensities. However, there are also cases where the lowering of the hip is due to other deficits. The first case is the lowering of the hip due to the appearance of a hollow back. The hollow back in this case occurs when your abdominal muscles give in to gravity and the pull of your latissimus and can no longer hold enough tension to stabilize your spine and hips in a neutral position. If this compensation occurs relatively early and you can still hold the front lever even longer, without your back giving up, this is an indication that your abdominal muscles and to some extent your hip flexors are the limiting factor here. To avoid this compensation in the future, it makes sense to train these structures more specifically. The following exercises are suitable for this.

Lowering of the legs in the Front Lever due to too weak abdominal muscles.

Dragon flag

The dragon flag itself is considered a lever skill. However, when you place your upper back on the floor, it significantly reduces the leverage on your shoulder joint while maintaining a similar load on your abs. This makes the dragon flag a valuable complement to front lever training. By performing dragon flags, you can develop proper control and technique for the front lever, focusing on the positioning of your spine and hips. Additionally, it helps prevent the abdominal muscles from becoming a limiting factor in the front lever due to their excessive involvement. You can incorporate the dragon flag as either an isometric hold or a full range of motion assist, depending on your preferred approach.

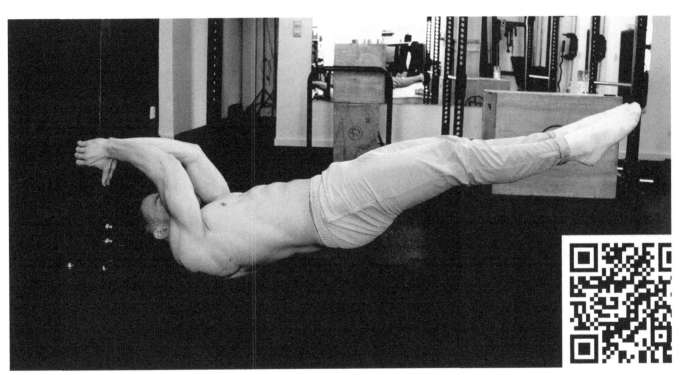

Dragon flag

Knee/Leg raises/Toes to bar

These compression exercises are highly effective for training hip flexion and spinal flexion. You can adjust the intensity by extending or flexing your legs. The greater the leg extension, the higher the load on your hip flexors and abdominal muscles, resulting in a more intense exercise. It's important to note that during the exercise, you should not only lift your legs but also round your lumbar spine. By creating flexion in both the hips and the lumbar spine, you maximize the training benefits of these exercises.

Another possible compensation occurs when you are unable to fully extend your hips. As a result, you may experience a slight angle in the hips or resort to a hollow back to compensate for the lack of hip extension. This can be caused by limited flexibility in the hip flexors, as discussed in the one leg front lever section, or by poor control of the gluteal muscles, which are powerful hip extensors in the body. It could also be a combination of both factors.

Glute bridges

Glute bridges and their variations are excellent for improving the activation of your glutes. To perform this exercise, lie on your back and bend your legs. Before extending your hips, engage your abdominal muscles. Make sure that your lower back is flat and not arched. Tilt your pelvis posterior and engage your glutes, lifting your buttocks slightly. A lift of around one to two centimeters is sufficient. From this position, push your hips upward and extend them fully. Contract your glutes strongly without losing the tension in your abdominal muscles. The goal is to feel a strong contraction in your glute muscles and develop a sense of proper activation. This exercise will help you improve your ability to control hip extension correctly, even in the front lever.

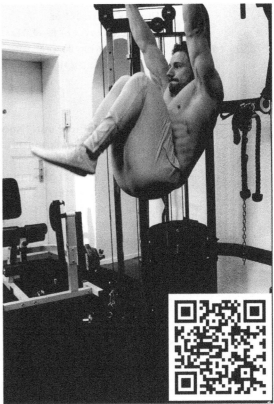

Knee raises

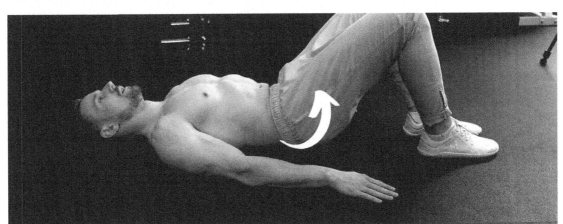

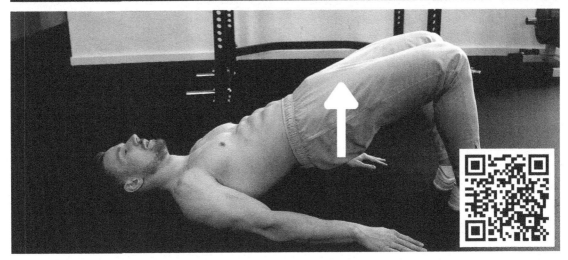

Glute bridge

Hip flexor stretches

To ensure that your flexibility does not limit your hip extension, you can additionally stretch your hip flexors. To stretch these structures, there are countless exercises, two of them are presented here.

1. **Reverse nordic curl (Kneeling sissy squat)**

   The reverse nordic curl is a great way to improve the flexibility of your hip flexors and train your knee extensors at the same time. Therefore, it's a great exercise to incorporate into a training without having to spend extra time stretching. To do this, you bring your rectus femoris into active insufficiency. You accomplish this by bending your knees but keeping your hips extended by tightening your gluteal muscles. Advanced athletes can perform full sissy squats. For beginners, the kneeling version, supported by a resistance band, offers more control. A slow and controlled eccentric phase is very important in this exercise. Use only the range of motion that you can control and increase it progressively. Take your time to avoid strains.

2. **Hip flexor stretch, standing**

   For this stretch, place one foot on a slight elevation. Next, tighten your core and butt and tilt your pelvis posterior. From this position, push your hips forward. You should feel a stretch in your groin area. Hold this stretch for a few seconds and if necessary increase the pressure if the stretch decreases.

Before considering compensation, it is important to assess your training intensity carefully. It is not advisable to rush through your lever skill training at the expense of proper execution. In many instances, additional assistance exercises may not be necessary. Instead, taking a small step back and practicing patience can be more beneficial.

Kneeling Sissy Squats

Hip flexor stretch, standing

3.2

Planche

3.2
Planche

The planche is a straight arm strength (SAS) lever skill from the push category. In this exercise, you essentially perform an isometric push-up using only your hands, supporting almost your entire body weight while maintaining a horizontal position parallel to the floor. As if that wasn't challenging enough, you execute the movement with your arms fully extended. Unless you possess exceptional genetic traits or extraordinary talent, expect to dedicate several years to learning the planche, depending on your current level of training. It's important to note that this information is not meant to discourage you but rather to emphasize the immense difficulty of achieving a clean and proper planche.

To help you grasp the planche and gain a clear understanding of the execution and targeted muscle groups involved, you will approach it gradually, step by step. Even in the initial stages, many athletes struggle to comprehend how to lift their legs off the ground. In order to comprehend this process, the analysis of the planche begins a few steps earlier.

Step 1: Quadruped push up hold

You start in a quadruped push up. Your arms are extended, your core is tight, your pelvis is tilted posterior and you keep your body in line. You push your shoulder blades apart and away from your ear. So you are forcing a shoulder protraction and depression.

Step 2: Move into balance

In the second phase, focus on achieving an equilibrium above your hands. This entails shifting your center of gravity over the area of contact with the floor. Throughout this process, maintain extended arms, engage your core muscles, and ensure proper alignment of your body. It's important to note that many individuals without a background in calisthenics will likely struggle at this stage, as it is often their first realization of the immense difficulty of the planche.

Step 3: Shoulder flexion / „lift off"

You have achieved a state of balance where the weight distribution on both sides of your hands is relatively equal. Your legs are still in contact with the floor, and to change this, you must lift them. Understanding the mechanics behind this movement requires conceptualizing your body from the shoulders downward as a rigid and inflexible unit. The actual effort required to raise your legs or body is concentrated on the shoulders. To lift your legs, you need to flex your shoulders, which involves pushing forward against the floor with your arms. This shoulder flexion movement is executed by the muscles surrounding the shoulder joint.

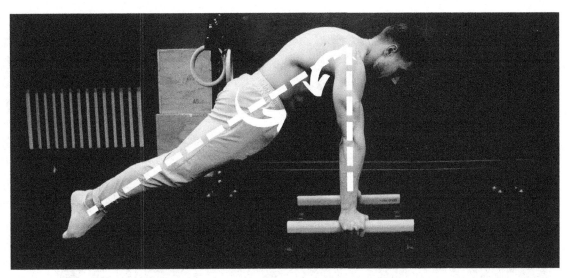

Quadruped push up hold

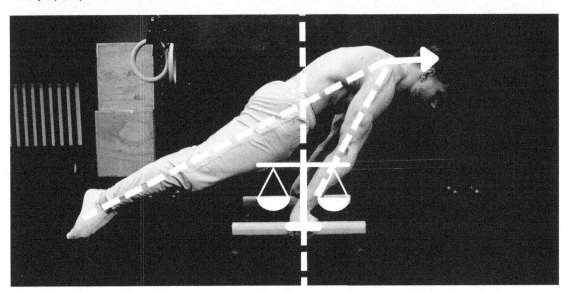

Weight shift in the quadruped push up hold. You bring your center of gravity over your wrists to achieve an equilibrium.

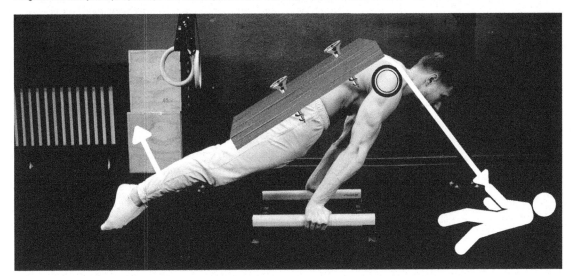

Symbolically stiffened body in the planche lean. The liitle male represents your shoulder flexors and the pulley represents your shoulder.

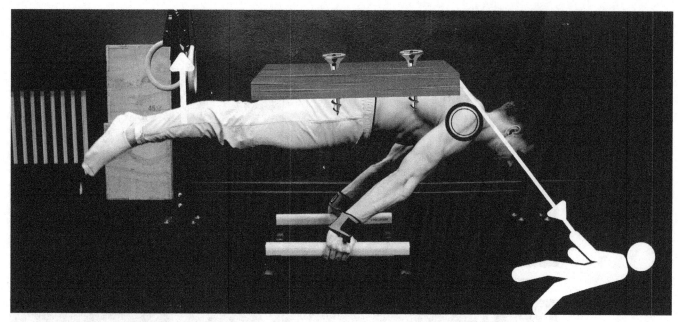

If you generate enough strength in shoulder flexion, your body will lift off.

A useful analogy is to envision your shoulder muscles as a pulley system, where the contraction of the muscles pulls your body upward. Your shoulder serves as the axis of rotation for the planche. By pressing your arms against the floor, you can elevate your legs. Throughout this process, your core muscles play a crucial role in stabilizing your body as a rigid unit. Once you have successfully lifted your legs while maintaining balance and extended arms, you have achieved the planche position.

Now that we have clarified the fundamental mechanics of the planche, we can utilize the lever skill conventions to delve into the precise joint positions and muscles involved.

3.2.1

Execution and anatomy

Since you have some practice from the front lever section, you can apply the first two conventions combined.

Convention 1: The body is stabilized in a line as perpendicular to gravity as possible.

Convention 2: All joints, that are perpendicular to gravity, are aligned in such a way that they can be muscularly stabilized as actively as possible against gravity.

During the analysis, we begin by examining your connection to the floor. To establish balance, you lean forward, and this requires your hands and forearms to secure you to the parallettes while maintaining a stable wrist angle. This action is known as ulnar abduction in your forearms. Failing to do so would result in falling forward when attempting a planche on handles. The ulnar flexors and extensors are responsible for maintaining this movement. Among these extensors is the extensor digiti minimi, which also extends your little finger. Consequently, you might have experienced difficulty exerting sufficient pressure on the grip on this side of the hand when leaning further forward in a planche. To address this, it is recommended to emphasize balance in planches and apply pressure primarily on the thumb side into the parallettes.

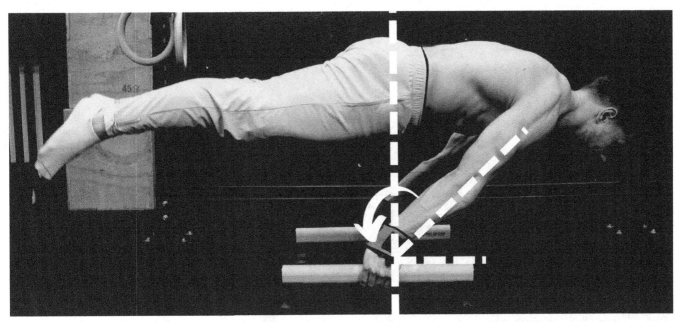

Planche grip with focus on an equilibrium and thumb-side directed force

There, the thenar muscles of your thumb fix you to the parallettes and provide appropriate stability. Depending on the degree of abduction in the wrist, there is a very strong stretch and large forces on the structures on the ulnar side (the side where the little finger is).

In this area, excessive intensity or training volume can quickly lead to overload or injuries such as cubital tunnel syndrome, causing compression of the ulnar nerve, which can lead to pain and numbness in the fingers. Therefore, please pay attention to the influencing factors and load variables as outlined in the lever skills section. Developing better equilibrium reduces the compensatory work required by your forearms and lowers the risk of injury. Therefore, maintaining balance during the planche hold is crucial to minimize forearm stress. The next joint you'll look at is the elbow. At this point you need a little briefing on ‚SAS' for further understanding.

The planche is the first real SAS element of this book. SAS stands for straight-arm-strength. The term SAS refers to skills/exercises that require the elbow joint to be actively stabilized in extension against hyperextension due to gravity or external loads. This means that gravity or external load wants to ‚break' your elbow joint.

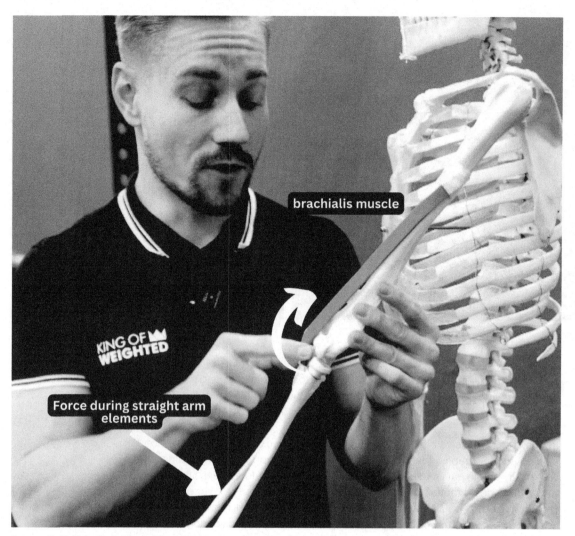

brachialis muscle

Force during straight arm elements

Force applied to the extended arm and the contraction of brachialis.

To counteract this external force, you stabilize your elbow through muscular effort and the assistance of passive structures while maintaining an actively stretched position. SAS elements pose considerable difficulty due to two main factors. Firstly, the muscles responsible for stabilizing the elbow joint in this position have a limited force arm due to the extended position. Secondly, the lever arm of the external load on the shoulder joint increases as a result of the extended arm. To better grasp this concept, let's consider the brachialis muscle in the elbow as an example.

The brachialis is the strongest flexor of the elbow and is located directly underneath your biceps brachii. As your elbow joint becomes more extended, the distance between the joint's axis of rotation and the muscle attachment decreases, known as the force arm. A longer force arm allows the muscle to generate greater torque with the same amount of force. Conversely, if the joint's position reduces the force arm, more force is required to achieve the same torque. Therefore, in the planche, as your arm becomes more extended, greater muscular force is needed to stabilize it against hyperextension. Furthermore, the challenging nature of SAS elements in the elbow stems from analyzing the strength components. By breaking down the muscle's resulting strength into its X and Y components, a notable observation emerges. With an extended elbow joint, a substantial portion of the brachialis' strength cannot actively contribute to flexion and joint stabilization. Instead, it leads to joint compression.

To maintain joint stability, the total muscle force must be sufficiently high to ensure that the specific strength component responsible for elbow flexion remains big enough.

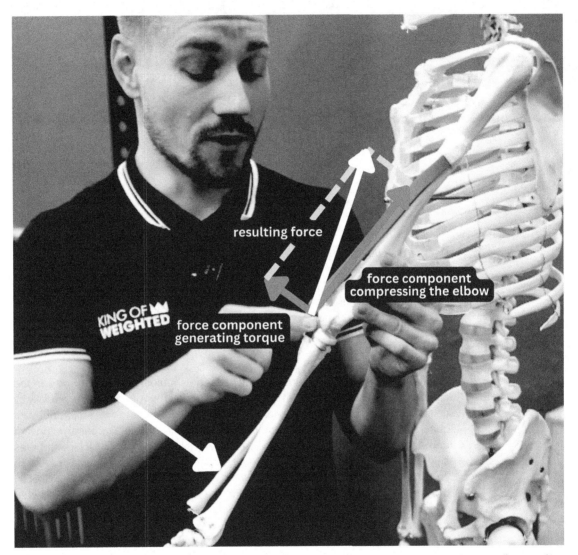

resulting force

force component compressing the elbow

force component generating torque

Strength components in the brachialis during SAS exercises. The strength component that generates torque in flexion is very small compared to the strength component that compresses the joint.

From both perspectives, it becomes evident that the arm flexors face unfavorable conditions for performing flexion and thus must exert immense forces to counterbalance these limitations. Consequently, athletes with exceptional SAS skills often possess remarkably developed arm flexors, even without dedicated isolated arm training.

! The important and legitimate question you are probably asking yourself now is: Why should I subject my elbow joint to large forces in a position that is difficult to stabilize? Unfortunately, I can't answer that question for you either. „Don't hate the player, hate the game" is probably the right saying in this case.

Back to the planche in particular. A large number of muscles are active in the elbow joint. The extensors of your wrist pull the elbow into extension when the wrist is fixed, whereas the flexors pull the elbow into flexion. Your arm flexors brachialis, biceps brachii as well as the brachioradialis stabilize the elbow joint and prevent an unwanted hyperextension by their contraction. The triceps brachii, as the antagonist of the flexors, stabilizes and, if necessary, extends the elbow in the case of unintentional flexion.

You're performing a flexion against gravity in the shoulder to lift your body. In the planche position, this movement is primarily performed by your deltoid, especially by its fiber part attached to the clavicle. Furthermore, your pectoralis major, i.e. your chest muscle with its fiber parts attached to the clavicle, pulls the upper arm forward and stabilizes the arm inward via its horizontally running fiber parts, which contributes significantly to the stability of the element, especially with wider parallettes. Your biceps brachii acts not only on your elbow but also on your shoulder. It is thus directly involved in the flexion of the shoulder joint. Another important and often neglected muscle related to the planche is your coracobrachialis. It assists during the flexion of your shoulder and stabilizes your arm into adduction along with your chest during wider holds.
During a planche, gravity pushes your shoulder blades into retraction. The angle of the arms also pushes them slightly into an elevation. To conform to convention two, and thus also to optimally stabilize the upper arm in its socket, you perform a protraction and depression. This means that you push your shoulder blades down and apart.

Planche with a protraction and compressed scapulae (top) compared with retracted and slightly winging scapulae (bottom).

The protraction is performed by the serratus anterior. Indirectly, the protraction and depression are supported by your chest. The trapezius and latissimus act as antagonists to the serratus anterior and deltoideus and therefore have a slight stabilizing effect and at the same time support the depression in the shoulder. However, the strength effect of these muscles on the planche is negligible and therefore these muscles have no relevance in planche training. To support the protraction of your shoulder blades and to prevent a possible winging of the shoulder blades, you retract your rib cage. This compresses your shoulder blades against your rib cage and makes your planche more stable. A slight natural rounding of the thoracic spine is completely sufficient. A very strong rounding would be a compensation according to the lever skill convention, as this would lead to your body position no longer being straight.

Natural, slightly rounded posture in the thoracic spine (top) compared to a strong rounding (bottom).

You should keep your lumbar spine neutral to create a straight planche line. The degree of extension and flexion of your lumbar spine is defined by the interaction of your back extensors and abdominal muscles.

Proper stabilization of the lumbar spine and hips is probably the most difficult part of the planche to learn. Gravity pushes you, and therefore your hip, down. The natural reflex to raise your hips is to tense your back extensors. By doing this, however, you not only raise your hips, but you bring your lumbar spine from its neutral position into hyperextension. This is not a bad thing by itself, but it does not result in a nice shape. Your planche will look more like a banana instead of nice and straight.

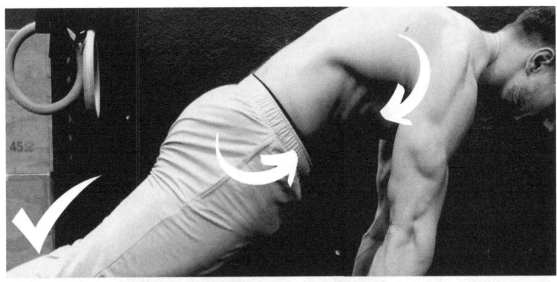

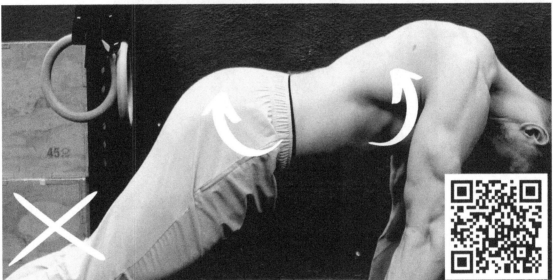

Correct control of the hip and abdominal muscles

In the planche, you have to learn to stiffen your lumbar spine by tensing your abdominal muscles and back extensors at the same time and to control the level of your hips by a flexion in your shoulder. This feels very wrong and unnatural, especially in the beginning, but it is the only way to keep your lumbar spine neutral and therefore the planche in line. To maintain a stable, neutral lumbar spine, you must tilt your pelvis backward into a posterior pelvic tilt (PPT). You can achieve this position by tensing your gluteal and abdominal muscles at the same time. Imagine that you want to pull your pelvis into your ribs to get your abdominal muscles really tense.

The hip joint itself is actively extended so that your legs are in line with your body. The load on the hip-extending muscles is limited to the weight of the legs and is therefore not a great challenge. These sometimes opposing joint rotations of the spine, pelvis and hip will make it difficult to control and understand the correct position. The pelvis is tilted backward (PPT), which feels like a downward rotation. The hip is extended at the same time, which feels like an upward rotation. So you need to rotate your pelvis in the opposite direction of your hip, or femur in your hip, while not moving your lumbar spine. Finally, you extend your knee and ankle joint to position yourself in a line.

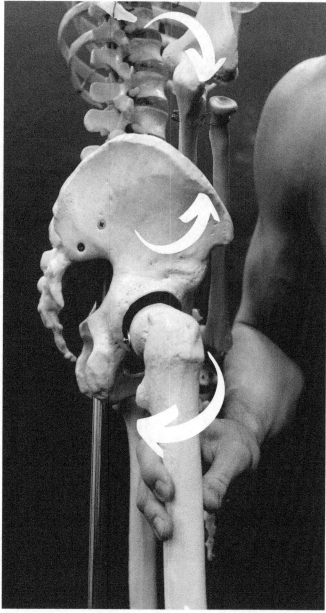

Different rotations in the pelvis, hip and spine.

3.2.2

Progressions

Through the use of different progressions, you have the ability to adjust the angular position of various joints in order to maintain an appropriate center of gravity based on your strength level during the planche. Similar to the front lever section, we will now discuss six commonly utilized progressions. Once you grasp the form and execution of these six progressions, you will be able to derive various combination forms from them with ease.

It is worth noting, albeit repetitive, that each progression allows for varying levels of difficulty. Depending on your execution and unique body proportions, the following sequence of progressions may not necessarily represent a linear increase in intensity. The transitions between progressions are fluid and individualized. The order is selected based on the coordination required for each progression relative to the size of the lever. Therefore, it is entirely possible that your training chronology may differ from what is presented here. This is perfectly acceptable and does not imply any error or suboptimal approach.

Planche lean

Definition: Toes on the floor, spine extended, hips extended, knees extended.
Scaling: pushing the shoulder forward over the wrists
Recommended assistance/variation: Ring support hold, progression holds with assistance, pseudo planche push ups
In contrast to the front lever, this section introduces a regression prior to the tuck holds in order to accommodate the unique challenges of the planche. The planche

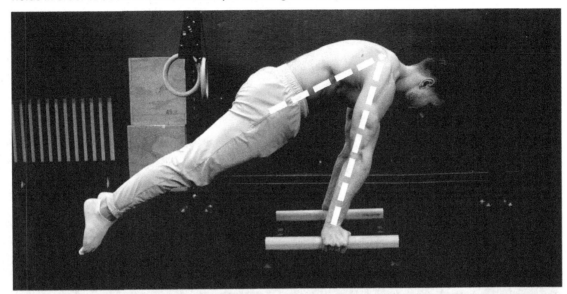

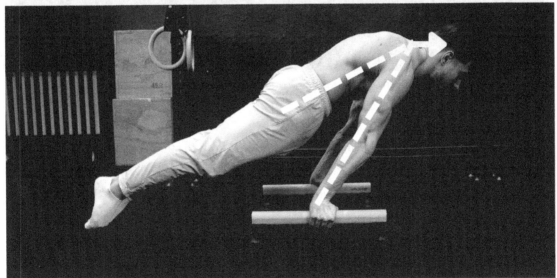

Planche lean in two different intensity levels. Little forward lean with a lot of weight on the feet (top) and a lot of forward lean with a lot of weight on the shoulders (bottom).

involves smaller muscle groups that are relatively weaker and requires more extreme positions. Therefore, if you have no prior experience, it is recommended to start with a gentle and safe progression known as the planche lean. The planche lean is suitable for beginners as well as slightly advanced athletes. With the planche lean, you can adjust the intensity of the hold by distributing your weight between the two points of contact with your body. By exerting more force through your feet, the hold becomes lighter, while shifting more weight onto your hands increases the difficulty. You can effectively scale the hold by gradually in creasing the forward movement of your shoulders. One way to measure progress is by measuring the distance to a wall and progressively increasing it from one workout to the next.

During the planche lean, it is important to focus on aligning yourself not along a horizontal line, but rather along the line connecting your shoulders and feet. This will ensure proper form and engagement of the target muscles.

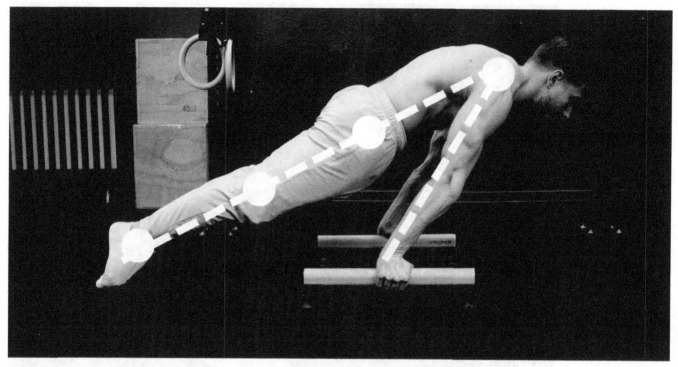

During a planche lean, you align yourself not horizontally, but rather along the line that connects your shoulders and feet.

It is essential to maintain fully extended arms, a strong abdominal tension, and a posterior pelvic tilt (PPT) throughout your practice. By establishing a solid technical foundation in these aspects, you will significantly enhance your ability to adapt to future progressions with greater ease.

Tucked planche

Definition: Hip angle up to < 90°, knees flexed
Scaling: spine extension, hip angle
Recommended assistance/variation: Progression holds with assistance, lever change holds, planche leans, pseudo planche push ups

Scaling of the tucked planche via the extension of the spine and hips.

The tucked planche serves as the initial and easiest progression, where your feet are completely lifted off the ground. At the start, your lumbar spine is rounded, and your hips and knees are maximally bent. The first step in scaling the tucked planche involves extending the lumbar spine. This requires the interaction between the back extensors and abdominal muscles to straighten the spine and increase the hip angle through lumbar extension. Once the spine is straightened, you can further scale the hip angle by extending your hips. This level of control can be challenging, and it is beneficial to utilize the control exercises outlined in the "assistance exercises" section. It's important to note that any change in the hip angle affects the entire planche position. To maintain balance and keep your center of gravity above your hands, the shoulder flexion angle must also be adjusted. This requires leaning further forward. Failure to do so may result in dropping your hips, losing the proper alignment, or even falling over if you lean too far forward. It's common to encounter these challenges in the beginning. The progression of the tucked planche concludes when you achieve a hip angle of just under 90°, transitioning to what is known as the advanced tucked planche.

3.2.2.3   **Advanced tucked planche**

Definition: Extended spine, knees bent, hip angle approx. 90–120°.
Scaling: hip angle
Recommended assistance/variation: Progression holds with assistance, regression holds, ballistic holds, lever change holds, tucked planche push ups.
The advanced tucked planche is a progression that is likely to be a significant part of your planche journey. As you increase the hip angle in the advanced tucked planche,

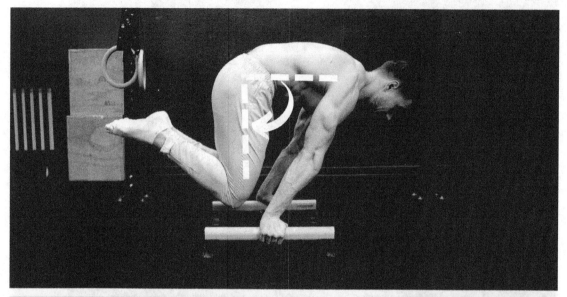

Advanced tucked planche with a hip angle of approx. 90° and 120°.

it can be challenging to avoid falling into a hollow back position, especially in the beginning. Patience and meticulous attention to technique is crucial at this stage. It's important to note that compensating with a hollow back becomes even more difficult to correct in the subsequent progressions, making it essential to address and master this issue in the advanced tucked planche.

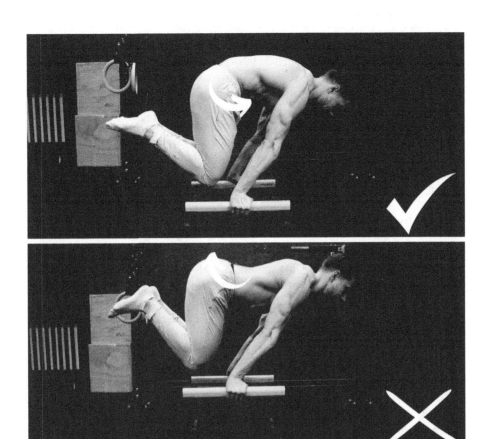

Advanced tucked planche without hollow back (top) and with hollow back (bottom)

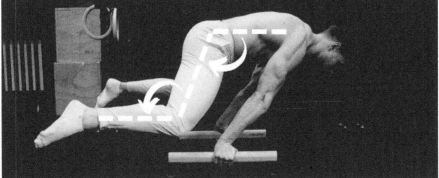

Tucked straddle planche with scaling of hip and knee angle

To establish a consistent hip angle and promote stability in your hips during the advanced tucked planche, actively pull your heels toward your buttocks. This action engages your leg flexors, aiding in the stabilization of your hips in their more extended position. It also allows you to scale the progression primarily through the hip angle rather than excessively through the knee. As you reach a certain hip angle, it is common for the knee to naturally open up slightly due to the active insufficiency of the rectus femoris muscle. This should not be a cause for concern. As long as you can maintain stability in that position, there is no need to forcefully resist it in order to reduce the number of joints involved. Keep in mind that as you progress towards the straddle planche, you will need to control and scale multiple joints simultaneously, making this knee deviation insignificant by the end of the advanced tucked planche.

3.2.2.4   Tucked straddle planche

Definition: hip angle 90°- 120°, knee angle up to 90°
Scaling: hip angle, knee angle, hip spread
Recommended assistance/variation: Progression holds with assistance, regression holds, ballistic holds, lever change holds, tucked planche push ups

The tucked straddle planche progression offers significant benefits, particularly during the transition from the advanced tucked planche to the straddle planche. As you train the advanced tucked planche, you may reach a point where it becomes challenging to further open your hips with the heels tucked. Instead of aiming for a half Lay planche, you can use the tucked straddle progression to work towards a straddle planche more effectively.

In the tucked straddle position, you spread your legs apart, forming a wider angle compared to the advanced tucked planche. This reduces the intensity while allowing for progressive work towards the straddle planche. It introduces a new and more challenging form of hip stabilization. However, it's important to maintain proper posterior pelvic tilt (PPT) and abdominal tension, as some of your hip flexors and extensors may be in an unfavorable position for hip flexion/extension when the legs are spread wide.

Mastering control in the tucked straddle position will help prepare you for the proper straddle planche. The wider you spread your legs, the more difficult it becomes to maintain PPT and abdominal tension due to the position of your hip flexors and extensors. This progression allows you to work specifically towards the straddle planche, but you must ensure that the intensities remain progressive. Simply spreading your legs without adjusting your hip and knee angles from the previous advanced tucked planche progression may unintentionally reduce the intensity. If reaching the straddle planche is important to you as an intermediate step or as your ultimate goal, the advantages of higher training specificity outweigh the challenges of less clear scaling in the tucked straddle planche progression.

One leg planche

Definition: Spine extended, one hip extended, one knee extended, one hip flexed at an angle up to < 180°, one knee flexed > 0°.
Scaling: hip angle, knee angle
Recommended assistance/variation: Progression holds with assistance, conditioning holds with assistance, regression holds, ballistic holds, lever change holds, (adv.) tucked planche push ups.

One leg planche

The one leg planche, similar to the one leg front lever, offers clear settings for adjusting the intensity. However, it is less commonly used in practice compared to the straddle planche. One reason for this could be that the straddle planche is already highly regarded as a standalone element and is therefore preferred.

Another reason is the disadvantage of the one leg planche, as it can only be executed effectively on high parallettes for most athletes. Otherwise, the bent leg may come into contact with the floor, or the hip would need to be raised, which would violate lever skill convention 1. Generally, the higher the parallettes, the more challenging it is to achieve a clean entry into the planche, as explained in the "Entry" section. This makes the one leg progression more difficult to initiate compared to the straddle planche, often leading to poorer execution technique.

Additionally, the stabilization of the hip in the one leg progression poses difficulties, as there is only one gluteus muscle available for active control. Unlike the front lever, where the back position aids in stabilization, the prone position in the planche makes it much more challenging to maintain posterior pelvic tilt (PPT) and a neutral lumbar spine.

For athletes who struggle with leg spreading due to poor hip mobility, which can hinder scaling via the straddle planche, scaling via the one leg planche can be a viable alternative. However, in the advanced progressions, such as the one leg front lever, these mentioned disadvantages become less significant, and the one leg planche can be executed without major issues. The gradual scaling of the one leg planche can be directly adapted from the front lever section.

Straddle planche

Definition: spine extended, hips extended, knees extended, hip spread
Scaling: hip spread, hip angle if necessary
Recommended assistance/variation: Progression holds with assistance, conditioning holds with assistance, regression holds, ballistic holds, adv. tucked planche push ups.

Straddle planche

The straddle planche is indeed a significant milestone for many athletes striving to achieve the full planche. Ideally, the intensity of the straddle planche is scaled primarily through the spread angle of the legs. The wider the legs are spread, the less intense the execution becomes, as the center of gravity is shifted closer to the shoulders.

However, in practice, it is common to introduce a secondary scaling method. In the initial attempts of the straddle planche, it is often challenging to maintain full extension in the hips. Therefore, scaling via the hip angle becomes necessary for most athletes. This means that the hip angle is gradually increased over time as the athlete gains strength and stability. By gradually opening the hip angle, athletes can progress from a more tucked position to a more extended position, ultimately achieving a full Straddle Planche.

This secondary scaling allows athletes to gradually adapt to the demands of the straddle planche and work towards achieving full extension in the hips while maintaining balance and stability.

Straddle planche with hip flexion

As the straddle angle increases, there is a greater tendency for the pelvis to rotate forward into an anterior pelvic tilt (ATP), and the legs may drop. This is a natural compensation of the body to reduce the intensity and manage the load of the planche.

In the wide straddle position, the gluteal muscles and many of the hip flexors have their fibers aligned in a direction that is less advantageous for generating power for hip extension. As a result, maintaining hip extension and a posterior pelvic tilt (PPT) becomes more difficult. This makes achieving a clean straddle planche technically challenging, even more so than a full planche. To achieve a technically clean straddle planche, it is crucial to prioritize technique training. High emphasis should be placed on refining the form and execution of the movement. Conditioning holds with assistance systems, such as bands or counterweights, can be effective in developing the required strength and stability while maintaining proper technique. By consistently working on technique and gradually increasing the difficulty, you can improve your ability to hold a clean straddle planche.

In addition, make sure that you enter properly and use the assistance systems the correct way, as described in the following section.

Conditioning hold of the straddle planche with a resistance band

3.2.3

Entry

Using low parallettes for the correct entry into the planche hold is highly recommended. Standardizing your entry allows you to consistently achieve the most optimal form possible, which is crucial for maintaining proper technique throughout the hold. Making corrections while already in the hold can be more challenging and may compromise the quality of the position. By focusing on the correct entry, you can ensure that each hold starts off with the best possible form. This, in turn, allows you to accumulate higher-quality hold time during your training sessions. The more quality hold time you accumulate, the faster you will progress in your planche training.

It's worth noting that there may be exceptions for athletes who require specific entry positions due to the nature of their sport or performance requirements. For example, freestyle athletes who incorporate the planche into a choreography may need to practice different entry variations, such as entering the hold on a high bar. However, even for these athletes, it is still beneficial to include a majority of their holds with the standardized entries discussed in order to improve the form and quality of their holds.

3.2.3.1

Entry tucked planche progressions

Position your hands on the parallettes, ensuring they are roughly shoulder-width apart. Extend your arms completely and bring your shoulders into depression and protraction. Push your shoulders over your wrists, creating tension in your shoulder muscles. Pull one knee towards your chest while engaging your core. Check the height of your hips and make any necessary adjustments to keep the hips on shoulder level. Before lifting the second leg, ensure that your hips are already at the correct height. With the tension and balance you've established, carefully lift the second leg, minimizing the need for further adjustments.

Entry into tucked planche progressions.

Entry adv. tucked planche progressions

3.2.3.2

Place your hands on the parallettes. Extend your arms fully and bring your shoulders into depression and protraction. Push your shoulders forward over your wrists, creating tension. In this step, there are some changes compared to the tucked planche. Instead of pulling your knee towards your chest, pull it towards the hip angle required for your chosen position. Keep your hips at shoulder height throughout. Rotate your hips into a posterior pelvic tilt (PPT) and engage your core to maintain this position. Additionally, pull your heel towards your buttocks to further stabilize your hips. Hold this position and find balance with the leg that remains on the floor. Shift your weight towards the thumb side of your hand, minimizing the weight on your supporting leg before the final entry. Once you have achieved balance, position your second leg beside the first leg, which is already lifted.

Entry into advanced tucked planche progressions.

3.2.3.3 Entry straddle planche progressions

Begin your entry in a planche lean position, ensuring that your hips are already positioned at the desired spread angle. Stretch your toes so that the top of your foot rests on the floor. Then, extend your arms, depress, and protract your shoulders. Push your shoulders forward over your wrists, creating tension. Instead of raising your hips to shoulder height, lower them to align with the line connecting your shoulders and feet. This will allow you to achieve a horizontal position once you lift your legs. In this position, rotate your hips into a posterior pelvic tilt (PPT) and maintain this posture by engaging your core and glutes.

Next, pull yourself through your arms to find balance and smoothly transition into the planche position. Your body should maintain the same alignment as before and will be lifted by the increasing tension in your shoulder flexion. Shift your weight towards the thumb side of your hands as much as possible during straddle planches to maintain balance. Strive to keep yourself as stable and balanced as you can throughout the movement.

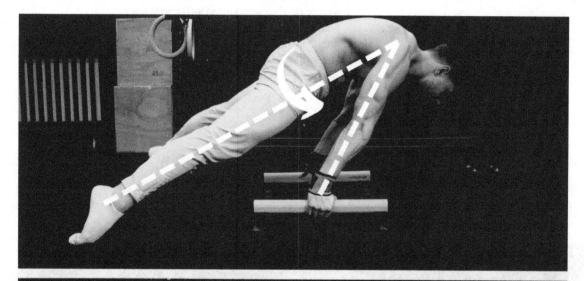

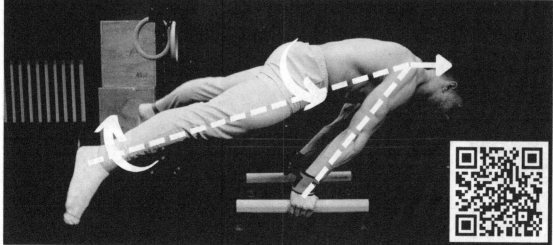

Entry into straddle planche progressions.

Entry full planche progressions

For the full planche, you will follow the same entry technique as the straddle planche, utilizing the planche lean. The difference is that you keep your legs closed together. Just like in the previous description, it's important to focus on aligning your hips with the line connecting your shoulders and feet and maintaining stability in that position. From there, smoothly transition into the hold by "sliding" progressively as described earlier.

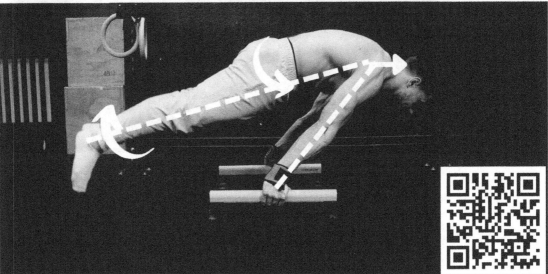

Entry into full planche progressions.

3.2.4

Assistance systems

When using resistance bands for planche training, there are different positions that offer advantages and disadvantages. In this discussion, we will focus on resistance bands attached to the body. Here are two common positions:

Band on the lumbar spine
You attach the band with a loop to a pull-up bar this method, the band is attached to a pull-up bar or similar suspension, and you step into the loop with the band positioned above your hips on your lower core.

This position has the least impact on your planche and is recommended for planche training. The band is positioned close to your body's center of gravity and pulls it upward, reducing the effective weight and making the planche easier. However, since

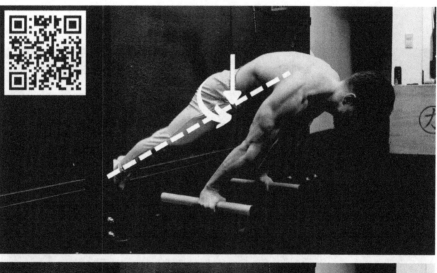

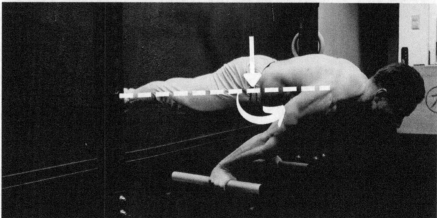

Planche with the band at the lumbar spine

the band is in front of the hips, you will need to stabilize them on your own. This allows for a high level of specificity and helps you develop a proper technique for planche holds without the band. It's important to ensure that the angle of the band is as vertical as possible, as larger angles can affect your balance. Smaller angles have a negligible impact.

Band on the shin / below the hip

In this method, the band is positioned below your hip, either at your thigh or even at the bottom of your feet. This type of support is more related to a planche lean rather than a free hold, and it is typically used with full progressions. If you require assistance with a full progression using this type of band position, it usually indicates that you are not advanced enough to work with that progression. Additionally, this type of band assist can distort the position of your center of gravity, so it's generally not recommended for planche holds.

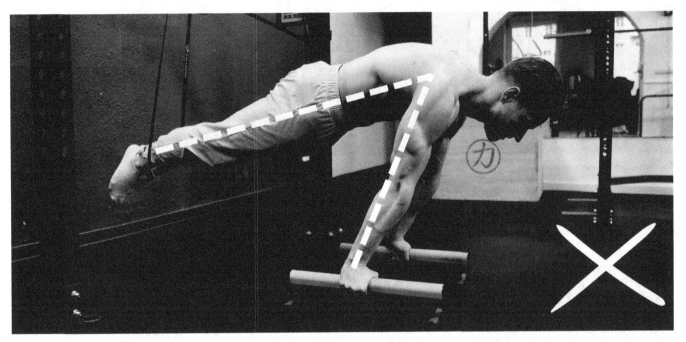

Full planche with a band on shins

3.2.5

Grip

The grip technique for shifting your weight to the thumb side has already been covered in the previous sections. You've learned in the „Entry" chapter why low parallettes are usually the better choice for your planche workout. In this section, you'll focus on grip width, the shape and width of the parallettes, and possible helpful angles at which to set them up. For the grip width, you should work with your shoulder width and adjust the parallettes from there to fit your needs. A slightly externally rotated position of the parallettes reduces the necessary abduction in the wrist and is therefore often perceived as somewhat more comfortable and less stressful in the forearm and wrist. The more you rotate the parallettes into external rotation, the more you rotate your arm flexion in the direction of loading. This means that the SAS load becomes significantly greater.

Parallettes with parallel grips, 30° rotation and 90° rotation.

If you are not accustomed to handling such a load, it is advisable to avoid using this position without proper preparation. A slight incline of the parallettes, where they slope towards the shoulders, can help alleviate stress on the wrists and forearms.
In cases where forearm overload is a concern, you can temporarily use this grip to

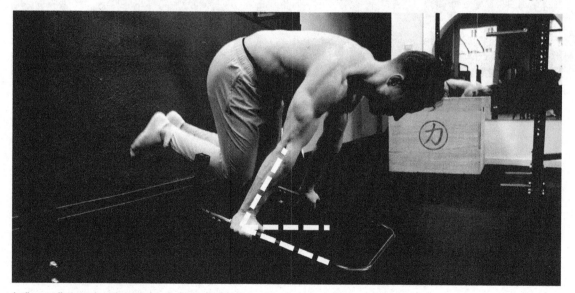

Incline parallettes reduce the necessary inclination in the wrist.

reduce strain on your wrists. However, it is important to work towards using a straight grip in the long run. If you rely too much on the sloped grip, you may lack the necessary forearm strength when transitioning to straight grips, which are essential for maintaining balance in the planche. It is recommended to use parallettes that provide a comfortable contact area with out being too narrow. Distributing the pressure over a larger surface area on your hand can enhance comfort during the planche. While the little finger may not contribute much force, having the ability to grip the parallettes with your entire hand, including the little finger, offers a stability advantage as you lean further forward in the planche. Therefore, a good parallette width is one that allows for ample contact surface while still enabling you to grip the parallettes with your little finger.

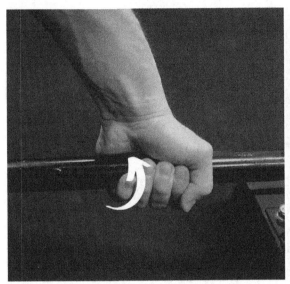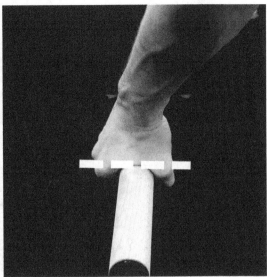

Different grips for the planche. A small handle on the left, which you can grip well but offers little support, and a broader handle on the right, which is harder to grip but offers more support.

3.2.6

Progress backup

The planche is in a broad perspective a shoulder flexion exercise. Accordingly, you should also choose a progress backup in which this movement is performed. In the context of this book, the weighted dip is obviously a good choice. The dip, especially when performed in the technique described in this book, has many exciting similarities with the planche. Firstly, the shoulder-dominant execution, the movement of the shoulder flexion itself, and the stabilization of a shoulder depression and protraction under high load.

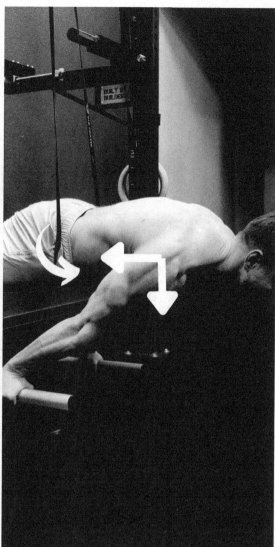

In both the planche and dip, the shoulders are pushed into protraction and depression under load.

Athletes specializing in push lever skills often exhibit remarkable strength in dips, sometimes reaching up to 200% of their own body weight, even without specific 1RM training. However, the transfer from dips to push lever skills is limited, as the technique and conditioning components specific to lever skills are not adequately addressed in dips. Nevertheless, this observation provides clear evidence that using dips as a progress backup can be a beneficial approach. By incorporating dips alongside specific planche training, you can capitalize on the advantages offered by dips compared to lever skills.

In case dips are not feasible or suitable for various reasons, there are alternative progress backups that I have found effective in my coaching career. The overhead press and bench press with a barbell are good alternatives. The overhead press targets the front and side shoulders, as well as the upper chest (particularly in the lower range of motion). Using a barbell allows for higher intensity work compared to dumbbells, which may be limited by stability issues without appropriate racks. The overhead press also provides the benefit of training the serratus anterior throughout a wide range of motion, which can have a positive impact on protraction in the planche. Similarly, bench presses, which share similarities with dips as discussed in the dips chapter, can serve as an effective progress backup. However, it is important to avoid using an excessively wide grip in order to maintain the ability to perform shoulder flexion.

Assistance exercises

Your chosen progress backup serves as the primary means for strength and hypertrophy assistance in your planche training. It allows you to regulate the volume and intensity of your workouts, supplementing your holds. By incorporating this progress backup, you can maintain a relatively high level of intensity in your planche training, even with moderate to shorter total hold times during the week.

If you opt for less strength and hypertrophy assistance through your progress backup, you will need to increase the number of holds and extend the total hold times throughout the week. This allows for a more balanced approach to your training.

In addition to your progress backup, there are other beneficial assistance exercises within the categories of ballistic holds and full range of motion (ROM). These exercises are further discussed in the „Dynamic lever skills" chapter, which provides detailed analysis and guidance for incorporating these exercises into your training regimen.

Ballistic Holds   3.2.7.1

L-Sit to planche/planche swings
Execution: L-Sit to planche or planche swings are performed on higher parallettes or a p-bars. You start in the static L-Sit or swinging from the support hold. Through the L-Sit or swing you accelerate into your chosen progression and briefly hold it isometrically.

Application: The swinging motion allows you to engage in repetitive and intense progressions, enabling you to accumulate hold times in a challenging progression. This approach can be beneficial for increasing your hold time in a new progression, allowing you to incorporate it into your workout with multiple sets of longer hold times.

L-Sit to planche

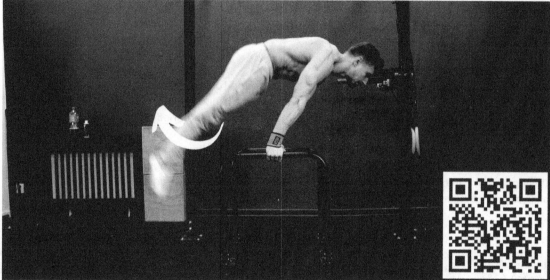

Planche swings

Planche lean to hold

Planche lean to hold
Execution:

Planche leans to hold are executed using low parallettes. Begin by assuming a planche lean position and gradually reduce the weight supported by your feet to a minimum. With a slight momentum generated from your feet, lift off into the planche position and maintain the hold for a brief duration.

Application: This exercise is particularly effective for straddle and full planche progressions. The initial planche lean places you in an optimal starting position, allowing you to enter the intense holds with excellent technique and quality. By focusing on shorter hold times, you can accumulate valuable training volume and refine your planche skills in advanced progressions.

Planche negatives

Planche negatives
Execution:

Planche negatives are ideally performed using low parallettes. This exercise requires a strong foundation in handstands. To execute planche negatives, lower yourself in a controlled manner into a planche position with extended arms. Lower your hips and shift your shoulders forward over your wrists while maintaining a rigid body throughout the planche progression.

Application: Planche negatives are highly challenging, not only in terms of strength but also coordination. Therefore, they are primarily recommended for advanced athletes who are already working on straddle and full planche progressions. Planche negatives are more of a skill on their own and are particularly beneficial for athletes looking to incorporate various elements into a single set. This exercise involves transitioning between handstands and planches. If your main focus is on achieving and holding the planche position itself, planche raises and negatives may not be necessary for your training.

Full ROM assistance   3.2.7.2

Planche push ups

Execution: You start in your planche regression and then lower yourself to the ground by bending your elbows, without leaving the planche position parallel to the ground.

Application: Planche push ups can be used in conjunction with planche hold training to accumulate additional specific training volume without having the direct hold position as a limiting factor.

Planche push up

Zanetti press

Execution: The Zanetti press is a SAS assistance exercise that you can perform with dumbbells or on the cable. To do this, lie down on a bench and stiffen up in a hollow body position. Rotate your pelvis into a PPT, tighten your core and butt, and slightly lift your thoracic spine. Grab two dumbbells and bring them together in front of your body with your arms extended. Your shoulders are protracted and depressed. In this position, with arms still extended, perform a shoulder extension followed by flexion.

Application: The Zanetti press is particularly useful for preparing the elbows for the demands of SAS elements. It serves as an effective warm-up exercise for planche training or as additional conditioning after your hold workouts. The supinated grip used in Zanetti presses is wrist and forearm-friendly. This exercise provides valuable assistance, especially if you experience limitations in your forearms or wrists when performing other planche assistance exercises.

Zanetti press

Activation exercises

Achieving proper control of the hips, shoulders, and core during a planche can be highly challenging. As you progress through the different stages, the difficulty only increases. To develop and enhance this control, there are beneficial activation exercises that you can include in your warm-up routine or use as pre-activation exercises before your planche holds.

Hollow body hold

The hollow body hold is a fundamental calisthenics position. In the context of planche training, the hollow body hold can assist in stabilizing your spine while under load, similar to the planche, and help maintain proper form. To perform this exercise, lie on your back. In the first step, engage your abdominal muscles and buttocks, tilting your hips into a posterior pelvic tilt (PPT). Lift your legs and thoracic spine slightly off the floor, so that only your lumbar spine maintains contact with the floor. The difficulty of this position can be adjusted by the placement of your arms. The higher you raise them above your head, the more challenging the hold becomes. This exercise aids in developing the ability to maintain body tension under load, which can then be applied to the planche.

Hollow body hip extension

To develop the ability to extend the hips while maintaining a fixed spine and pelvis, a variation of the hollow body hold with a lever change can be beneficial. Begin by assuming the hollow body hold position, but with your hips flexed. Use your arms for balance if necessary. Now, focus on extending your hips while keeping your lumbar spine in the hollow body position. This exercise helps you gain control over the movement of your hips independent of your spine, which is crucial for performing advanced variations like the advanced tuck planche or various front lever progressions. Mastering this control will make these movements much easier for you.

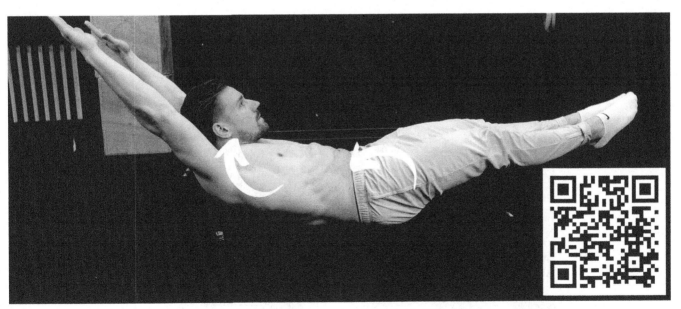

Hollow body hold

Hollow body hip extension

Planche lean hip extensions

Preparatory exercises are valuable for building strength and control, but they can never fully replace specific training in the target position. To enhance hip control in the planche while under load, you can perform a specific exercise. Find a surface that allows your feet to slide easily. Assume a planche lean position with extended arms, depressed and protracted shoulders, hips and feet aligned, and a tensed core. Lean slightly forward to engage your shoulders. In this position, maintain your hollow body tension while pulling your feet toward your body. You can also lift your feet off the floor at the end of the hip flexion and transition into a tucked or advanced tucked planche. Then, extend your hips and return to the starting position in a controlled manner. Throughout the exercise, it is crucial to maintain core tension without compromising it. This exercise targets hip control specifically within the context of the planche, helping you develop the necessary strength and technique.

Planche lean hip extension

Lever change holds with band assist

Irrespective of the progression you are working on, you can repeatedly practice activation using a stronger resistance band. It is particularly beneficial to focus on mastering the correct technique when working with new progressions. Simply use a stronger band and perform lever change holds into your desired progression, paying close attention to hip position and core tension. This exercise is particularly valuable for training the activation required for a straddle planche, as the difficulty increases when the legs are spread apart. By consistently practicing this exercise, you can improve your technique and strengthen the necessary muscles for the specific planche progression you are aiming for.

Lever change hold with band assist

Forearm training

If you experience forearm, wrist, or elbow pain during high-intensity or high-volume planche training, incorporating additional forearm exercises into your routine may be beneficial. While the extensors of the wrist are primarily stressed during the planche, I recommend including a comprehensive forearm training regimen. This should involve a combination of exercises that target the flexors, extensors, and pronators/supinators of the wrist. In other words, exercises that involve flexion, extension, and rotation of the wrist against an external resistance in various directions. By incorporating these exercises, you can provide balanced and holistic training for your forearm muscles, reducing the risk of imbalances or overuse injuries. You can find recommended exercises at the end of the pull/chin up chapter.

"Winging" of the shoulder blade

Shoulder blade winging, also known as scapular winging, can have an impact on the stability of your shoulder girdle during the planche. However, it's important not to panic immediately. If your shoulder blades are slightly misaligned and you don't experience any issues or pain under load, there may not be a need for immediate action. In cases where the winging is pronounced, it is advisable to consult a professional for further evaluation. Winging occurs when the attaching muscles fail to properly secure the shoulder blades to the rib cage. This can be due to factors such as inactive or weak rhomboids or trapezius muscles, as discussed in the front lever chapter. In such cases, the shoulder blades may protrude laterally, away from the body's midline. Refer to that chapter for information on addressing this issue.

303

Another potential cause is inactivity or weakness of the serratus anterior muscle. When the serratus anterior is inactive, the scapulae may be slightly more centered on the rib cage, as limited protraction occurs. In practical terms, mild winging is often not a significant problem. Your first step should be to determine if the issue arises only when using very challenging progressions. If this is the case, additional assistance may not be necessary, and simply reducing the intensity of your training can be beneficial. However, if the serratus anterior requires attention, activation exercises for this muscle can help improve scapular stability. Similar to the protraction to retraction front lever exercise, you can perform this movement during a planche lean. Unlike the front lever, the protraction in this exercise is against gravity. During the movement, push your shoulder blades apart as much as possible in the upper position. It's important to note that this should not involve excessive, but just slight rounding of the thoracic spine. You should feel activation in the serratus anterior, which is located beneath the latissimus muscle. If you sense muscle activity in that area during protraction, you are likely performing the exercise correctly. Additionally, when planning your workout, include overhead presses to train your serratus anterior effectively, as described in the progress backups. This can reduce the likelihood of the muscle limiting your performance in the planche.

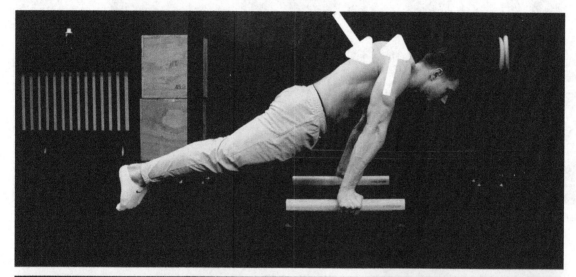

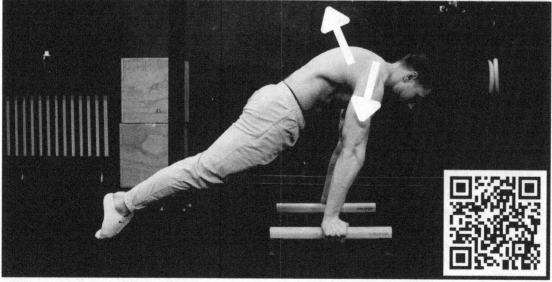

Planche lean protraction to retraction

3.2.8

Correctly classify local compensations

In practice, movements occurring in a joint during a planche that are unintended are often associated with muscle weakness in that joint. In this section, you will apply the knowledge you have gained to test your understanding. By analyzing the external forces acting on your body during a planche, you can identify the most common compensatory movements and draw conclusions about their underlying causes.

Lowering/folding/lifting the legs

If you struggle to keep your legs and hips aligned with your body during a planche, it's a common misconception to think that you need to strengthen your back extensors and glutes to keep your legs up. However, this assumption is flawed. While there may be athletes who have difficulty supporting the weight of their own legs at the hip, that would be comparable to individuals who rely on a walker and struggle to climb stairs independently.

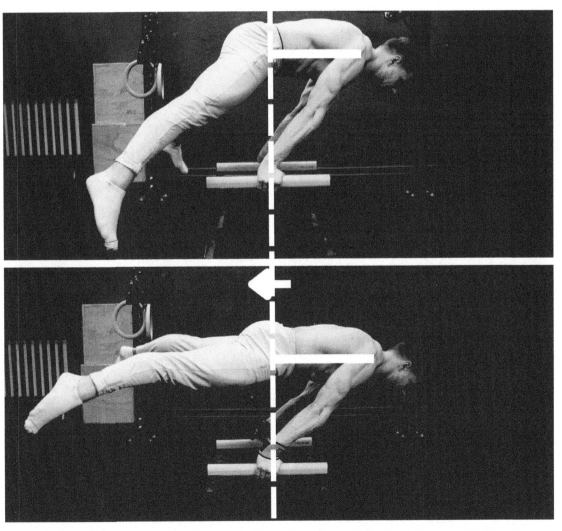

Flexing the hip moves the center of gravity closer to the shoulder. The resulting load arm on the shoulder joint becomes smaller. Thus, the resulting load on the shoulder is significantly smaller in the upper image than in the lower one.

By analyzing the torques exerted on your joints during a planche, you'll notice that as the torque on the hip extensors increases, the torque on the shoulders also increases proportionally. However, it's important to recognize that the shoulders are already subjected to a significantly greater torque. Therefore, the more plausible explanation for the compensation in the hip is that your body instinctively tries to deload the shoulders, not the hip itself. This suggests that the issue lies not in having weak hip muscles, but rather weak muscles in the shoulder girdle, which play a crucial role in maintaining the planche position.

When observing deviations from the lever skill conventions in your planche, it's advisable to analyze the applied load arms on the involved joints. This analysis can help identify which joints are experiencing the greatest load and are likely contributing to compensatory movements. However, it's important to note that individual cases may have unique limiting factors that go beyond this analysis. In such cases, seeking guidance from an experienced trainer is recommended to address specific concerns and develop an appropriate training approach.

4.

Dynamic
lever skills

4.
Dynamic lever skills

In previous chapters, we discussed various dynamic assistance exercises such as planche push ups, front lever raises, and front lever pull ups in relation to lever skills. These exercises are all categorized as dynamic Lever skills, as they involve performing dynamic movements within the lever skill position. Rather than providing a detailed analysis of each individual exercise, we can establish a concept based on conventions that allows you to develop a clean execution on your own.

When a dynamic lever skill begins in the lever skill position, such as planche push ups or front lever pull ups, the lever skill conventions apply to the starting position. Similarly, if an exercise like a planche negative ends in a lever skill position, the lever skill conventions also apply to the final form of that exercise. It's important to note that these conventions pertain to the ultimate form of the exercise.

Deviations from the execution according to these conventions can be seen as compensatory movements. By observing these deviations, you can identify potential weak points in the movement and take appropriate measures in your training to address them. It's crucial to understand that it's not about determining what is right or wrong in a strict sense, but rather utilizing the analysis tool to make informed decisions in your training and strive for the most optimal form possible.

1. **During the entire movement, the total body center of gravity is moving on the normal between the contact surface from your hands to the device and the floor.**

In dynamic lever skills, it is crucial to maintain the body's center of gravity approximately above or below the contact surface with the device/floor. This ensures that the load arm remains consistent throughout the exercise and allows for optimal execution. By keeping the center of gravity stable and avoiding any deviations, you work with the biggest leverage and strive for the most perfect form of the progression you are working on. This convention helps identify compensations and deviations that may occur when the center of gravity shifts, allowing you to address any weaknesses and make appropriate adjustments in your training.

2. **Joints that are not involved in the movement are actively stiffened and stabilized in a line.**

In combination with convention 1, all dynamic lever skills are defined in such a way that you have to execute them as cleanly as possible. The used load arm remains constant and the movement path of the negative and positive movement remains congruent. Evasive movements through ‚uninvolved' joints result inevitably in a conflict with convention 1 or 2 and can thus be interpreted as compensation.

Using two common dynamic lever skill exercises, you will learn to apply the principles correctly. With the help of these examples, you can then easily apply the conventions to all other exercises. The first example is the planche push up along with the front lever pull up. The starting point for the exercise in each case is the desired lever progression. The shape of this progression is defined by the lever skill conventions. At this point, you also apply the first convention for dynamic lever skills so that you know exactly what to focus on during the movement initiation.

During the entire movement, the total body center of gravity is moving on the normal between the contact surface from your hands to the device and the floor.

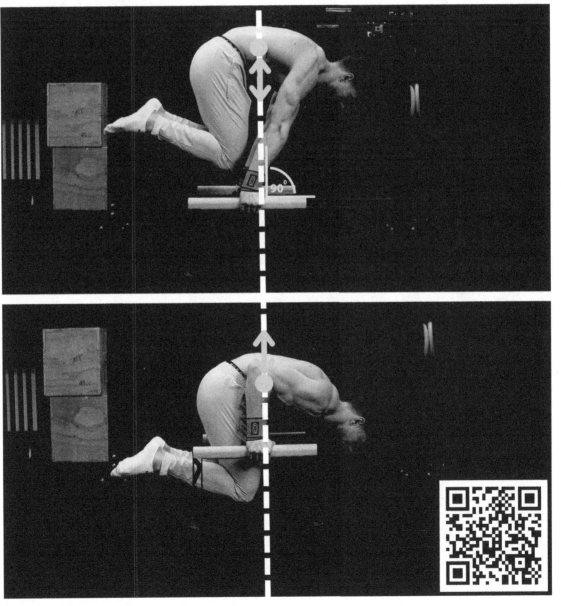

Analysis example planche push up

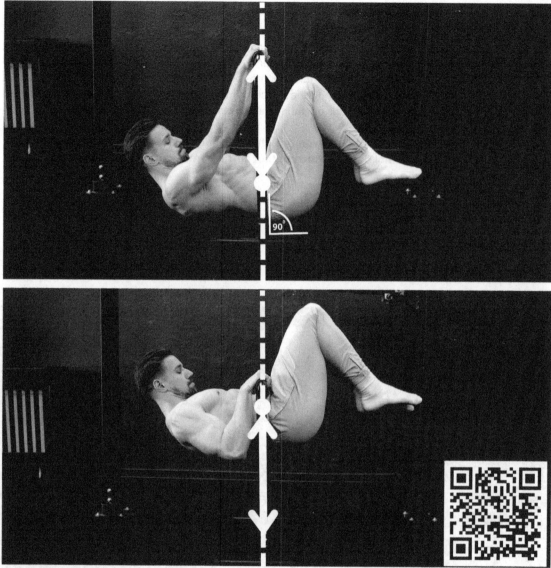

Analysis example front lever pull up

The normal refers to the perpendicular line connecting your overall body center of gravity to your hands. It represents the center of gravity of the chosen progression and should be maintained throughout the entire range of motion of the movement. Any deviation from this line, such as changing the progression mid-movement, indicates a compensatory action that should be addressed and trained out in the short to medium term. For instance, if you excessively raise your hips during planche push-ups, causing a shift in your center of gravity, it inevitably decreases the load arm on your shoulders and reduces the intensity and specificity of the skill.

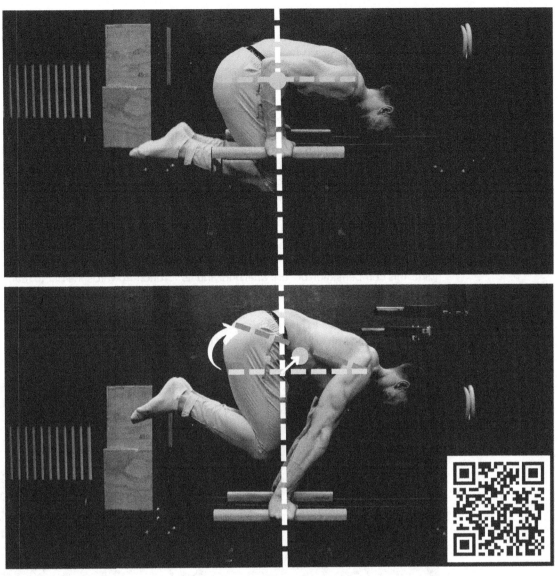

Analysis example planche push up with raised hips.

To identify compensatory movements, it is crucial to have a clear understanding of the optimal and final execution of the exercise. In the case of planche push ups and front lever pull ups, convention 1 states that your overall body center of gravity should remain unchanged throughout the entire movement. This means that unintentional changes in your chosen progression should be avoided during execution. However, intentional progression changes for specific training purposes are acceptable and reasonable.

Detecting shifts in the center of gravity or the center of gravity itself can be challenging since it is estimated rather than precisely measured. To identify a shift in the center of gravity, observe changes in joint angles that define the chosen progression. Pay attention to any "shrinking" of your body, where body segments move closer to the estimated normal. These movements are compensatory actions employed by your body to reduce stress on certain structures or muscles. Recognizing these compensations allows you to focus your training on strengthening the weak muscles and prevent such compensations in future movements.

This is where the second convention becomes important. It regulates under which conditions you can change your body position during dynamic lever skills after you have left your starting position.

Joints that are not involved in the movement are actively stiffened and stabilized in a line.

In both front lever pull ups and planche push ups, only the shoulder, elbow, and wrist joints are actively involved in the movement, while the spine, shoulder blades, hips, and knees remain actively stabilized and aligned based on the chosen progression. There may be instances where the shoulder blades need to be released from their position to achieve a specific range of motion, such as achieving depth in a planche push up. However, it is crucial to promptly return the shoulder blades to their initial position once the end ranges are surpassed. One common compensation observed in these exercises is spinal flexion, which reduces the range of motion in the shoulder joint. This compensation occurs when individuals "crunch" towards the bar to reach the desired pull height or depth in planche push ups. This movement involves the spine deviating from its actively stiffened position, resulting in a compensatory action. Additionally, this leads to body segments moving closer to the normal, leading to a reduction in load arm length and thus relief on certain joints and muscles.

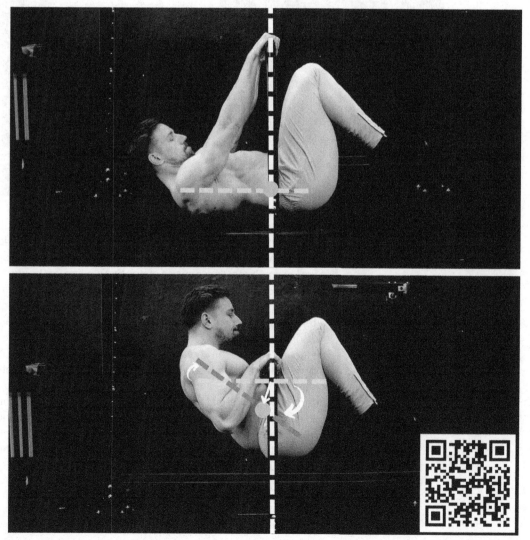

Analysis example front lever pull up with crunch

By recognizing these compensations, it becomes apparent which joints and muscles are being relieved during different parts of the range of motion. Armed with this understanding, adjustments can be made to the chosen progression, range of motion, or even assistance exercises during training to address specific weaknesses or imbalances.

These dynamic Lever skill conventions apply equally to exercises such as negatives or raises. By utilizing these conventions, you can easily assess and improve your execution of these exercises, leading to better long-term training results. It is important to incorporate the lever skill conventions to determine the desired position to reach during raises or negatives. This ensures that your shoulder blades and hips are properly positioned throughout the movement, aligning with the target lever skill position. The sooner you can achieve and stabilize this position, the less corrective movement will be required.

Let's consider the example of a front lever raise on the high bar starting from the hang position. Visualize the line connecting your hand to the center of gravity, known as the normal line. Your center of gravity should move along this line during the raise. To achieve this, it is crucial to maintain even hip movement alongside shoulder extension. This creates a vertical trajectory of your center of gravity along the normal line, satisfying the first convention.

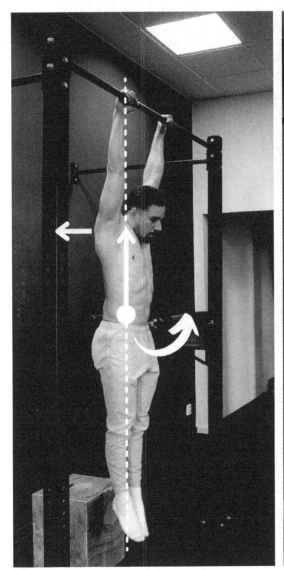

Analysis example front lever raise

The same principles apply when transitioning from a handstand to a planche. This transition is particularly sensitive as it requires a high level of balance. So, if you move your hips out of sync with the shoulder extension during the front lever raise, such as by tucking your legs to decrease the progression, it alters the position of your center of gravity in relation to your shoulders, making the raise easier. Additionally, excessive momentum can cause your center of gravity to deviate from the normal line, as the high acceleration temporarily allows for a lack of balance dependency. In such cases, these movements can be considered compensation.

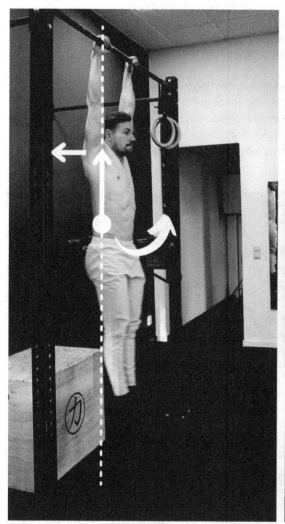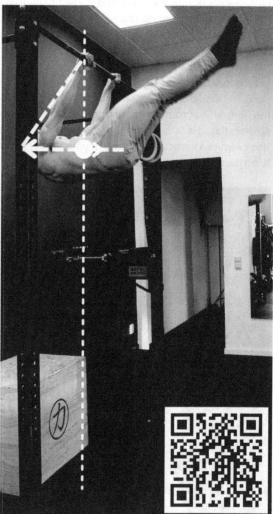

Analysis example front lever raise with crunch

The second convention is very important, especially in raises or negatives, as the movement should occur solely in the shoulder joints and shoulder blades. Any additional movement in other joints should be avoided. With some practice, it becomes relatively easy to determine whether you are executing lever skills and dynamic lever skills correctly, or if you are employing compensatory movements that deviate from the optimal technique. Regularly analyzing your own movements using this framework will help you avoid adopting improper movement patterns that hinder your progress.

4.1

Handstand
push up

4.1
Handstand
push up - HSPU

The handstand push up is one of the most popular skills in our King Of Weighted Coaching and, together with the muscle up, the most frequently requested skill. It represents the combination of strength, coordination, balance, and mobility like no other skill. Only an athlete who sufficiently combines all these qualities can perform a clean handstand push up. In this chapter, we will not only analyze the movement itself but also delve into the progressive training methods that will enable you to develop your HSPU abilities.

4.1.1

Execution and anatomy

The handstand push up (HSPU) is not considered a true, dynamic lever skill because the underlying element, the handstand, does not fall under the lever skill category. However, the HSPU can create a lever-like effect through the process of performing push-ups while in a handstand position. With some adjustments, we can apply the dynamic lever skill conventions to discuss the ideal technique and execution of the HSPU. There are various variations of the HSPU, each with its own level of difficulty. In the first step, we will determine the most challenging position for a regular HSPU and use that as a basis for analyzing the full movement. To determine this position, we will establish some definitions and provide factual reasoning. In this book, I will provide definitions that you can use to guide your training and understanding of the HSPU.

1. The most challenging and desirable execution of a regular HSPU is one
   in which the athlete maintains a range of motion where the forearms are
   approximately perpendicular to the ground consistently. In this position,
   the upper arms should be as parallel as possible when viewed from
   above, allowing for maximum shoulder extension and keeping the upper
   arms as 'long' as possible when viewed from a sagittal perspective. At
   90° elbow flexion, the athlete reaches the point with the greatest load
   arm on the shoulder, making this execution the final and ideal form to
   strive for.

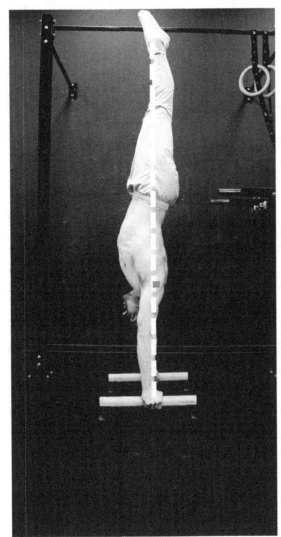 

Defined final form of the HSPU

From this perspective, we can consider a very upright HSPU with a wide
grip or flared arms as a regression from the regular HSPU. In this variation, the
effective length of the upper arms is reduced, resulting in a significant decrease
in the load arm on the shoulder joint. Additionally, the range of motion is reduced.
The movement shifts more towards the frontal plane rather than the sagittal plane.
This type of execution emphasizes shoulder adduction rather than shoulder flexion.
It's important to note that this variation is not considered incorrect or wrong in itself!

2. If the forearm leaves its vertical position to allow the athlete to go deeper into the HSPU, this is called a deep or a deficit HSPU. This, therefore, is a progression of the regular HSPU.

Flaring the arms reduces the load arm on the shoulder joint, provides a much more upright body position, and tends to shift the movement to the frontal plane.

Indeed, performing an HSPU with a wide grip or flared arms can have its own benefits and serve specific training goals, as it places different demands on the shoulders compared to a regular HSPU. However, it's crucial to recognize that this variation represents a regression from the final form of an HSPU. Understanding this distinction is important for your analysis, as it helps you differentiate between different execution variations and their respective levels of progression.

3. **If the forearm leaves its vertical position to allow the athlete to lean further forward to lower his body to the horizontal, this is called a 90° HSPU or its regressions.**

As you progress with more ROM in handstand push-ups, you'll encounter additional components beyond the basic overhead exercise. These include increased load on the extensors and flexors in your forearms, as well as greater

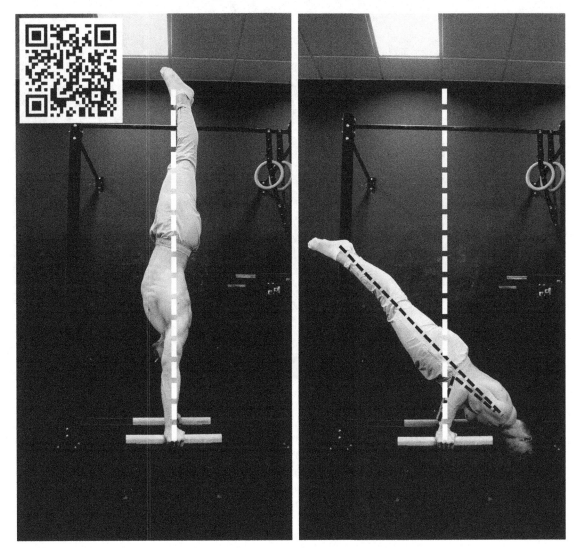

Deficit/deep HSPU

demand on your arm flexors. The combination of these additional components, along with the increased range of motion and coordination required, makes this execution a progression of the regular HSPU. In other words, it represents a more challenging variation that builds upon the foundational skills of the regular HSPU.

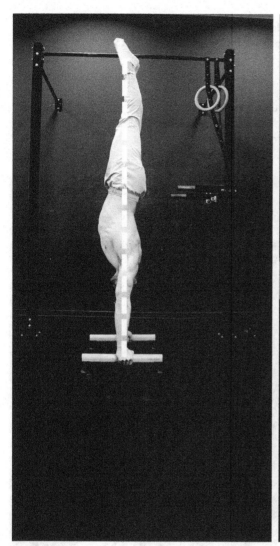
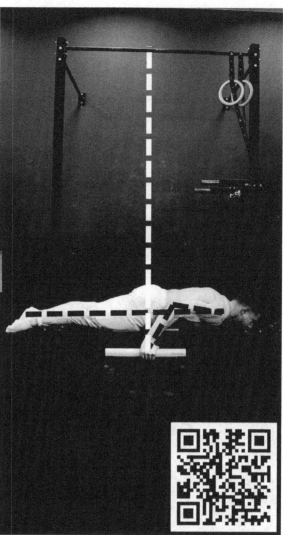

90° HSPU

As you continue to lower your hips and push forward over your wrists, the handstand push-up transforms into a 90° HSPU. This represents a further progression of the regular HSPU, as it introduces a significantly increased load on the shoulder and forearms. The 90° HSPU involves additional components beyond the overhead exercise, making it a distinct skill that should be treated separately.

Understanding the boundaries between the progressions as well as the progressions of the HSPU itself allows you to analyze your HSPU and develop effective training strategies to improve your specific variation. By recognizing the unique challenges and demands of each HSPU progression or regression, you can tailor your training approach accordingly.

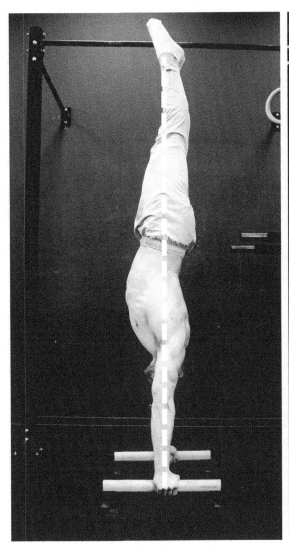

Balance in handstand works with many different body shapes.

The handstand as a starting position

4.1.1.1

The handstand can be easily explained in theory. It involves balancing your body's center of gravity over your hands, similar to how you balance on your feet. In the beginning, your posture is not as important as maintaining balance. The crucial aspect is positioning your center of gravity along the normal to the contact area with the floor. There are various body shapes and positions that can achieve this condition. It's important to note that this book does not provide the final solution for a perfect handstand. The handstand serves as an essential intermediate step that you must master well enough to ensure that balance does not limit your progress in HSPU training.

As you progress further, it becomes important to focus on your body position in the handstand. The ultimate goal is to align all body segments vertically in a straight line. This alignment involves stacking your wrists, elbows, shoulders, spine, and hips on top of each other. Achieving this alignment requires not only balance but also proprioception, which is the ability to sense and understand the position and movement of your body in space. Maintaining this alignment overhead is particularly challenging and requires dedicated practice over time. To attain the desired alignment, you also need adequate overhead mobility. You should aim to open your shoulders sagittally to approximately 180°, allowing you to move your arms fully overhead without compensating by hy-

Lack of overhead mobility is compensated in other joints

perextending your thoracic spine. Only when you achieve this level of mobility will you be able to achieve a straight handstand position. Developing overhead mobility and maintaining proper alignment are ongoing processes that require time, consistent effort, and practice.

If you have limited mobility, as I have, compensations need to be made in other areas of your body. These compensations can occur in your thoracic spine, lumbar spine, leg position, or with a bent elbow. The ability to maintain a straight handstand is therefore closely tied to your overhead mobility. Improving your overhead mobility is primarily achieved through progressive strength training that focuses on the full range of motion. Additionally, incorporating passive stretches for flexibility can expedite your progress. However, it's important to note that stretching alone cannot re-

place active training in this joint area. What makes the handstand even more challenging is that flexibility alone is insufficient. You must also be able to stabilize the position under the full load of your body weight. This requires active engagement from the muscles responsible for the upward rotation of the scapula, which allows your arms to move overhead, as well as the shoulder abductors. These muscles actively hold you in the position and provide the necessary stability. Even with excellent mobility, if these muscles cannot maintain the position and your arm deviates from the desired alignment, holding a straight handstand becomes difficult. It's important to prioritize both overhead mobility and stability in your training.

To learn how to incorporate handstand training into your workout effectively, refer to the "Modular-system training" section for guidance.

HSPU - The 2-line model

Based on the handstand, it logically follows that the center of gravity of your entire body must remain above the contact surface with the floor in order to maintain balance. Deviating from this alignment would result in falling over. In practice, there are tolerances that allow for slight corrections using your hands and forearms. When observing the handstand from a sagittal perspective, you'll notice that your center of gravity moves up and down in a line above your wrists. This movement is essential for maintaining balance. This line is referred to as line 1 in the 2-line model, and it represents the center of gravity line.

Both conventions for dynamic lever skills also apply to the handstand push up. The convention 2 states that all joints not involved in the movement should be actively stiffened and stabilized in a line against gravity. This ensures that you maintain the straight handstand line and avoid compensatory movements. The joints involved in the movement are the elbow and shoulder joints, as well as the wrist joints for balancing or regulating the range of motion. All other joints, including the spine, hips, and knees, should be stiffened and stabilized in a line. However, if you have deficits in your overhead mobility and are unable to hold a straight handstand, you may need to adjust the stabilization of non-involved joints based on your mobility limitations. Typically, you would stabilize these joints in a line against gravity shortly after initiating the downward movement.

Moving on to the second line of the 2-line model, you define it by jumping to the end position of the HSPU where your forearm is still approximately perpendicular to the ground. At this point, draw a line connecting your ankles and shoulder joint. This line represents the position where all non-involved joints should be in the final HSPU position if you have followed the second convention. It is referred to as the Range Of Motion line.

 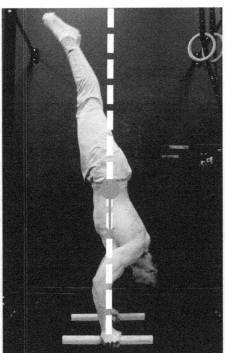 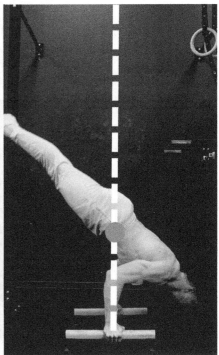

Center of gravity line of the HSPU

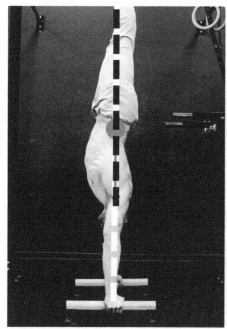
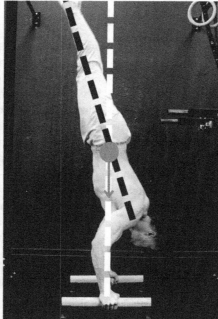
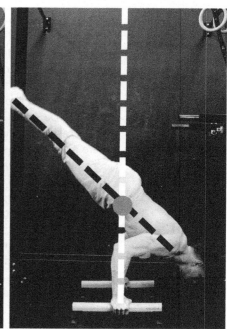

Range of motion line of the HSPU

At this point, you are justified in asking yourself what all the effort is for. The two lines, the center of gravity line and the Range Of Motion line provide valuable insights into the technique and process of an HSPU. By observing these lines, you can understand the simultaneous movements that occur during an HSPU.

The upper and lower angles between the two lines represent the range of motion of your shoulder. This range of motion involves shoulder extension as you lower down and shoulder flexion as you push up. To maintain balance and prevent fall-ing over, you must bend your elbows simultaneously and evenly as you lower your hips. This coordinated movement of arm flexion and shoulder movement allows the shoulder to follow the path traced by the upper arm around the shoulder joint. Meanwhile, your center of gravity moves vertically along the center of gravity line from the starting point to the intersection of the two lines. By analyzing and understanding the interaction of these movements, you can better grasp the mechanics and techniques required for an HSPU.

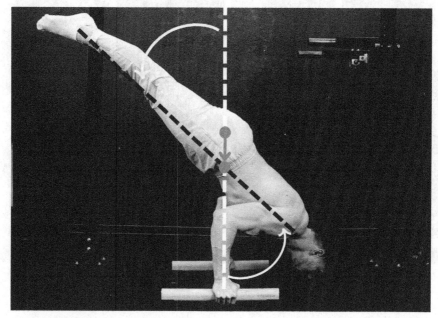

2-line model HSPU

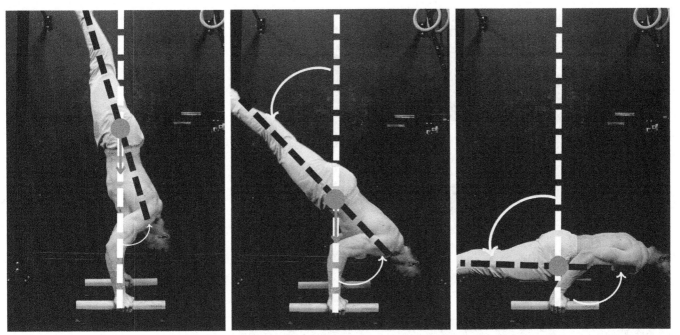

2-line model using the example of a 90°HSPU. The concept remains the same. The range of motion in the shoulder reaches it's maximum here at 180°.

In reality, this is not always one hundred percent correct, since the forearm would have to be held completely stationary, which rarely happens. In the end, the model is only a model to illustrate the execution of the exercise. Therefore, you will now see how you can use this model to find your individual HSPU technique. As you will see, the HSPU technique varies greatly from athlete to athlete. The negative movement is completed with your body being on the ROM line. To complete the two defined conventions, you must then press up the same way you took down in the negative. This is the only way you can guarantee that your center of gravity remains on the center of gravity line and that all non-involved joints remain actively stiffened. The positive movement and negative movement must therefore be congruent. For the positive, this means that you simultaneously per-

form an extension in the elbow and flexion in the shoulder. This causes your center of gravity to move straight up on the center of gravity line and the shoulder to move around the radius of the upper arm around the elbow, back to the center of gravity line into a handstand.

Depending on the location of your individual total body center of gravity and the length of your upper arms, the angle between the two lines changes significantly for the same depth of HSPU. Thus, an athlete with long upper arms must perform more movement in the shoulder for the same depth, thus completing more work to achieve an equal depth. An athlete with short upper arms can perform the HSPU much more upright and thus has less movement completed in the shoulder at the same depth.

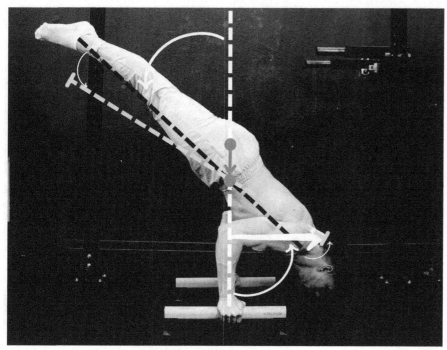

If the upper arm is lengthened, the athlete must complete more range of motion.

So his HSPU is usually less intense and the work the athlete has to complete per repetition is less. So the shape and also the difficulty of the HSPU changes with your individual anthropometry. So your HSPU probably looks different than my HSPU on the graphics because the interaction of the movement of the shoulder and elbow must differ from mine. This is important to understand because otherwise, you may be aiming for a form that is not achievable for you because your individual perfect form looks different.

The model makes it easier for you to estimate the loads acting on your shoulder. The normal distance from the center of gravity line to the shoulder joint determines, at least in our simplified 2D model, the load arm on your shoulder joint. The greater this distance, the greater the load on your shoulder. So the more horizontal your personal ROM line is and the greater the sagittal distance between the center of gravity line and the shoulder in your final position, the heavier an HSPU will be for you compared to other athletes who have a steep ROM line with a smaller distance of the shoulder to the center of gravity line.

So only compare your HSPU to athletes who have similar conditions. Otherwise, the comparison will not add any value to you. The same applies to the design of your training. The more intense the HSPU becomes due to your individual conditions, the longer it will take to learn the skill. Because of the interaction of intensity and volume, you can accumulate less training in the same period of time compared to someone for whom the HSPU is less intense. In the next step, you use the model to analyze the common compensation movements that occur during an HSPU. To do this, you first take a look at the theoretical heaviest position. This occurs when the upper arm is parallel to the ground. In this position, the largest load arm is applied on the shoulder. Above and below it, it becomes smaller again. Therefore, the sticking points of the HSPU are usually located around this point.

If the sagitally distance between the center of gravity line and the shoulder joint significantly controls the load on the shoulder during the HSPU, you can interpret any voluntary or involuntary reduction of this distance as compensation. These compensations thereby indicate a weakness in the shoulder muscles responsible for this movement. To reduce the distance between the shoulder and the center of gravity line, there are three different compensation strategies in practice, which occur individually and in combination.

1. Abduction and internal rotation of the elbows

Moving your elbow outward during the lower position of the handstand push-up (HSPU) results in a shorter sagittal length of your upper arm and a decreased distance between the line of gravity and your shoulder. This shift in elbow position redistributes the load from shoulder flexion to other movements and structures.

2.+ 3. Pushing the elbows backward and hyperextension of the lumbar spine

Since these two compensations almost always occur together in practice, they are also mentioned together. If you move your elbow backward at the lower reversal point when pressing up, you reduce the distance between your shoulder and the center of gravity line. To prevent you from falling backward, you must inevitably perform a compensatory movement in the spine or hips leading to a hyperextension in your lumbar spine. This is why these two compensations often occur together.

Here you can find all compensations to reduce the distance to the center of gravity line.

Scorpion HSPU with reduced ROM in the shoulder extension.

Using a strong hollow back as a compensation strategy in the HSPU results in a slightly different form of execution. This approach significantly reduces the range of motion in the shoulder right from the start, making the HSPU easier to perform. In this variation, known as the Scorpion HSPU due to its resemblance, the shoulder is not initially aligned with the center of gravity line. As a result, the shoulder has less range of motion to cover. The relative position of the arms to the thoracic spine in this movement is more related to an Incline push-up rather than a traditional HSPU.

Another compensation used unconsciously by athletes to reduce the range of motion in the shoulder is a strong adduction of the shoulder blades or retraction of the shoulder. If you shift the position of the shoulder joint relative to the rib cage, you also shift your center of gravity. More protraction inevitably means a shift in the center of gravity toward the head as you push your body further forward, away from the center of gravity line. In order to stay balanced and compensate for this shift, your hips must drop further. This causes your ROM line to flatten and the HSPU becomes more intense. The opposite happens in a retraction. If you push your shoulders into a retraction, you push your center of gravity over the center of gravity line and have to compensate with a hollow back to avoid falling over. This means you have to do less range of motion in the shoulder. So your ROM line becomes steeper again and the HSPU less intense.

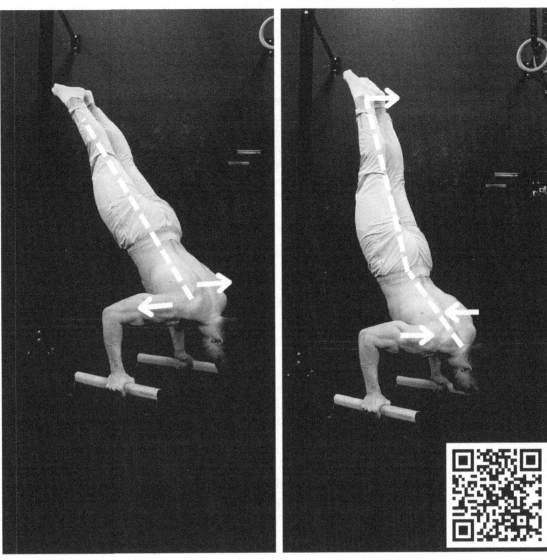

Retraction of the shoulder creates a hollow back because retraction shifts the body's center of gravity backward.

In most cases, the retraction of the scapula in the HSPU is not solely due to an inactive or weak serratus anterior muscle, but rather indicates overall weakness in shoulder flexion. Therefore, the limiting factor for these compensations is your shoulder flexion ability. If you find yourself relying on these compensations, it is important to prioritize shoulder flexion in your training to address this weakness. Occasionally, the triceps may also be a limiting factor, although this is less common as they typically experience less stress compared to the shoulder. However, it is important to note that compensations affecting the triceps may not be solely attributed to the triceps themselves. At this point, the 2D model has its limitations, and you should consider oth-er exercises and your individual perception of muscle fatigue to draw further conclusions. If you notice that fatigue in your triceps is limiting your performance in related exercises and you struggle to recover between sessions, it may indicate that the triceps are a limiting factor in your HSPU. You can consciously utilize these compensations to some extent in your training to control the intensity of the HSPU and adapt the exercise according to your specific needs.

4.1.2

Modular-system training

To master the HSPU, you need to combine several qualities: balance, strength, and coordination. Depending on your level and talent in each of these qualities, the structure of your training will change. An athlete who already has enough strength and only lacks coordination and balance will train with a different approach than someone who has great balance but is missing the strength component.

To help you find the right way to achieve your first HSPU, no matter what situation you are in, you will be given a modular system. Depending on your starting point, you can put together the right training for your needs. The system provides you with three different categories of exercises. Please note that there are always overlaps between the categories. The classification is therefore only based on the main focus of the exercise.

4.1.2.1

Basic exercises: strength

This category includes all the basic exercises that will help you build up sufficient relative strength for the HSPU. These exercises work just like the progress backups of the lever skills or pull/chin ups in phase 0 of the muscle up training. Therefore, these exercises should be as specific as possible, but not limited by high coordination or balance requirements. Additionally, it should be exercises that are adaptable in volume and intensity without losing their specificity. The HSPU is an overhead movement. You are performing shoulder flexion. So for strength building, you ideally use shoulder flexion exercises in a similar or at least related range of motion.

Overhead press

The overhead press is the gold standard. It is easy to scale, offers you a high specificity, and therefore has a very good carryover to your HSPU. However, when performing the overhead press, make sure to perform it with your elbows in front of your body and not with a wide grip next to your body. This will keep the movement pattern specific and increase the transfer to your HSPU.

 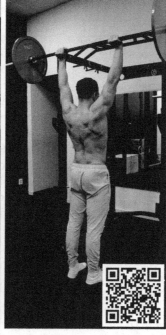

Overhead press for HSPU

(Elevated) Pike push ups

Pike push ups are the calisthenics counterpart to the overhead press. However, unlike the overhead press, there are some disadvantages in everyday training when you decide to use pike push ups as your basic strength-building exercise. One of the biggest downsides is the flexibility needed in the hips and leg flexors. Many athletes cannot perform a proper overhead movement with pike push-ups because they cannot place their feet close enough to their hands without excessively bending their knees. A second disadvantage is that they are much harder to progressively overload. Weighted pike push ups are feasible and work in practice. However, comparing the effort and convenience to the overhead press, the pike push up would not be my first choice. The final disadvantage to the overhead press is the ability to separate shoulder flexion from arm extension in a pike push up. As a result, many athletes are tempted to first perform a sort of normal push up from the lower reversal point before pushing themselves back into the pike position. However, with this compensation, you, unfortunately, miss the overhead component that HSPU training is all about. Should you decide to do pike push ups because the exercise simply excites you more, make sure you are flexible and technically confident enough to truly train overhead with this exercise.

Pike push ups

Elevated pike push ups

Weighted dips

The weighted dip is also an excellent basic exercise for building strength. In contrast to the previous exercises, however, you make sacrifices here in the specificity, because you do not perform an overhead movement. Especially for advanced athletes who can already accumulate a lot of overhead volume with the basic exercises from the category strength & coordination, the dip is a useful addition without running into the risk of overloading the same structures with too much volume.

Incline bench press

Incline bench presses with a stronger incline angle reflect HSPU very well, especially in the lower position. So this exercise is a good alternative for you if you have problems with core stability during heavy overhead presses. Also, athletes with spinal injuries can use incline benches or seated overhead presses to reduce the axial load on the spine and continue to train with high specificity at lower risk.

Incline bench press

4.1.2.2

Basic exercises: balance

This category includes all exercises that are primarily intended to improve your balance on your hands for the HSPU. Note that the relative strength and coordination requirements are not zero here either. These exercises are sorted in ascending order by their estimated relative strength requirement.

Incline wall handstand → wall handstand

For incline wall handstands, you stand with your stomach at a slight angle to the wall. This reduces the force on your shoulders slightly and allows you to progressively get used to the load without overloading yourself. Over time, reduce the angle until you are standing straight with your stomach close to the wall in a wall handstand. Be sure to actively press against the floor and keep your body tension at a maximum. Your butt, core, and thighs should be tight enough to keep your body aligned. Only your feet should touch the wall.

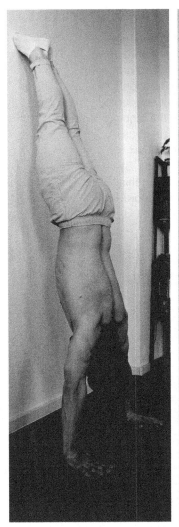
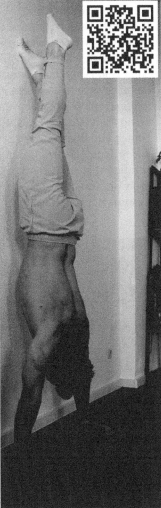

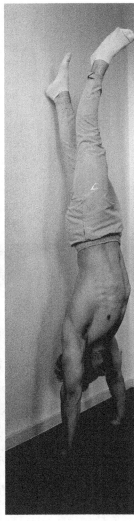

Incline wall handstand   **Wall handstand, floaters**   **Handstand kick & hold**

Wall handstand, floaters

In the next step of the wall handstand, release one foot from the wall and position it with your extended leg over the center of your body. Take your time and find your balance. Then switch legs and repeat the procedure with the other leg. Once you feel balanced and secure with only one leg on the wall, the next step is to briefly release both feet from the wall and stand freely for short pulses. As you do this, try to distribute your weight across the entire palm of your hand and get a feeling for the way it feels to balance your entire body freely. Grab your finger slightly into the floor to be able to make balance corrections. The more practice you get, the longer your freeholds close to the wall will be. The close distance to the wall ensures that you have to stand in a relatively straight line, so you're already learning good form.

Handstand kick & hold

To learn the proper entry technique for the handstand, it is essential to practice kicking yourself into free handstands. Initially, this can be a bit intimidating as there is a risk of falling on your back if you lose control. It is recommended to start practicing against a wall or, even better, with a training partner who can assist and provide corrections until you find the right amount of kick. However, it is important to venture out on your own relatively quickly and attempt unassisted kicks. If you happen to fall over, you can release one arm from the ground, allowing you to land safely on your feet. The goal is to gradually reduce the frequency of errors from session to session and increase the duration of your handstand holds.

Shoulderstand

The shoulderstand is a valuable exercise for developing strength and balance in the lower position of the handstand push-up (HSPU). It involves holding this position isometrically, with an emphasis on keeping the upper arm as parallel to the floor as possible. To benefit from this exercise and have a carryover to your HSPU, it is crucial to actively engage your muscles while in the shoulderstand position. Simply resting your upper arm on your forearm with full arm flexion will result in a minimal training effect.

L-Sit to shoulderstand

The more dynamic version of the shoulderstand can be likened to ballistic holds in lever skills. This exercise involves accumulating short hold times in the shoulderstand position, which enhances your strength ability in that position. The slight swing from the L-Sit assists you in transitioning into the shoulderstand, allowing you to accumulate longer hold times. By combining strength and balance in this exercise, you also enhance your coordination for the handstand push-up (HSPU).

Shoulderstand

L-Sit to shoulderstand

Basic exercises: strength & coordination

4.1.2.3

For this particular set of exercises, a certain level of relative strength and coordination is required. The exercises in this category are arranged in increasing order of specificity and difficulty for the handstand push-up. This implies that the more relative strength and coordination you possess, the more options you have to choose from within this category, as they become more closely aligned with the specific demands of the HSPU.

Floating pike push ups Lvl. 1

In this variation of the pike push-up, you begin by achieving a full balance at the bottom reversal point, ensuring that your entire body weight is supported by your shoulders and your center of gravity is

directly above your wrists. Once you have stabilized yourself in this position, you lift your feet off the floor and hold this balanced position just before initiating the positive (upward) movement.

Floating pike push ups Lvl. 2

In level 2, you follow the same negative movement as in level 1, bringing your entire body weight onto your shoulders and aligning your center of gravity over your wrists. However, at this level, instead of simply raising your legs, you perform a full hip extension to bring your body into a complete shoulderstand position. Hold this position briefly before lowering your legs and initiating the pressing-up phase

Floating pike push ups Lvl. 1

Floating pike push ups Lvl. 2

Wall HSPU negatives

Position yourself approximately one forearm length away from the wall, assuming a wall handstand position. From here, initiate a negative movement following the execution rules of a free HSPU. Lower yourself slowly and in a controlled manner, focusing on maintaining control throughout the descent. Try to minimize the transfer of your body weight onto the wall, keeping as much of the load on your shoulders and wrists as possible. If you have developed sufficient strength, you can hold the lower reversal point isometrically before proceeding with the movement.

HSPU negatives

In this exercise you perform only the negative of the HSPU following all executions rules from the 2-line model.

Back to wall HSPU

Assume a wall handstand position with your back facing the wall, positioning yourself approximately one forearm length away. Bend one knee to approximately 90 degrees and release the other leg from the wall, allowing it to hang freely. This variation allows you to avoid excessive hyperextension and benefits from the stability provided by the wall, while still providing some assistance through the use of your legs. Generally, this variation is slightly easier to perform compared to the belly-to-wall variation. The slight hyperextension of the spine reduces the load on the shoulders, and the position requires less overall body tension, resulting in lower fatigue per repetition. However, it should be noted that this variation is slightly less specific to the HSPU in terms of movement mechanics compared to the belly-to-wall variation.

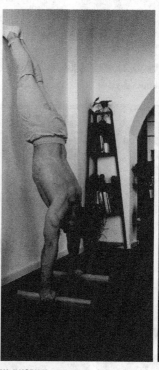

Back to wall HSPU   **Wall HSPU Negatives**

Wall HSPU

Assume a wall handstand position with your core facing the wall, positioning yourself approximately one forearm length away. Fully extend your toes and ensure that the wall surface is smooth and slippery. During the exercise, maintain contact with the wall only through the tips of your feet and avoid any walking movements. It is crucial to maintain high body tension and minimize weight transfer to the wall. As you reach the bottom reversal point, focus on pushing upward rather than pushing back against the wall at an angle, mimicking the movement of a regular HSPU.

Pike push up to HSPU

In this exercise, begin by performing a pike push up Level 2. Then, utilize the acceleration generated from the hip extension to execute a slightly easier positive movement of the HSPU and transition into a handstand position. This allows you to practice the full positive motion of the HSPU with the assistance of momentum.

It is important to note that achieving the right amount of momentum may require some practice. Initially, you may experience difficulties such as falling over if you generate excessive momentum or failing to complete the positive movement if you generate insufficient momentum.

HSPU, partial reps

Incorporate partial repetitions into your training routine to focus on the portion of the HSPU that you can effectively control. This exercise variation allows for a high degree of specificity. However, it's important to use this approach only when you can achieve a reasonable range of motion. You have the option to perform partial repetitions freely or artificially limit the range of motion using tools like yoga blocks. Partial repetitions are also beneficial as a way to gauge your progress and determine how close you are to performing your first full HSPU.

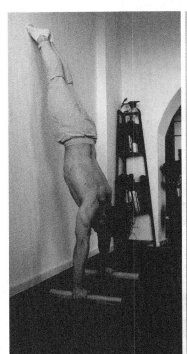

Wall HSPU   **Partial HSPU**

Straddle HSPU

Straddle HSPUs are an effective training method for targeting the full range of motion of the HSPU with a high level of specificity while reducing the intensity. By positioning your legs in a straddle angle, the distance sagittally from the center of gravity line to the shoulders is reduced. This allows you to maintain a more upright posture and alleviate some pressure on your shoulders. It's important to ensure that you maintain proper form during this regression exercise, adhering to all the form conventions. This will facilitate a smoother transition to performing full HSPUs in the future.

Wall HSPU with deficit

To train a larger range of motion in your HSPU, you can increase the height of your hand position. By placing your hands on elevated surfaces, such as parallettes or yoga blocks, you create a greater depth in the movement. This increased range of motion can be particularly beneficial when transitioning from wall-assisted HSPUs to performing them freely. By incorporating this intensification through an extended range of motion, you can make the transition more efficient and improve your overall HSPU technique.

To create a training plan for yourself using the three categories, it's important to assess your current abilities. To assist with this assessment, I have defined milestones for the first two categories that can serve as a guide.

Straddle HSPU

These milestones indicate that you have reached a level of development sufficient to begin specific HSPU training. However, it's important to note that these milestones are based on estimations derived from experience and do not directly reflect your HSPU performance. They are meant to provide you with load variables for your training and can be adjusted in the future based on further research and studies.

Milestone relative strength: 90–100% bodyweight e1RM in the overhead press / 5–8 pike push ups.

This milestone is intended to help you to assess whether it makes sense for you to already integrate specific HSPU training into your plan, or whether you would be better advised to invest this time in further building your relative strength. The values in relation to your body weight are only an estimation. It is assumed that you need an overhead relative strength of about 90–100% upwards to perform at least one repetition of the basic exercises from the strength & coordination category. An e1RM, a calculation from a normal working set, is sufficient for this. The actual implementation of a 1RM attempt with this weight is not necessary. Your e1RM will be much higher than your real 1RM, especially in the beginning, because you have no practice with maximum attempts. Technical details and psychological factors are very decisive here, which is why the e1RM and the 1RM differ greatly, especially for beginners.

To provide a comparison, data from studies on normal push-ups can be used. It has been found that during a normal push-up, approximately 66–75% of body weight is moved on the way down and 53–70% on the way up, with variations depending on load distribution across body segments. Trained athletes who can better concentrate the load on their shoulders tend to fall towards the higher end of these ranges (32). Therefore, considering that pike push-ups involve additional load distribution challenges, it can be inferred that to effectively perform exercises from the strength & coordination category where your legs lift off or provide only partial load through friction (such as wall HSPU), you should theoretically be able to move 90–100% of your body weight overhead. This can be achieved by having an e1RM of the overhead press within that range or by performing 5–8 pike push ups where your shoulders are loaded with over 80% of your body weight. However, it's important to note that these values are only valid if the pike push ups are performed with proper hand and foot positioning, and the center of gravity is adequately shifted over the wrists during the negatives.

Milestone balance: 10s+ handstand

The milestone provided aims to guide you in setting the right parameters for your balance training. Having a solid and secure handstand is crucial, as it allows you to concentrate and focus on the regression of the HSPU. If you are constantly struggling to maintain balance, it will be difficult to apply strength effectively. A good starting point for your handstand proficiency is being able to hold a safe standing position for an average of 10 seconds, with a very low error rate. This means that even with 10 handstand attempts, you should still be able to average 10 seconds or more. Once you have achieved this level of confidence, you can reduce the frequency and practice time for handstand training in your workout, focusing more on maintaining your current level.

It's important to note that this recommendation applies if your primary goal is to learn the handstand exclusively for the purpose of the HSPU. In this case, having an average good handstand is sufficient. Once you have reached this milestone, a frequency of 1–2 balance training sessions per week will be enough to maintain your level. However, if you have not yet reached this milestone, it is recommended to train your balance 3–4 times per week. Start with a frequency of 1–2 sessions per week in the beginning and gradually increase to allow your passive structures and muscles enough time to adapt to the new load. This approach will help prevent issues in your forearms, wrists, shoulders, or elbows that may arise from excessive training intensity without proper adaptation periods.

Creation of the training plan:

Once you have assessed your starting point and determined the training variables based on the milestones, the next step is to integrate them into a training plan along with the regressions from the strength & coordination category. Here is a guide on how to create a table with possible combinations:

Ensure coverage of the entire range of motion of the HSPU: When integrating regressions, make sure to combine them in a way that covers the full ROM of the HSPU. For example, you can combine exercises like floating pike push ups with free HSPU negatives to target different parts of the movement.

Emphasize free and unassisted work: while regressions on the wall can be useful, it's important to integrate exercises where you don't rely solely on assistance. This helps develop the necessary strength and coordination for performing unassisted HSPUs. For example, combine partial HSPU reps with wall HSPUs in your training plan.

Choose appropriate intensity: select regressions that are challenging enough to train in the repetition range of 1 to a maximum of 5 reps per set. This ensures that you are working with sufficient intensity to build strength. Beginners should split their volume approximately 1/3 of the time between reps 1–5 and approximately 2/3 of the time between reps 6–12. Advanced athletes can reverse this ratio.

Volume and sets: the volume should range between 10 and 20 sets per week. This includes the sets of basic exercises from the relative strength and coordination categories. Distribute the sets across the selected regressions and exercises to ensure balanced training.

Handstand holds: Aim for at least 5–10 successful handstand holds per session. This will help improve your balance and stability in the handstand position, which is crucial for HSPU progression.

By following these guidelines, you can create a structured training plan that includes the necessary regressions, sets, and volume to progressively develop your HSPU strength and coordination. Remember to listen to your body and adjust the plan as needed based on your individual progress and recovery.

By using this table, the described exercises per category and the starting values for your load variables, you can now put together the right training for the HSPU according to your level.

Cases	Milestone relative trength	Milestone balance	Basic exercises strength & coordination	Basic exercises relative strength	Basic exercises balance
1	Not reached	Not reached	None	2–3x per week	3–4 per week
2	Reached	Not reached	2–3x a week, cover full ROM, choose regression heavy enough that you can do a maximum of 1–5 reps per set	1–2x per week	3–4 per week
3	Not reached	Reached	None	2–3x per week	1–2x per week
4	Reached	Reached	2–3x the week, cover full ROM, choose regression heavy enough that you can do a maximum of 1-5 reps per set	1–2x per week	1-2x per week

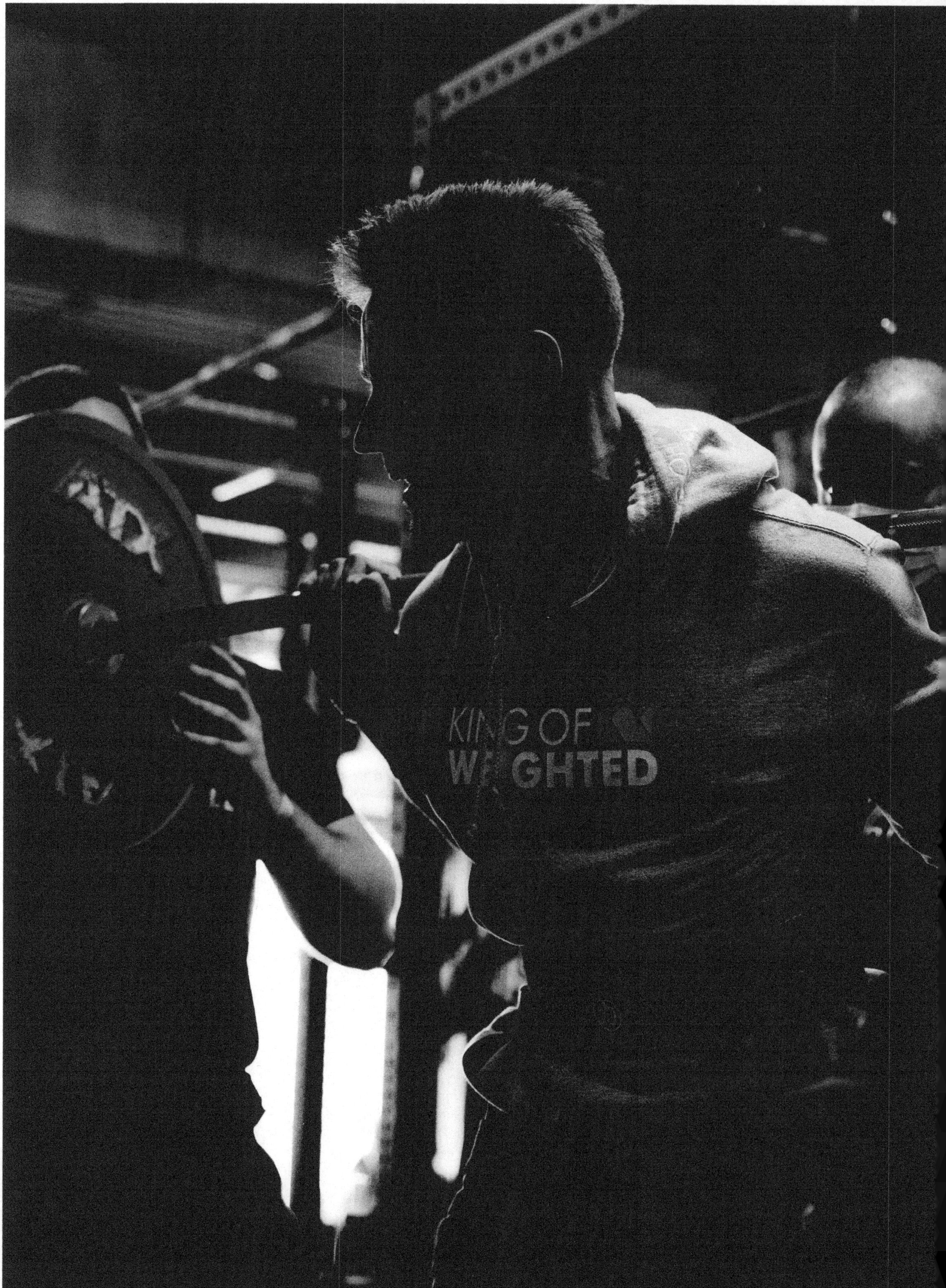
KING OF

5.

About the author

5.
About the author

It is very uncomfortable to write about yourself and to promote yourself with numbers and titles. Therefore, I would rather give you my own calisthenics and weighted calisthenics journey as an athlete and trainer in a nutshell, so that you can better understand my expertise and also my ideas and concepts of training and hopefully also identify with them.

My training career began when I was 17. It was the last phase of school, just before graduating from high school. I joined a gym and started training. At first, I only worked out on machines because I was given a sample program by a co-worker at the gym, which consisted of a simple machine circuit. I did this for probably half a year before I was confident enough to step into the free weight area. Once there, weight training became my absolute passion pretty quickly. Looking back, however, I could have used that time much more efficiently. If I would show you the program that I trained in those first two years, you would probably laugh your ass off. I then trained for about four years in the gym and mainly on a classic bro split. In those four years, I have already incorporated many pull-ups, dips, and push-ups into my training program without knowing what ‚calisthenics‘ is and without knowing the full potential of these exercises and the sport. Then one hot summer in 2014 changed everything and got me into calisthenics. It was simply the bad air at my local gym that made me search for „outdoor workouts“ on Google. Luckily, there was a hit. In Berlin-Mitte, in Monbijou-park, there was a kind of calisthenics facility back then. It was half children‘s playground, half bar park. I went there without much expectation. When I first got there, I met a group of mostly Russian guys and girls who were working out there. They told me that they were training calisthenics. The group called themselves Barliner Workout and organized daily open group workouts. I trained with them once, then a second time, and was quickly accepted into the group then trained with them almost daily. Whether it was windy, rainy, or snowy. In any weather on any day. Looking back, I am incredibly grateful for that great time that brought me so close to this sport.

That‘s actually the story of how I got into the sport of calisthenics: a Google search plus a group of like-minded people. A short time later I learned my first bar muscle up, and a year later my first full planche and my first front lever, I had my first experience with handstands and handstand push ups and started weighted calisthenics training in addition to skill training. Then in October 2017, I did my first 100kg dip, which was quite a sensation at the time. Over time, as one of the now experienced athletes, I began to coach the group as well as lead my own workouts. I started writing my own programs, reading books on bodybuilding and powerlifting, and applying all the concepts that I liked and that worked to calisthenics. I watched everything about calisthenics on YouTube and started my own channels to share my journey and insights. In 2016, I also completed my bachelor‘s degree in electrical engineering. My engineering education probably explains the more theoretical, mechanical approach to calisthenics exercises. I then started my master‘s degree in mechatronic systems but dropped out after only one semester to start my own business as a calisthenics coach and pursue my passion.

Since then, I have written over 3000 different training programs for my coaching clients, given over 500 hours of training video feedback, and worked with over 350 athletes personally in coaching and helped thousands of athletes who bought my pre-designed programs at the time. In the meantime, I've won the German Weighted Calisthenics Championship four times (2017, 2018, 2019, 2023), finished third at World Championships, and won or finished in the top 3 at several other national and international competitions. Almost all of these competitions are documented on my YouTube channel if you want to accompany my story with pictures from that time. To date, I've built King Of Weighted™, a world-renowned brand of weighted calisthenics coaching and equipment, and one of the first calisthenics coaching companies in the world along with a team of great coaches. So without being an all-knowing person when it comes to calisthenics and weighted calisthenics, there's a very high probability that what I'm telling you in this book is reasonable, proven hundreds of times, and backed by a lot of experience. Hopefully, that makes you feel good about reading this book and being able to trust in my words!

@kingofweighted

@micha_bln_

Reference List

1 Final Rep Ventures UG (2022) https://final-rep.com/regelwerk.html Zugriff 15.12.2022

2 Pat Davidson, PhD: A Coach's Guide to Optimizing Movement Rethinking the Big Patterns S.61–65

3 Phil Page (2011). Shoulder muscle imbalance and subacromial impingement syndrome in overhead athletes. International Journal of Sports Physical Therapy 6(1), S.51–58.

4 Król H., Golas A.. (2017). Effect of barbell weight on the structure of flat bench press. Strength Cond Res.(5), S.1321–1337.

5 Brigatto FA, Lima LEM, Germano MD, Aoki MS, Braz TV, Lopes CR. (2022). High Resistance-Training Volume Enhances Muscle Thickness in Resistance-Trained Men. J Strength Cond Res. 36(1),S. 22–30.

6 Lempke L, Wilkinson R, Murray C, Stanek J.(2018). The Effectiveness of PNF Versus Static Stretching on Increasing Hip-Flexion Range of Motion. J Sport Rehabil. 27(3), S.289–294.

7 Page p., Frank C., Lardner R. (2010) Assessment and Treatment of Muscle Imbalance. S.192

8 Dickie JA, Faulkner JA, Barnes MJ, Lark SD (2017) Electromyographic analysis of muscle activation during pull-up variations. J Electromyogr Kinesiol. 32, S.30–36.

9 Caryn A. Urbanczyk, Joseph A. I. Prinold, Peter Reilly, Anthony M. J. Bull (2020) Avoiding high-risk rotator cuff loading: Muscle force during three pull-up techniques. Scandinavian Journal of Medicine & Science In Sports, Volume 30, Issue 11, S.2205–2214

10 Prinold JA, Bull AM. Scapula kinematics of pull-up techniques (2016) Avoiding impingement risk with training changes. J Sci Med Sport. 19(8) S.629–35.

11 Youdas, James W, Amundson, Collier L, Cicero, Kyle S, Hahn, Justin J, Harezlak, David T, Hollman, John H. (2010). Surface Electromyographic Activation Patterns and Elbow Joint Motion During a Pull-Up, Chin-Up, or Perfect-Pullup™ Rotational Exercise. Journal of Strength and Conditioning Research 24(12), S 3404–3414

12 Complete Anatomy Application (2023) 3D4Medical from Elsevier

13 Graichen H, Bonel H, Stammberger T, Haubner M, Rohrer H, Englmeier KH, Reiser M, Eckstein F. (1999) Three-dimensional analysis of the width of the subacromial space in healthy subjects and patients with impingement syndrome. AJR Am J Roentgenol. 172(4) S.1081–6.

14 https://flexikon.doccheck.com/de/Musculus_latissimus_dorsi Zugriff: 05.01.2023

15 Baechele T., Earle R. (2008), Essential of Strength Training and Conditioning, Third Edition by NSCA S.66–81.

16 http://wiki.ifs-tud.de/biomechanik/muskel/mus03 Zugriff: 13.11.2022

17 1. Hill, A.V. (1970), First and Last Experiments in Muscle Mechanics. London: Cambridge University Press

18 Steinbeck J, Brüntrup J, Greshake O, Pötzl W, Filler T, Liljenqvist U. (2003) Neurohistological examination of the inferior glenohumeral ligament of the shoulder. J Orthop Res. 21(2) S.250–5.

19 McKenzie A., Crowley-McHattan Z., Meir R., Whitting J., Volschenk W. (2022), Int. J. Environ. Res. Public Health 19, 13211 S.2–11

20 Wolf M., Androulakis-Korakakis P., P. Fisher J., J Schoenfeld B., Steele J. (2022) Partial vs full range of motion resistance training, A systematic review and meta-analysis, SportRχiv

21 Friedrich W. (2021) Optimales Sportwissen Grundlagen der Sporttheorie und Sportpraxis, Spitta Verlag, S.137–162

22 Ikai, M., and T. Fukunaga. (1968) Calculation of muscle strength per unit cross-sectional area of human muscle by means of ultrasonic mea-surement. Int Z Angew Physiol Arbeitphysiol 26, S.26–32.

23 Schulz M. (2022) The correlation of the 1RM Pull/Chin Up and the ability to perform a muscle up, King Of Weighted GmbH

24 Lum D, Barbosa TM. (2019) Brief Review: Effects of Isometric Strength Training on Strength and Dynamic Performance. Int J Sports Med. 40(6) S.363–375

25 Helms E., Morgan A., Valdez A., (2018) The Muscle & Strength Pyramid, Second Edition S.47

26 Lanza MB, Balshaw TG, Folland JP. (2019) Is the joint-angle specificity of isometric resistance training real? And if so, does it have a neural basis? Eur J Appl Physiol. 119(11–12) S.2465–2476.

27 Pürzel A, https://intelligentstrength.net/peak/programmvariable-intensive-ness-in-bezug-auf-maximalkrafttraining/ Zugriff: 29.03.2022

28 Ilkai, M., and T. Fukunaga. (1968) Calculation of muscle strength per unit cross-sectional area of human muscle by means of ultrasonic mea-surement. Int Z Angew Physiol Arbeitphysiol 26, S.26–32.

29 Nuckols Greg (2019), https://www.strongerbyscience.com/strength-train-ing-women/ Zugriff: 09.02.2023

30 Nuckols Greg (2018), https://www.strongerbyscience.com/predict-strength-gains/ Zugriff: 09.02.2023

31 W. Pschyrembel (2014) Klinisches Wörterbuch. 265. Auflage

32 Suprak, David & Dawes, Jay & Stephenson, Mark. (2010). The Effect of Position on the Percentage of Body Mass Supported During Traditional and Modified Push-up Variants. Journal of strength and conditioning research / National Strength & Conditioning Association. 25. S.497–503

33 Vigotsky AD, Halperin I, Trajano GS, Vieira TM. (2022) Longing for a Longitudinal Proxy: Acutely Measured Surface EMG Amplitude is not a Validated Predictor of Muscle Hypertrophy. Sports Med. 2022 52(2) S.193–199

34 Nuckols Greg (2016), https://www.strongerbyscience.com/emg-amplitude-tell-us-muscle-hypertrophy/ Zugriff: 09.02.2023

35 Ackland DC, Pak P, Richardson M, Pandy MG. (2008) Moment arms of the muscles crossing the anatomical shoulder. J Anat.213(4) S.383–90

36 Graichen H, Bonel H, Stammberger T, Englmeier KH, Reiser M, Eckstein F. (1999) Subacromial space width changes during abduction and rotation--a 3-D MR imaging study. Surg Radiol Anat. 21(1) S.59–64

37 Wade, P. (2018): Power Calisthenics – Das Bodyweighttraining für maximale Muskelkraft, Beweglichkeit und Schnelligkeit mit über 100 Übungen. riva Verlag

38 Kuechle DK, Newman SR, Itoi E, Morrey BF, An KN. (1997) Shoulder muscle moment arms during horizontal flexion and elevation. J Shoulder Elbow Surg. 6(5) S.429–39

Made in the USA
Las Vegas, NV
03 January 2024

83827041R00195